Doubt's Boundless Sea

SKEPTICISM AND FAITH
IN THE RENAISSANCE

Doubt's Boundless Sea

SKEPTICISM AND FAITH
IN THE RENAISSANCE

by

DON CAMERON ALLEN

THE JOHNS HOPKINS PRESS, Baltimore, 1964

© 1964, by The Johns Hopkins Press, Baltimore, Maryland 21218
Printed in the United States of America
Library of Congress Catalog Card Number 64-10939

This book was brought to publication with the
assistance of a grant from The Ford Foundation.

Preface

IN AN EARLIER book about the fortunes of the Noah legend in the Renaissance, I wrote, I suppose, the prologue and epilogue for this volume. At that time, I described the debate about the proper language, text, canon, and interpretation of the Old Testament, and illustrated the confusion of the literalists by tracing their efforts to find successful evidence in support of a Universal Deluge and the salvation of clean and unclean animals. Their constant controversies (mirrored, I thought, in the literary and artistic treatments of "the second Adam and first Christ") nurtured more weeds in the garden of faith than they hoped to uproot.

The men who started the trouble, who pointed to the variations in the texts of the Old Testament, who questioned the divine inspiration of passages, even books, of the Bible, who uttered ridiculous doubts about Eden, the Flood, the career of Moses, these men were often called "atheists." It was these men, too, whom the literal interpreters sought to unperplex. The Bible, unfortunately, is the stumbling block of theology; and the literalists finally fell on their faces and admitted that "the Deluge was universal only in terms of the then inhabited world." They reached this sorry conclusion because solid geometry was unable to provide enough water to drown the globe and to build a boat large enough to transport all those birds and beasts and their provender. Faith, the evidence of things not seen, succumbed to mathematics. For a moment the literalists thought that history might be of some help. All peoples, those who wore feathers and those who slanted the eye and twisted the queue, had a flood story. But there was darkness in the light. Not all the survivors were named Noah or had the same career or lived in the same millenium; in other words, the proposed historical proof of the veracity of Genesis proved that Genesis was another chapter in the mythology of man. The atheists were, ironically enough, finally supported by the orthodox.

In the present volume I hope to display the profiles of some of these atheists and record the beliefs of unbelievers. For the Renaissance, in general, an atheist was one who could not accept any religious principle shared by all Christian creeds. A Jew, a Mohammedan, a deist was an atheist, and the definition could be narrower: to many Protestants, the Pope was the chief of Roman Catholic atheists; to many a Roman Catholic, Canterbury was head of the Anglican atheists. None of the men in my present study called himself an atheist, none denied the existence of God. With very few exceptions, this statement holds true for all the atheists indicted by the orthodox opposition. I have not had the space or patience to write about all of them; but here, as a preliminary illustration, I should like to bring forward the views of that Royalist, Episcopal atheist, Thomas Hobbes, who was detested and attacked both at home and abroad for his irreligion.

Hobbes attempted to climb the logical ladder to God, but he quickly realized, as had many of his metaphysical predecessors, that demonstrations of this nature always ended in many first causes (I, 411–12); [1] nevertheless, he states flatly

---

[1] All references are to Molesworth's edition (London, 1839–45).

that reason suggests the existence of God (IV, 59; III, 383) and therefore all must agree with "the heathen philosophers" that there is "a first and eternal cause of all things," which is what men mean by "God" (III, 95). The infallible testimony of reason indicates there are no atheists (IV, 294), but should there be, they are fools (II, 199). As finite creatures, we cannot know what God is; hence, we can only accord him attributes that are negative, superlative, or indefinite (II, 215–16; III, 352). In spite of our ignorance of God, we know he is just because he is powerful. Power justifies action; and, hence, when weak men complain about the injustice of God, it is they, not he, who are unjust (V, 116).

If there is a God, Hobbes says, there is a divine Providence, "a natural dictate of right reason" (III, 345). To deny the presence of Providence is to own "a wretched apprehension of God" (II, 214). Having philosophically admitted both God and Providence to his philosophy, Hobbes also admits immortality, but it is the immortality of his own metaphysical cogitations. Adam was created with an incorruptible body, which became corruptible when he fell. As a consequence of this metamorphosis, Adam and his descendants died and will remain dead until the final resurrection. At that time, those worthy of salvation will live eternally in this earth (III, 452). There is for Hobbes no post-mortem retribution. Hell is a metaphor (III, 446), but at the Last Day, those who merit a "second death" will be simply sponged out (III, 449–50). One can see that Hobbes' religious creed might have disturbed ardent believers, but he goes a little further. Even then, he is a religious eccentric rather than an atheist.

Taking sides with Thucydides, one of his favorite Greeks, who was also called "atheist" in his own generation, Hobbes refuses to put up with superstitions or ridiculous religious notions; consequently, he was not one to approve revelations or miracles (III, 316, 362–65; 416, 424). Likewise, he could not believe that Moses wrote the *textus acceptus* of the Pentateuch; he is, however, ready to allow that "the Old and New Testaments, as we have them now, are the true registers of those things which were done and said by the prophets and apostles" (III, 376). None of this, he says, really matters. A belief in Jesus Christ is all that is necessary for salvation (III, 590); we shall not believe "an angel from Heaven, nor the Church neither," if they speak contrary (II, 310). The author of these words is clearly not an atheist, not even an anti-Christian. If orthodox Protestants were dismayed by any of these views, they should have been reassured by Hobbes' strictures against the atheist Catholics.

The Pope, Hobbes writes, takes his title from the pagan, Roman Pontifex Maximus (III, 660–61), and derives his "fulmen excommunicationis" from Jupiter (III, 509). The Roman Madonnas and Bambini are only the pagan Venuses and Putti (III, 660). In the same fashion, one may equate holy water with heathen "aqua lustralis," wakes at funerals with bacchanalia, maypole dancing with the rites of Priapus, and the Papacy itself with the ghost of the deceased Roman Empire (III, 663). The Catholic priesthood finds its pagan analogies in British faery lore.

> The ecclesiastics are spiritual men and ghostly fathers. The fairies are spirits and ghosts. Fairies and ghosts inhabit darkness, solitudes, and graves. The ecclesiastics walk in the obscurity of doctrine, in monasteries, churches and church yards. . . . The fairies are not to be seized on and brought to answer for the hurt they do. So also the ecclesiastics vanish away from the tribunals of civil justice. . . . The fairies marry not, but there be amongst them incubi that have copulation with flesh and blood. The priests also marry not. . . . What kind of money is current in the kingdom of fairies is not recorded in the story. But the ecclesiastics in their receipts accept of the

same money as we do, though, when they are to make any
payment, it is canonizations, indulgences, and masses.

The utterances of Hobbes, the gentile Spinoza of England,
while not utterly Anglican are hardly atheistic. With Herbert of Cherbury and John Toland, he furnished for the
godly the trinity of atheism; yet any one of these men could
occupy a modern seminary chair, although he might not be
liberal enough for some of his colleagues. What can be said
for and against these atheists can be repeated about the others
whose theologies I have surveyed in the following pages.
None of them has been selected for the uniqueness of his
opinions; each has been chosen because his unpopularity with
orthodox believers was enormous. I have tried to present
them fairly. I always let them speak for themselves; in fact,
to use a seventeenth-century expression, I am simply the *tuba*
through which their voices come. I have not consciously employed my stops; their measures breathe forth according to
their interpretation of the score.

Although I have centered my attention on nine men, I
have occasionally quoted others—Bruno, Telesio, Campanella, Cuperus—for illustration rather than emphasis. Twelve
years ago when I began to read all of this literature, I imagined a wider canvas; the passage of time showed me the
absurdity of this plan. Some of my reading has gone into the
waste of footnotes; most of it has gone into the waste. With
it went essays on other atheists who have, in my opinion,
been well treated elsewhere. I have done similar destruction
to many of the apologists; but I have carefully divided my
book between both sides. I hope that I have allowed the
orthodox opponents of atheism enough space to make their
attitudes clear.

Actually, it is the orthodox thinkers who trouble me most.
How can their spiritual panic be explained? Why must the

existence of God and human immortality be expounded every thirty days for almost two centuries? Religious men let the heathen rage and never raged back at them. The answer to my questions may in some instances be the natural lation of professional vanity, but the real reason, I expect, was otherwise. The dike of faith was going down as the sea of rationalism burst through. Christians realized that when it had overwhelmed the steeples and drowned the cocks, it would sweep all men into a materialistic skepticism or, at best, into a rational theism. For many of them the prospect was undoubtedly frightening, because the sea that roared without the wall roared more violently in their minds. They had to fight the atheist within them! Some of them dug in their heels and shouted for the dike-menders; others would gladly have gone with the tide, but they had never learned to swim. My sympathies go out to these spiritual ambivalents. They might give Bruno and Vanini a hot hour at the stake, but they, in their turn, must burn for a lifetime.

The trepidation of the orthodox is, I suppose, the theme of my book, but I also intend to provide a background for students of literature, who may find passages that elucidate the poetry and prose of the Renaissance. Originally, I planned to adorn my text with illustrations from European *belles lettres*, but I decided against this idea. Poetry and theology are not great bedfellows, and I shall not force them to sleep together. In my last chapter, however, I have attempted to show how all that had previously been thought and said by atheists and orthodox can be knotted together in the career of Rochester, the atheists' laureate.

Following the inner light, I have gone in for some bibliographical heresies. Full bibliographical information about each source is supplied at the first reference; thereafter, unless two or more books by the same author have to be considered, I print only the page references. The terminal book lists will have to be consulted, but the harvest of *ibids., op. cits.,* etc. is, consequently, reduced. In all direct quotations and in titles, I have modernized the spelling, but I have never altered the syntax or changed a word for which there is no modern equivalent. The retention of old spelling and printers' abbreviations is deliciously nostalgic and amusing to some, but I see no gain in the practice. I have also bowed to my critics of the past and translated all quotations from non-English texts.

This book came into being when, as a very young man, I read the great Lecky and later the industrious Busson. I began to read my authors in 1950–51 when I worked at the Bodleian and British Museum libraries. The opportunity to bring my material into some form waited until 1960–61 when I was appointed Herbert F. Johnson Professor at the Institute for Research in the Humanities at the University of Wisconsin. I happily acknowledge my great debt to Mr. Herbert Johnson and the officers of the Johnson Foundation of Racine, to the members of the Department of English at the University, and to Professor Marshall Clagett and my other companions in the Old Observatory. Thanks to all, I was freed for the first time in my life from temporal and material restrictions and provided with books, encouragement, and learned but, nevertheless, cheerful companions.

Easter, 1963

Contents

Doubt's Boundless Sea

**SKEPTICISM AND FAITH
IN THE RENAISSANCE**

Chapter One

Atheism and Atheists
in the Renaissance

~~~~~~

I

THE WORD "atheist," almost unknown to the Middle Ages, was rediscovered by the Renaissance as a majestic term of reproach and condemnation.[1] Roman Catholics, convinced that doctrinal disagreement ended in unbelief, called the views of their opponents "atheism."[2] Protestants pointed up

[1] F. T. Perrens, *Les Libertins en France au XVIIe Siècle* (Caen, 1884); J.-Roger Charbonnel, *La Pensée Italienne au XVIe Siècle et le Courant Libertin* (Paris, 1919); Fritz Mauthner, *Der Atheismus und seine Geschichte im Abendlande* (Stuttgart and Berlin, 1921); Henri Busson, *Les Sources et le Développement du Rationalisme dans la Littérature Française de la Renaissance* (Paris, 1922; revised edition, 1957), *La Pensée Religieuse Française de Charron à Pascal* (Paris, 1933), and *La Religion des Classiques* (1660–1685) (Paris, 1948); Julien-Eymard d'Angers, *L'Apologétique en France de 1580 à 1670* (Paris, 1954); and G. Spini, *Ricerca dei Libertini* (Rome, 1950). More modern studies of the situation in England are George T. Buckley, *Rationalism in Sixteenth Century English Literature* (Chicago, 1933); M. C. Bradbrook, *The School of Night* (Cambridge, 1936); Ernest Strathmann, *Sir Walter Raleigh* (New York, 1951), pp. 1–98; Paul H. Kocher, *Christopher Marlowe* (Chapel Hill, N.C., 1946), pp. 1–68, and *Science and Religion in Renaissance England* (San Marino, Calif., 1953).

[2] Guillaume Assonleville, in his *Atheomastix* (Antwerp, 1598), puts the blame for atheism on the Reformation (pp. 22–26) and marks Henry VIII and Elizabeth as atheists (p. 110). *Calvin* is an anagram of *Lucian* (p. 124). Catholics regularly implied that Protestantism was simply a stage on the road to atheism: see Marin Mersenne, *L'Impiété des Déistes, et des Plus*

their case against Rome by counting the alleged atheists in the Catholic hierarchy.[3] Some Christians heard the bellow of atheist laughter in every street; others doubted the existence of a convinced atheist or held that atheists, if they did exist, were fearful and solitary.[4] Almost all authors of books

---

Subtils Libertins Découverte, et Réfutée par Raisons de Théologie et de Philosophie (Paris, 1624), II, 280–81; J. Maldonatus, *Commentarii in Quattuor Evangelistas* (Paris, 1596), p. 572; Charles Poullet, *Réponse aux Athéistes de Tours* (s.l., 1590), pp. 1–8; A. Barclay, *Argenis* (Rouen, 1643), II, 161; and Jean Cousin, *Fundamenta Religionis* (Douai, 1598), pp. A2v–A3, 12–14.

[3] Protestants quote the irreverent and irreligious remarks of Cardinal Perron or Popes Clement VII and Alexander VI. Johannes Micraelius, *Historia Ecclesiastica* (Magdeburgh, 1699), pp. 887–88, reports a typical series of Roman blasphemies. A broadsheet, *The Voice of the Nation*, hawked about London in 1675, claimed that if the "Emissaries of Rome" sent to England failed to convert men to Popery, they then taught "the principles of Atheism." See Thomas Good, *Firmianus and Dubitantius* (Oxford, 1674), pp. 1–3.

[4] In his *L'Incroyance au XVIᵉ Siècle* (Paris, 1942), L. Febvre argued contra Busson, who replied in his revised volume of 1957 (pp. 1–13), that atheist was a "smear word" and that no Renaissance man, Rabelais in particular, was an atheist. Febvre's conclusions are supported by Paul Kristeller in "El Mito del Ateismo Renacentista y la Tradicion Francesa del Librepensamiento," *Notas y Estudios de Filosofia* (San Miguel de Tucman), IV, 1–14. Some theologians held that there were multitudes, swarms, crowds of atheists: see Moise Amyraut, *Traité des Religions contre Ceux Estiment Toutes Indifférentes* (Samur, 1631), pp. 2–3; Jean de Neufville, *De Pulchritudine Animi* (Paris, 1556), p. A1; Charles de Bourgueville, *L'Athéomachie* (Paris, 1564), pp. 6–8. Mersenne's estimate of 50,000 atheists in Paris appears in the first form of col. 671 of *Quaestiones in Genesim* (Paris, 1623) and vanishes when cols. 669–74 change to an attack on deism. On the history of this alteration see Mersenne, *Correspondance*, eds. C. de Waard and R. Pintard (Paris, 1945), I, 121–22. When Mersenne made this statement, he named Cardano, Bonaventure des Périers, Charron, Machiavelli, Campanella, Vanini, and Fludd, some of whom were in hell, no doubt, but none in Paris. English estimates were similar. Bishop Latimer has heard that there were a great many in England who had atheist ideas (*Works*, ed. G. E. Corrie [Cambridge, 1844], I, 187); John Case found clouds of these "scorpions and locusts" at Oxford (*Ancilla Philosophiae* [Oxford, 1599], pp. A–Av). See also Walter Charleton, *The Darkness of Atheism Dispelled by the Light of Nature* (London, 1652), pp. A–Av; John Edwards, *Some Thoughts concerning the Several Causes and Occasions of Atheism* (London, 1695), pp. 1–2; and Seth Ward, *A Philosophical Essay towards the Eviction of the Being and Attributes of God* (Oxford, 1677), pp. 1–2, 4–5.

against atheism believed no man died an atheist, and some (Clement Ellis is an example) said all men turned to God in the dark and that atheism set with the sun; [5] nonetheless, book after book persuading, convincing, or castigating the atheist streamed from the presses of Europe during the sixteenth and seventeenth centuries. In few of these volumes was the word "atheist" used correctly,[6] and atheism was seldom separated from heresy or even theological disagreement.[7] This intolerant confusion in basic definition is not

Opposing this estimate of the number of atheists are those who think real atheists few in number and secret in practice: Leonardus Lessius, *De Providentia Numinis et Animi Immortalitate Libro Duo adversus Atheos et Politicis* (Antwerp, 1613), pp. 4–5; J. B. Bossuet, *Sermons* (Paris, 1929), I, 157; Yves de Paris, *La Théologie Naturelle* (Paris, 1640), I, 48; J. B. Morin, *De Vera Cognitione Dei ex Solo Naturae Lumine* (Paris, 1655), trans. by H. Care as *The Darkness of Atheism Dispelled by the Light of Reason* (London, 1683), pp. B–Bv; Louis Cappel, *Le Pivot de la Foi ou Preuve de la Divinité contre les Athées et Profanes* (Samur, 1643), pp. 1–2; and Franciscus Turretinus, *Theologiae Elencticae Institutio* (Geneva, 1688), pp. 175, 184. For English views see William Bates, *Considerations of the Existence of God and of the Immortality of the Soul* (London, 1676), pp. 3–4; Thomas Manningham, *Two Discourses* (London, 1681), pp. 2–3; William Towers, *Atheismus Vapulans, or a Treatise against Atheism* (London, 1654), pp. 4–5; and Joshua Bonhome's preface (p. A3v) to his translation (*The Arraignment and Conviction of Atheism* [London, 1679]) of David Derodon, *L'Athéisme Convaincu* (Orange, 1695).

[5] *The Folly of Atheism Demonstrated to the Capacity of the Most Unlearned Reader* (London, 1692), pp. 70–71.

[6] For proper definitions of atheism see C. Cheffontaines, *Novae Illustrationis Christianae Fidei adversus Impios, Libertinos, Atheos* (Paris, 1586), pp. A2v–A3v; and Baruch Canephius, *Athéomachie ou Réfutation des Erreurs . . . des Athéistes, Libertins, et Autres Esprits Profanes* (Geneva, 1582), p. 1. For other definitions see John Weemse, *A Treatise of the Four Degenerate Sons*, in *The Works* (London, 1636), IV, 5; John Dove, *A Confutation of Atheism* (London, 1605), pp. 1–5; Laurence Pollot, *Dialogues contre la Pluralité des Religions et l'Athéisme* (Rochelle, 1595), pp. 98–99; Samuel Parker, *Disputationes de Deo et Providentia Divina* (London, 1678), p. 3; and Heinrich Tietzmann, *Atheismi Inculpati Monstrum* (Wittenburg, 1696), p. B1v. The most farfetched definition is found in Frederick Voigt, Συν Θεω *De Atheismo* (Leipzig, 1695), where anyone who "does not believe that God created out of himself is styled 'an atheist' " (p. B3).

[7] On the slow discovery of the use of the term see Busson, "Les Noms

mitigated by the fine and elegant discriminations established by the Christian theologians who wrote about atheists and atheism.

The Renaissance apologists recognized two faces of atheism. There were practical atheists, who lived intemperately and were careless of salvation. They were rogues and rascals, not especially dangerous to the Christian faith. On the other hand, there were speculative atheists, who often lived decorous lives but who tested every religious notion and were, consequently, very much to be feared. Some of these men, it was said, thought the world eternal or the chance product of a fortunate confluence of atoms. Others believed in a divine creator who used coeternal matter or part of his own substance to make the universe. Some went wrong on Providence, believing in the Nature which supervised birds but not in the Grace which noted the sparrow's fall. A few of them went almost all the way to orthodoxy but could not accept the idea of immortality or that of heaven and hell. The orthodox expressions of these concepts were regarded as rationally acceptable, but they were also known to be supported and perfected by the testimony of revelation. Revelation was the Old and New Testaments interpreted by Roman authority and tradition, Anglican right reason, or the inner voice of Puritanism. Ascending the steep stair of revelation, many a speculative atheist had a bad fall.

The facts of Christian revelation, though not finely expressed, were found by some orthodox scholars in the books of the pagans; men were, however, urged to be cautious, because the natural light that showed Socrates one God, also disclosed to Democritus the reckless atoms, which drifted and fell into ordered universes. Some of the Fathers and a few Renaissance Christians saved from eternal dam-

---

des Incrédules au XVIe Siècle," *Bibliothèque d'Humanisme et Renaissance*, XVI (1954), 272–83.

nation the wiser pagan philosophers whose natural speculations approximated Christian doctrine, but such easy redemption was not widely approved. Plato might be touched with
holiness, but his scholar Aristotle believed the world to be
eternal and obnoxiously insisted that nothing came of nothing. Close to almost impious Aristotle was impious Epicurus,
patron saint of medieval heretics, who concluded that mind-
less atoms could swirl without divine direction into a splendid
living universe. In his essay on atheism, Francis Bacon contends that a "contemplative atheist is rare," but he denounces
Leucippus, Democritus, and Epicurus, who held "that an
army of infinite small portions or seeds unplaced should have
produced this order and beauty without a divine marshal."
Bacon's contemporary John Weemse added Diagoras and
Protagoras to the list of Greek professors of irreligion,[8] and
the number of the proscribed ancients increased until Bishop
Parker, a man not infamous for tolerance, exonerated a few
Attic atheists so that his case against others of them might
seem more judicious.[9] As the seventeenth century moved
toward its conclusion, it became decent to acquit many
philosophers of antiquity who were forced to read the Book
of Creatures under the moonshine of natural light. Outright
scoffers against the truth, such as Celsus, Porphry, Julian,
Lucian, Pliny, and Lucretius,[10] men who refused to see even
in the twilight of nature, were naturally not pardoned. They
were exhibited as men made arrogant by their trust in hu-

[8] P. 5.
[9] Pp. 14–56; for another list see Daniel Colberg, *Unicum, Proprium,
Adaequatum Remedium Therapeuticum Atheologiae* (Rostock, 1680), p.
Bv.
[10] Pierre Viret takes reasonable pleasure, as other men do after him, in
noticing that like all atheists the classical ones died poorly: Pliny choked
on ashes, Lucian was eaten by dogs, and Lucretius committed suicide.
Exposition de la Doctrine de la Foi Chrétienne (Geneva, 1564), p. 894.
In his *God's Arrow against Atheists* (London, 1622), John Smith observes
that Aristotle finally acknowledged the existence of one God and said
gods were invented to explain his multiple attributes and powers (p. 19).

man reason, and it was frequently observed that they would have been forgotten if modern rationalists had not invented "humanism" and "learned times," prime causes of atheism.

Athenian atheism, which audaciously opposed its feeble counternotions to the revelations of a divine truth naturally perceived, came to Rome and propagated. The two-headed monsters it begot slept during the wise Middle Ages but awakened in Renaissance Italy and were nourished by the new secular learning. Melchior Canus, an Iberian, is horrified to meet fellow Catholics who have read Aristotle and consequently have "unhealthy doubts about the immortality of the soul and the divine supervision of Providence." [11] Roger Ascham, no Roman, knows men who value Petrarch more than Moses, Cicero more than St. Paul, and Boccaccio more than the Bible. "They count as fables the holy mysteries of Christian Religion; they make Christ and his Gospel only serve civil policy." [12] The same sour opinion of Italian rationalism is expressed in the next century by Dr. Gui Patin, who describes Italy as a land of "pox, poisoning, and atheism." [13] His friend, Gabriel Naudé, not too famous for simple piety, denounced the Italians for their cynical denunciations of atheism; they convince no one and "make their readers disbelieve everything." [14] Clavigny de Sainte Honorine traces Italian atheism to the transmission of learning after the fall of the Byzantine Empire and French atheism to the cultural results of Francis I's Italian ventures.[15] So the Greeks infected

[11] *Opera* (Padua, 1727), p. 276.

[12] *English Works*, ed. W. A. Wright (Cambridge, 1904), p. 232. It is this sort of contamination that is described in the discussion between Pamela and Queen Cecropia in Book III, chap. X of the *Arcadia*.

[13] *Lettres*, ed. J. H. Reveille-Parise (Paris, 1846), III, 80, 333.

[14] *Naudaeana et Patiniana* (Paris, 1701), pp. 38–39.

[15] *Le Discernement et l'Usage que le Prince Doit Faire des Livres Suspects* (Paris, 1672), p. 82. The unhealthy spiritual condition of France during the latter years of Henri III is reported by Pierre Crespet in his *Instruction de la Foi Chrétienne* (Paris, 1589): he puts the blame on Pomponazzi and Machiavelli (p. 246v) and says that Epicurus would

the West with an antispiritual ulcer that was diagnosed in Italy and then cauterized in France and England.

John Calvin, who burned the "speculative atheist" Gruet and beheaded the "practical atheist" Monet,[16] wrote on the disease of disbelief in *Des Scandales* and *Contre la Secte des Libertins*.[17] During the next hundred years, the art of morbid spiritual diagnosis was studied and perfected by the scores of men who wrote books against atheists and atheism. Charron, himself accused of atheism, divides disbelievers into three groups;[18] Weemse finds four classes; and other men find more.[19] One of the better taxonomists was Robert Burton, who observed numerous forms of this "monstrous melancholy." But more to be praised for his extraordinary modesty in this anatomy is Richard Hooker, who thought an atheist to be nothing more than an atheist. Let a man but think his soul immortal, Hooker wisely observes, and a belief in the creation of the world, the Providence of God, the resurrection of the dead, the joys of heaven, the endless pains of the wicked, and the authority of the Bible comes after "as a voluntary train." [20] With this sane conclusion one may

---

get a larger congregation in France than Christ (p. 190v). His sour speculations are supported by Henri Estienne's bitter outburst: see *Apologie pour Hérodote*, ed. P. Ristelhuber (Paris, 1879), I, 179–206. Pierre Viret says that never had men been so open in their admission of atheism, although they might attempt to dignify their non-belief by calling it "deism." *De la Providence Divine* (Lyons, 1565), pp. 3–6.

[16] On these men see A. Roget, *Histoire du Peuple de Genève* (Geneva, 1870–83), II, 289–312, and F. Bonivard, *Chroniques de Genève* (Geneva, 1867), p. 103. Monet had a book of dirty pictures which he called "my New Testament."

[17] C. Schmidt, *Les Libertins Spirituels* (Paris, 1876); see also James Mackinnon, *Calvin and the Reformation* (London, 1936), p. 95, and R. N. Carew Hunt, *Calvin* (London, 1933), pp. 224–58.

[18] *Les Trois Vérités contre Tous Athées, Idolâtres, Juives, Mohammedans, Hérétiques, et Schismatiques* (Bordeaux, 1593), pp. 7–12.

[19] Pp. 5–7.

[20] *Laws of Ecclesiastical Polity*, ed. J. Keble (Oxford, 1888), III, 19–22. For other groupings see Martin Fotherby, *Atheomastix* (London, 1622), pp. B2–B3v; Jean Boucher, *Les Triomphes de la Religion Chrétienne*

compare the elaborate course in spiritual pathology of Gisbertus Voetius, whose professional advice was piously followed by antiatheists for almost a hundred years.

Voetius was a professor at Utrecht and famous in his time. His roars of theological rage make the treble of most religious quarrels of the early seventeenth century. His rhetorical blasts against rivals, especially the allegorist Cocceius, shook, to rephrase the Miltonic line, the arsenal of the Reformation. He wrote many books ornamented with prejudice and annotated with contumely. During June and July, 1639, he lectured on atheism to the students of the university.[21] He began by distinguishing between "proper atheists," who create doubts with their hypersubtle and overlearned theological disquisitions, and "participating atheists," who suppress their own and others' consciousness of God. The latter, dangerous group is composed of "practical" and "speculative" atheists. Practical atheists consider religion useless (Epicureans, deists, libertines), practice a wrong religion (heathen), fail to observe proper rites (indifferentists), attend worship for the sake of policy (Machiavellists and Politiques), or are merely careless sensualists. Speculative atheists are either "dangerous" or "mild." The first kind does not believe in Providence, scorns the Bible (or, as Catholics, regards it as unimportant), distrusts the natural light, and doubts some or all of the divine attributes. "Mild

---

(Paris, 1628), pp. 531-32; T. Campanella, *Atheismus Triumphatus seu Reductio ad Religionem per Scientiarum Veritates* (Rome, 1631), pp. 1-4; Cappel, pp. 3-10; and Derodon, pp. 148-50. Colberg (pp. Bv-D4v) follows Voetius' analysis; then makes a second grouping: Jews, Mohammedans, Catholics, heretics, neutralists, naturalists, skeptics, "atheist ministers who do not read the plain text but smother it in rhetoric, and mystics like Tauler." See also Pierre Poiret, *Cogitationes Rationales de Deo, Anima, et Malo* (Amsterdam, 1685), pp. 51-59, and J. J. Bircherod, *Exercitationes contra Atheos de Aeterna Divinae Existentiae et Providentiae Veritate* (Copenhagen, 1660), pp. 7-10.

[21] The lectures were printed in Voetius, *Selectae Disputationes* (Utrecht, 1648-60); I shall discuss them seriatim.

speculative atheists" refuse to believe in immortality or the resurrection of the body. But how do people born in Christian lands, Voetius asks, get in this godless state? [22] He answers his own question.

Some atheists learn their impiety from books; others are taught by their intellectual vanity and curiosity, their depraved affections, their laziness, ignorance, love of pleasure, avarice, and ambition. The social class or professional requirements of a candidate for atheism are sometimes responsible for his election; but next to the prompting of Satan, the main cause of religious disbelief is skepticism, a rigid intellectual attitude common to men who "hate the other kind of knowledge" and who reject all wisdom not approved by their reason. These men insist that knowledge win the certification of reason; yet they are invariably the sort of men who seek to know what is unknowable—the abstruse and forbidden. When they fail to obtain this improper knowledge, they fall into dejection and come to regard any notion transcending the direct testimony of sense, or the exact bounds of nature, as untrustworthy. To illustrate this intellectual inclination of atheists, Voetius recalls Pomponazzi's

[22] Voetius was not the first to explain the causes of atheism. Canephius, in a simpler age, ascribes it to Satan and original sin (pp. 2–3). Dove thinks it comes from a disbelief in special Providence, failure to hear preaching, the fact that God does not strike atheists down, Satan's malice, and the law's laxness (pp. 7–14). Weemse lays the blame on the smoothness with which the world runs, man's inability to imagine God, the frustration of those who cannot find God, and a desire to live wickedly (pp. 3–5). Mersenne lists pride as the main cause, but he finds innumerable minor causes (*Quaestiones*, cols. 715–16); see Philippus Faber, *Adversus Impios Atheos* (Venice, 1627), pp. 1–2. In the latter part of the seventeenth century, John Edwards devotes all of his *Some Thoughts* to the causes of atheism, but puts the blame mainly on "learned times," which he makes responsible for Unitarianism, Spinoza, Bible criticism, the new "mechanical philosophy," the exaltation of the Septuagint above the Hebrew Bible, and Mr. Hobbes, "their Great Master and Lawgiver"; in fact, an atheist said to Edwards (p. 128) that "his Leviathan is the best Book in the world next to the Bible: he himself was a man of great Piety, and is spoken against by none but the Priests."

refusal to accept the substantiality of angels and demons because it cannot be proved by mathematics.

If atheism is a disease, its spiritual ravages are increased by the mercurial nature of man's will. Impatient will plunges man into religious theories of no value; excited will pushes him toward spiritual novelty; and contemptuous or spider will enmeshes him in webs spun out of itself. As the will directs, men act. Men who are like Rabelais feel so comfortable and secure in carnality, they scorn anything spiritual. But among all doubters, "smug humanists" are the worst because they remake God in their own "perfect images" and treat his revealed word as if it were a humanly written book.[23] This is a serious religious crime because human books, as everyone knows, are a main cause of atheism. Some perilous volumes are well intended but badly argued defences of orthodox religion; others are plainly the seductive devices of evil men like Cardano, Vanini, Campanella, and other atheists. Naturalists, who wish to provide the supernatural with solid scientific explanation, write many outrageous books; whereas other books are put together by curious thinkers who work out cosmologies based on the feeble principles of astrology or magnetism. The literate are thus betrayed by books; but they, in turn, undo simple folk by voicing careless doubts about religion.

Though not a rigid antirationalist, Voetius objects to the "current pretense to a freedom to philosophize and prophesy." He finds grave fault with the humanistic notion "of progress and perfectability" and with "pansophism" with "its pride and hope in unknown and so-called admirable methods and dogmas which will make what man now knows seem in after ages no more than a candle in the sun." When he looked at all "these new discoveries which suggest all knowl-

---

[23] The same point is made as early as 1546 by De Bourgueville, who says some atheists liken the Bible to the stories of Lancelot and Roland (p. 33).

edge is filled with defect and error," he saw satanic traps for the unwary, "only old notions in new clothes." Behind all this new intellectual excitement, Voetius assured his audience, were the sly Roman Catholics, who had taken over the humanistic methods of textual criticism and were using it to discredit the Scriptures. The books of Cardinal Perron, Regourd, and Sebastian Francke that discuss textual problems are atheistically tainted and belong in the same library with those of the open atheist Vanini and the cryptic doubter Campanella. Voetius also informed his hearers how to unmask a cryptic atheist. Be wary, he said, of men who express doubts about the supernatural and speak lightly of miracles (fake Roman Catholic ones excepted), prophecy, and ghosts. A Christian should also be careful of men who point to contradictions in the Bible and then compare it to ordinary books. If someone describes clergymen as "fantastic" or "useless," believers should mark him, because atheists are usually hilarious fellows given to calling preachers "styxes, birds of ill-omen, Alastors, and dark clouds." One of their cleverer tricks is to attack an atheist, fully expound his Lucianic remarks, and then, after a tepid confutation, depart, "leaving certain subtle curiosities in the midst of things." Voetius observes that atheists are especially plentiful in those loosely run democracies that permit "liberty of conscience."

If this Clausewitz of orthodoxy had not printed his course of lectures, many an atheist hunter before the Lord would have had little to say. Gottleib Spitzel wrote three imitations of Voetius' *De Atheismo;* in the first of them, the *Scrutinium Atheismi Historico-Aetiologicum* (Augsburg, 1663), he attributes atheism to wicked books like the *De Tribus Impostoribus,*[24] Cardano's *De Subtilitate,* Vallée's *De Arte Nihil Credendi (sic),* Charron's *De la Sagesse,* the collected writings of Rabelais, Vanini, Fludd, and Campanella, and the

[24] See Appendix.

clandestine circulation of pernicious manuscripts.[25] He is a
true disciple of his master and attributes the spread of atheism
to openmindedness, the subordination of church to state, the
diversity of sects, the investigations of naturalists, Cardano,
and Descartes. His friend Anton Rieser follows the Voetian
scheme in his *De Origine, Progressu, et Incremento Anti-
theismi ad Spitzelium* (Augsburg, 1669), but he is wise
enough to agree with Hooker that atheism, a disease of lit-
eracy, is still atheism even if it is called "allotheism," "poly-
theism," "pseudotheism," "libertinism," "indifferentism," or
"syncretism."

With the publication in 1677 of Tobias Wagner's *Examen
Electicum Atheismi Speculativi* not only are the methods of
Voetius repeated, but Wagner, a Tübingen theologian, also
admits the whole contention is a struggle for minds. "There
has probably never been a practical atheist who did not have
a theory." Historians and opponents of atheism had never
hesitated to name atheists, but with Wagner's book the great
lists of atheists—Aretino, Vanini, Poggio, Pomponazzi, Cardano, Cremonini, Poliziano, Barbaro, Des Périers, Muret,
Vallée, and Rabelais—become customary adjuncts to the
conventional indictments. In his book we read of a German
atheist, Knützen of Schleswig, "who denied the existence of
God and Satan and urged men to live honestly giving each
his due." This man, we are told, preached that the Bible is
a mass of contradiction, that the soul is mortal, and that holy
matrimony is only sanctioned prostitution.[26] Wagner had
also read Browne's *Religio Medici*, in Moltke's critically

---

[25] Pp. 58–59. G. Spitzel's *De Atheismi Radice* (Augsburg, 1661) contains
a long attack on rationalism (pp. 24–60); his third book, *De Atheismo
Eradicando,* printed at Utrecht in 1669 and dedicated to Anton Reiser,
has nothing new. In his two dissertations, *De Scepticismo Profano et
Sacro* and *De Atheismo Praeprimis Socinianorum* (Strasbourg, 1665),
Gabriel Wedderkopf blames Satan for atheism because the human mind,
chief testifier to God's existence, could have no doubts.

[26] Pp. 4–12.

annotated Latin translation, and was offended by the physician's doubts and by the fact the book was on the shelves of public libraries.[27] But Wagner's book was among the last to wear full Voetian dress; times were changing and there was a faint brightness of tolerance, even for atheists, showing above the dark horizon of Christian orthodoxy.

II

Since they could not take oaths and lacked an "inner check," the atheist's rights to citizenship were challenged during the late seventeenth century. Henricus Petrus, having discovered that even the natives of Florida believed in God, argued that atheists were, consequently, untrustworthy citizens. The officers of state should undertake "their cure," [28] and men should be aware that "freedom of belief" is not freedom to believe nothing.[29] These views were seconded by J. G. Grosse, who equated atheism with advanced immorality,[30] and by G. H. Mencken, who demonstrated the worthlessness of an atheist's word.[31] In spite of such warnings, Heinrich Teitzman of Wittenberg, though not uninfluenced by Voetius, is cautious about accusations against atheists in his *Atheismi Inculpati Monstrum* (1696); [32] whereas J. L. Fabricius goes so far as to deny the existence of strict atheism

[27] Browne's "doubts," which are cited at length by Charles Blount in "A Letter . . . to Mr. Gildon," *Miscellaneous Works*, ed. C. Gildon (London, 1695), pp. 3–8, disturbed Wagner very much. Colberg (p. C4v) calls Browne "a doctor who writes in contempt of God's Word" and compares him with the Preadamite, Isaac de la Peyrere, as "an atheist in the church."

[28] *De Atheismi Eversione* (Helmstadt, 1689), pp. A3–B3.

[29] Pp. F2v–F3v.

[30] *An Atheismus Necessario Ducat ad Corruptionem Morum* (Rostock, 1696).

[31] *Dissertatio Moralis de Juramento Athei* (Leipzig, 1713).

[32] Pp. B3v–B4 repeat Voetius' basic classifications.

in his *Apologia pro Genere Humano contra Atheismi Calumniam*. Unwilling to be this liberal, J. C. Wolf simply maintains that Voetius' "Indirect atheists" (Chinese, Jews, Hindus) should not really be called "atheists." [33] In 1708 J. C. Hamm complained that the epithet "atheist" is too recklessly used; and shortly afterward, C. H. Schelling wrote an honest evaluation of unbelievers' morality and discussed the ethics of Hobbes and Spinoza without normal Christian repugnance.[34] It is possibly regrettable that the somewhat saner views of these early eighteenth-century theologians did not find a larger place in the exhaustive histories of atheism which began to appear.

The first modern history of atheism was written by an English clergyman, Jenkins Thomas Philipps, tutor to the children of George II. Philipps' *Dissertatio Historico-Philosophico de Atheismo sive Historia Atheismi* was published at London in 1716 and is the fruit of its author's extensive readings, not only in the books of well-established atheists, but also in those of British philosophers of the empirical school and those of empiricists who were also theologians. " 'Deus est' is inscribed in every heart," says Philipps, but there have been "speculative atheists" who painted out the inscription. He admits that the idea of God must come through the senses because, of course, innate ideas do not exist. "We are not speaking at this moment of revelation." Man learns much about God and his attributes from the creatures, but it is, nonetheless, almost impossible to define God. We may say he is a spirit, but we cannot define spirit. If we say that God is a thinking being, wise and good, all

---

[33] Preface to *De Atheo ex Structura* του εγκεφαλου *Convincendo* (Ratisbon, 1708).

[34] *Oeconomiam Systematis Moralis Atheorum* (Helmstadt, 1718). The atheists of antiquity find a solid champion in R. W. Boclo, who exonerates Anaximander, Anaxagoras, Homer, Virgil, Ovid, and others in his *De Gentilium Atheismi Falso Suspectis* (1716), and a learned advocate in J. G. Staedelen, author of the admirable *De Atheismi Origine* (Jena, 1720).

these adjectives must be humanly defined and understood. For this reason some men, "who believe nothing they cannot see," do not believe in God.[35]

"The philosophic idea of fate which had dogged man throughout his history" is, in Philipps' estimation, a major cause of atheism. "We Christians know better and avoid, as diligently as we can, those problems of philosophers which make men laugh."[36] A related cause of atheism is fear of a Supreme Being. Italian politicians capitalized on this fear; skeptics like Vanini built systems on it; the Roman Church exploited it for material advantage. From Italian cynicism, humanistic learning, and the discoveries of the naturalists have come most of the atheistic ideas rampant in Europe. The new concepts of the nature of the universe have also pushed the testimony of Moses into doubt, and new textual methods have induced men to scorn the Bible. The philologian Bembo, for instance, described it as "nonsense," and the critic Bonamici admittedly preferred the odes of Pindar to the Psalms. The result of this humanistic, literary prejudice is a disesteem of Scripture, but Philipps has high hopes for a renewal of Christian belief on the ground of the discoveries of scientists such as Boyle, Ray, and Derham.[37] He now begins a tour through the history of disbelief.

"I must first define an atheist because Julian, Erasmus, Grotius, and other men are lumped carelessly together under this title." An atheist has either never heard of God or has convinced himself God does not exist. Philipps knows it is also customary to call a man an atheist who does not believe in Providence, immortality, or the resurrection of the body.[38] He sees atheism as a product of urban life. Cain, the first city dweller, was an atheist; his example was followed by a long procession of Athenian infidels. Of these, Thales, Anaximander, and Anaximenes were not true atheists, but Anaxagoras surely was. The irreligious Democritus and Leucippus were merely materialists. Epicurus may have been an atheist, but it is also true that many things he never said are credited to his discredit. His poet laureate, Lucretius, was certainly an atheist.[39]

When the ruling religion of antiquity, Epicureanism, was disestablished by Christianity, atheism disappeared for a time from the world. The cult of fine letters vanished at the same time; but when humanists rediscovered the old literature, the old frivolities, scorned by Christians, gleefully returned. Italy is, of course, once again at fault. In that unfortunate land men swallow the idea of immortality with a grain of salt and are more easily convinced of a hereafter by Homer or Virgil than they are by the Bible. Philipps knows and repeats the tired anecdotes associated with the Italian atheists Bembo, Poliziano, Ficino, Pomponazzi, Simone Porzio, Caesalpino, Beauregard, Cardano, and Vanini.[40] He is probably the first theologian to proclaim Machiavelli, "whose commentary on Livy is filled with piety," as blameless of the charge of atheism; [41] and though he was one of the few historians to read Bodin's *Heptaplomeres*, he tags the Frenchman as nothing worse than a convert to Judaism. He writes Hobbes down as an atheist but spares Herbert of Cherbury. He concludes his book happily with a stirring account of the sinful life and deathbed conversion of the eminent atheist and libertine, the Earl of Rochester.

The authority of Philipps' book was superseded when Johannes Buddeus, a Jena professor, printed his *Theses Theologicae de Atheismo et Superstitione*. In this book, we read first that atheists are few in number; but Buddeus gravely predicts a large increase in their number unless the freedom of thought, now widely permitted and praised, is

[39] Pp. 31–75.   [40] Pp. 80–114.   [41] Pp. 92–93.

not immediately and rigorously suppressed.[42] The subjects of his book are "speculative atheists," whom, he admits, are usually men of virtue and honesty prevented by a blind passion from seeing how all things announce the existence of God. They think either that nothing divine can be known or that there is a natural explanation of all things.[43] Men of this sort existed before the Flood; they were at the court of Solomon; but the first known by name were Thales, Anaximander, and Anaximenes. But not all Greek thinkers were skeptics or mechanists, and Buddeus praises Socrates as "an opponent of superstition." He likes Plato because "although some think him a Spinozist, others think his opinions close to Christianity." [44] He reprints the conventional registers of atheists, inspects their religious ideas, and votes blackly against Aretino, Beauregard, Cremonini, Poggio, Bruno, Pomponazzi, Vanini, Cardano, Campanella,[45] and Rabelais. The charge of unbelief is not proved, he thinks, against Montaigne, Charron, and Descartes.[46] Dr. Thomas Browne was just an indifferentist; Herbert of Cherbury was merely a deist.[47] Spinoza was Satan's pope, and Hobbes was Spinoza's nuncio to Englishmen. In unhappy England, they now endure Toland, who "surpasses in impiety all the other atheists of all time." [48]

Buddeus distinguishes between several preatheist conditions of the mind such as naturalism, pantheism, indifferentism, skepticism, and Epicureanism. When one flirts with one of these philosophies, one accepts in the end one or more of their damnable beliefs.[49] Buddeus, like his predecessors, describes atheism as a disease. The man who has contracted it may attempt to hide his symptoms under an honest exterior,

[42] I have used *Traité de l'Athéisme et de la Superstition*, trans. Louis Philon (Amsterdam, 1740), pp. A8–A8v.
[43] Pp. B5, 105–8.   [44] Pp. 10–16.   [45] Pp. 51–53.   [46] Pp. 70–75.
[47] Pp. 87–90.   [48] Pp. 90–92.   [49] Pp. 106–48.

but, nonetheless, he inwardly scorns and disdains all Christians "with reasonable sentiments." If this ailment of the soul continues to spread, Buddeus foresees governments collapsing and the foundations "upon which rest the safety and tranquillity of society" in ruin.[50] Having frightened his readers with dire prophecy, Buddeus runs through the customary proofs of the Christian doctrine for the benefit of non-believers. His book is thick and learned, but it is only a preparative to J. F. Reimann's *Historia Universalis Atheismi et Atheorum Falso et Merito Suspectorum apud Judaeos, Ethnicos, Muhamedanos*, printed at Hildesheim in 1725.

Reimann, well known as a friend of Leibnitz, describes the atheism of all peoples in all times. He considers the nature of Virgil's unbelief. "Was he a Spinozist or Epicurean?" [51] He decides after careful study—he always supplies elaborate references—that Machiavelli, Ochino, and Bembo were not atheists.[52] The actual faith of Pomponazzi bothers him because Malebranche and Leibnitz think he was not spiritually affected by the anti-Christian demonstrations of his philosophy.[53] He considers the century-old attack on Cardano unfair and agrees with Reiser, Parker, and Naudé that he was mad, not bad.[54] He has no doubts about Vanini's unbelief; [55] but he maintains that Rabelais was "a not unlearned man with a dirty mind," who was unable to control his natural foulness when he talked of sacred things.[56] Bodin was a naturalist, and Charron was falsely accused of atheism. The Montaigne of the *Apology for Sebonde* appears to be an atheist, but he must be judged not on one book but on the basis of all his writings.[57] There are, to be sure, Spanish atheists; but Reimann refuses to echo the common complaints against Sanchez because he has been unable to secure a copy of his

[50] Pp. 163–64.   [51] Reimann, p. 252.   [52] Pp. 356–60.
[53] Pp. 361–63.   [54] Pp. 365–68.   [55] Pp. 369–76.   [56] Pp. 389–92.
[57] Pp. 403–7.

book.[58] What he has not read, he tolerantly refuses to condemn. In England, "home of sects and schisms," there is the suspicious hylozoist Francis Glisson, and the impious John Craig, with his theories about the mathematical probability against the exact transmission of Christian truth. Thomas Hobbes, Charles Blount, Anthony Collins, and John Toland are obvious atheists. Bernard Collins, who offered medical annotations on each of Christ's miracles, is probably of their company. Men have said that Herbert of Cherbury was a deist; perhaps so, but was he a Christian? Reimann, like others before him, records the wicked life and pious repentance of the Earl of Rochester. It is to his credit that he defends the much-abused Dr. Thomas Browne, a man "who confessed himself a skeptic in philosophy but not in religion," whose "life and words are pure piety." [59] There are, of course, many atheists in Holland, and Reimann "lacks paper" to list those in Germany. Reimann, like his predecessors, trembled before rationalism, but he should be congratulated because he attempted to exculpate many men continually accused of godlessness.

III

A connoisseur of atheism has no difficulty with Renaissance literary characters like Shakespeare's Edmund or Tourneur's D'Amville. They follow their instincts, have doubts about the immortality of the soul, live for profit and pleasure, and die the atheist's death. They may have more wit than superstitious Caliban's drunken, atheist gods, but they are essentially "practical atheists." Books written by "speculative atheists," on the other hand, are difficult to find.

[58] Pp. 432–34.
[59] Pp. 439–62; the defence of Browne appears on pp. 446–48.

When one reads the writings of named "atheists" like Pomponazzi, Cardano, Sanchez, Vanini, Montaigne, Charron, and other religious thinkers, one sees the orthodox reasons for the charges against them; but no one of them openly denies God's existence. The difference between these atheists, so tirelessly and tiresomely accused, and the full-scale, anonymous atheists mentioned in the books that set out to "evaporate," "strangle," "stamp out," or "overturn" atheism is very great. The "atheist" impaled in these annual volumes is a shadowy figure; and even when he is given a name like Knützen or Ram, information about him is slight. As one learns about Celsus from Origen, so one must in general learn about the Renaissance "atheist" from his orthodox assailants. To find the shadow of this dangerous but omnipresent infidel, one can turn to the book against atheism published by Campanella, a Catholic, in 1631, and the similar work of the Protestant Cuperus, which was printed in 1676. Both theologians were so successful at reporting the absurd ideas of the "atheist" that they were themselves accused of inventing him to propagate misbelief.

Campanella's *Atheismus Triumphatus seu Reductio ad Religionem per Scientiarum Veritates* begins with a résumé of carping atheist questions, the orthodox answers to them, and a series of reasonable theological problems that the rational Christian had to solve. Atheists ask, for example, how one God can be three gods or incarnate and at the same time not incarnate. They accept virginal conception, but they cannot understand how a woman could still be a virgin after childbearing. They must be told why God, after vilifying himself to save man, saved so few of them. They also want to know why Tartars, Japanese, Chinese, Hindus, Africans, and polar inhabitants were neglected by the dispensers of the New Dispensation. The method employed by Campanella to answer these speculative doubts is twofold; he either dispels them with one or more passages of Scripture or irons out the rough place in the Bible that brought about the confusion. When he is asked why neither Moses nor Christ mentioned the existence of a western hemisphere, he quotes John 10:16: "And other sheep I have." If, on the other hand, atheists point to Christ's statement that he would come quickly to judge men and ask why he is so slow, they are told that Christ used "quickly" only in terms of eternity.[60] After following the wiser method of basing his explanations on revelation, Campanella vainly attempts to establish a rational theology, and this effort undoubtedly made him a son of Satan.

The human mind, he writes, is a reflection of the Supreme Reason, the existence of which is affirmed when atheists try to reason it away. This intricate and complex universe is clearly controlled by a governing intelligence which restrains the warring elements, prevents the occurrence in nature of abhorred vacuums, and designs the splendidly efficient bodies of men and animals. The very inability of man to comprehend the nature or explain the functions of his body proves for Campanella the existence of a Supreme Reason. The existence of this supervising intelligence also makes it reasonably certain that the universe is neither eternal, as Aristotle said, nor a creature of chance, as Epicurus maintained. To the casual observer, chance seems to be real; but this apparent reality, says Campanella, is either *per accidens* or "in respect of man's ignorance of the whole."[61] But the atheist most often shelters himself in the shade of the multiform evils that darken a good world created by a benign God. Campanella, who had trouble enough, admits he is also puzzled by the omnipresent problem of evil.

He begins his rational consideration of this divine wrong

[60] Campanella, *Atheismus Triumphatus* (Rome, 1631), pp. 1–14.
[61] Pp. 16–31.

with death, the greatest of evils. Why must men die? What good is there in this? Man's body, Campanella writes, is composed of earth, of lettuces, of grain, of the flesh of cattle. No man is displeased to know this; but he enjoys his presence in the world so much, he hates the fate which makes his living substance into worms. Death is, however, not entity, but process, a transmutation. Once our flesh has become worms, the worms might in their turn loathe being transformed into man. The world is not only the living, but the living and the dead, and man lives by the death of bread. There is really neither good nor evil in the process of death, and God has absolutely no share in it. The atheist, satisfied by this reply, points to moral evil, which reduces man, alleged king of animals, to less than beast. Man, it is true, says Campanella, is not so strong as elephants, horses, and bulls. He is not sharp-eyed as eagles nor so keen in hearing as wolves. In these respects he is inferior, but he also has reason and a soul, and these possessions make him lord of all. Reason establishes the necessity of religion and proves the existence of the soul by sensing its immortality.[62] No animal has these rational or spiritual comforts. The elephant, said to worship the full moon, has only "a shadowy religion."

For Campanella there are four stages of religion: animal religion, known to birds and beasts; natural religion, known to animals and men; rational religion or the biblical "fear of God"; and the revealed religion, which leads men to Christianity.[63] Having reached this highest level of proof, Campanella defends the story of Christ, the veracity of the Apostles, miracles, and other Christian matters against the rational insinuations of the atheists; but by recording their arguments, Campanella got the reputation of a cryptoatheist who attractively spread the atheists' doubts about religion and

[62] Pp. 32–51.   [63] Pp. 64–118.

stumbled in his refutation. His Protestant successor walked into the same trap.

Franciscus Cuperus, one of the many men who piously attacked the works of the archatheist Spinosus Spinoza, was rewarded for his labors with the Order of Atheism, First Class. In 1681 G. H. Bredeholl [64] mentions him together with Thomas Browne, Vanini, Campanella, Rabelais, Machiavelli, and Knützen because he was a feeble defender of religion who covertly spread disbelief. Bredeholl's suspicion was warmly endorsed in 1710 when J. W. Jaeger of Jena, a strong Voetian, published his *Cuperus Mala Fide aut ad Minimum Frigide Atheismum Spinoza Oppugnans.* Cuperus' *Arcana Atheismi Revelata Philosophice et Paradoxe Refutata* (Rotterdam, 1676) intends to destroy Spinoza's *Tractatus* and restore the reputation of prophets and miracles, as well as the orthodox interpretation of the Bible, to pre-Spinozian condition.[65] The book also attempts to explain several hundred textual contradictions in the Bible that had furnished grain for the mills of atheism. With this effort, entirely Christian, Cuperus' renown as an atheist was made.

Atheists, Cuperus reports, notice that Genesis has God make man in his image, whereas Exodus states no one is similar to God.[66] Leviticus forbids marriage with a sister, a rule violated by Abraham.[67] Matthew relates the visit of the centurion to Christ, but Luke says he only sent some Jews to question Jesus.[68] In Mark there is one angel at the tomb, whereas Luke has two. This difficulty Cuperus avoids by proposing that the two Marys were together when they told Mark and separate when they saw Luke, who assumed that each woman spoke to a different angel.[69] Atheists are,

---

[64] *De Existentia Dei ex Lumine Naturae Cognoscenda* (Helmstadt, 1681), pp. D2–D3v.
[65] Cuperus, pp. 1–139.   [66] P. 144.   [67] P. 154.   [68] P. 168.
[69] P. 172.

Cuperus reports, amused by a God who was so exhausted after six days' work that he had to rest.[70] When they read about the Fall, they inquire about talking serpents (birds can speak), about the reason for the snake's punishment (allegorical), and about the need for eating apples to advance one's sexual education (Adam and Eve may have cohabited before the Fall).[71] These godless scoffers also describe Noah's Flood and Abraham's Sacrifice as pagan myths; [72] they question the justice of a God who preferred the enormous sinner David to the more righteous Saul or who struck a pious man dead because he steadied the falling Ark of the Covenant.[73] Atheists likewise doubt the virgin birth, observe that Jesus was not in the lineage of David unless he was Joseph's son, and wonder why Josephus, who writes at length about Herod, never mentions the slaughter of the innocents.[74] The work concludes dramatically with a dialogue between Philalethes, a Christian, and Misalethes, an agnostic.

Philalethes believes that Nature can teach man about its omnipotent, omniscient, and eternal cause; but Misalethes thinks no idea more absurd than this. All men know hunger and the pangs of sexual desire, but there are American nations with no knowledge of God. In fact, it is obvious that men were long without any idea of God. If this is true, Nature says nothing about its creation. One cannot learn of God from Nature, Misalethes continues, because if God created Nature, he is not in Nature, and if, as the orthodox state, the idea of God is innate, one need not look for it in creatures. He wonders whether or not a man born without senses could learn of God from Nature and asks Philalethes about the knowledge of God in the more intelligent animals. "You cannot teach animals the arts, to work in gold and paint

---

[70] Pp. 177–78.   [71] Pp. 179–80.   [72] Pp. 181–84.   [73] Pp. 187–88.
[74] Pp. 190–93.

pictures." "Ah," responds Misalethes, "man cannot be taught to make wax or honey." He imagines that if animals were provided with hands, they could do many things. "Why then," Philalethes asks cleverly, "are beasts called beasts?" [75]

When Philalethes attempts to prove God's existence by pointing to the beauty, harmony, and order of the world, Misalethes notes that most of the world is unavailable to man, a large part of it hostile to him, and the remainder totally indifferent.[76] He refutes Philalethes' idea that the world must be created because it decays by observing that air and water do not corrupt and that many things simply change into other things and leave part of their essence in their progeny. Philalethes opposes this observation by asking what would happen if all men died in an epidemic or if it was decided to end the human race by killing all women? Misalethes sees no end to Nature in either catastrophe, because other things would spring from the substance of the ruin.

To offset his opponent's obvious advantage, Philalethes suggests that the written history of man proves by its very shortness that creation is recent; but Misalethes thinks it a mistake to assume the world and man coeternal. When Philalethes states that Nature does nothing in vain, he is asked to explain the purpose of rainstorms at sea. Baffled in these efforts to persuade his unbelieving opponent, Philalethes repeats the henological argument of St. Thomas: God is either perfect or imperfect. He cannot be imperfect, so he must be perfect. Since nothing can be perfect without existence, God must exist. This logical gambit, says Misalethes, is pure sophistry. "If you ask me what I understand by God, I do not say 'a perfect being.' I say 'nothing.'" But how would men know about the perfect, Philalethes responds, if they were not informed by a God who was himself perfec-

[75] Pp. 220–23.   [76] P. 224.

tion? "Remove," Misalethes rejoins, "the imperfections from substance. . . . If you remove illness, deformity, stupidity, and similar defects from man, we have a notion of the perfect man. . . . The same rule holds for a dog, a lion, or a louse." [77]

Philalethes now marches out a whole regiment of arguments rationally establishing the existence of God. He marshals the proofs that depend on the hypothesis of the existence of the soul, but his wicked antagonist shows that the same arguments support the immortality of animals and even of plants. Frustrated in this attempt, Philalethes turns to the supernatural testimony of the human conscience; but he is told he must show how this remorseful organ works in men who have never heard of God and have naught to fear from men.[78] His succeeding proof from the ruins of the world, the mountains and deserts, may prove, says Misalethes, that the world had a beginning but not necessarily a creator; [79] and he chides him for always substituting the word "God" for "Nature." With this warning in mind, Philalethes attempts one more divine hypothesis that stems from the visible universe, which is finite in extension and duration and composed of contrary parts, faculties, and operations. He learns, for his argumentative pains, that theories based on the temporal finiteness of the world lead either to an atheistic pantheism or a dualism, that astronomy has eliminated the concept of finite extension, and that a harmony of contraries can arise as easily from Nature as from God. Misalethes, the reader gathers as the debate ends, is not an atheist as he has seemed but rather a fundamental scripturalist and revelationist who wants Philalethes to abandon his crude attempts at a rational theology and depend entirely on revelation.[80]

Misalethes may be sincere in his attempt to demonstrate the irrationality of rational theology; nonetheless, we have

[77] Pp. 227–33.   [78] Pp. 236–37.   [79] Pp. 239–40.   [80] Pp. 242–44.

no difficulty in understanding why his century considered his creator and Campanella atheists. Both apologists were too reasonable in their defences of orthodox Christianity. Their reporting of the other side is too accurate, and, consequently, their tone, in some respects, is not much different from that of the offensive mocker Vanini. Regardless of the piety or impiety of their intent, they emphasize the essential fact: in the demonstration of supernatural religion, the lamp of reason is a flame that destroys, not a light that reveals. Tourneur, the author of the seventeenth-century *The Atheist's Tragedy*, understood this only too well; at the conclusion of his play, when the godless D'Amville, about to execute another, accidentally brains himself with the ax, he has the atheist see in this ill-chance the command of God and the weakness "of natural understanding." Nature and the wisdom of men are subordinate to a "power above." In other words, the atheist must knock his brains out to understand the divine.

Chapter Two

Three Italian Atheists:
Pomponazzi, Cardano, Vanini

∿∿∿∿∿∿∿∿∿∿∿∿∿∿∿∿∿∿∿∿∿∿∿∿∿∿∿∿∿∿∿∿∿∿∿

THE NAMES OF Pomponazzi, Cardano, and Vanini appear in almost every Renaissance polemic against the atheists and their beliefs; they are accused of inciting men to godlessness and are regarded as the banner bearers of God's enemies. Very few of those who attacked them or entered their names on the lists of infamy knew what they really said. There are, of course, careful refutations of some of their dangerous works, but the average Christian who surveyed them with horror would have been tongueless if he were required to report their impious views. The better-informed historians of unbelief proscribe other Italians who rode in the same squadron. Bruno, burned for his doubts, was one of the hussars of hell; and Caesalpino,[1] Cremonini,[2] Poggio, Bembo, Poliziano, Ochino wave their satanic sabers with him. Ma-

---

[1] For a general account of Andrea Caesalpino, see F. Fiorentino, *Studi e Ritratti della Rinascenza* (Bari, 1911), pp. 195–231. His Aristotelianism and the attack on him by Taurellus, which got both philosophers in the wrong, are related by Charbonnel, pp. 100–1, 299–302; Guido de Ruggiero, *Rinascimento, Riforma, e Controriforma* (Bari, 1930), II, 15–16, 23–24, 34–35; and G. Saitta, *Il Pensiero Italiano nell'Umanesimo e nel Rinascimento* (Bologna, 1949–51), II, 226–47.

[2] For Cremonini, Charbonnel's account (pp. 230–74) is certainly the most complete, though Saitta's (*Il Pensiero Italiano*, pp. 422–40) is better at fixing his position in Italian philosophy.

chiavelli is never omitted from the roster, although he is finally redeemed. But the unholy trinity of Pomponazzi, Cardano, and Vanini was known to the least learned of the antiatheists. From the point of view of the historians, it was Pomponazzi who revived the Athenian disease of doubt, Cardano who grew virulent cultures of it, and Vanini who spread the contagion wherever he went.

I

Pietro Pomponazzi, who ended his life as professor of philosophy at Bologna and as the most distinguished of Italian Aristotelians, was educated at Padua, the great university of his generation, where he heard the lectures of Francesco di Nardo, a Thomist. At this university, rational examination of the doctrines that were central to both philosophy and theology, such as that of the immortality of the soul, was revived after two centuries of silence by a coterie of learned and clever men, Paolo Veneto, Tommaso de Vio Cajetan, and Nicoletto Vernia, who, in response to the requests of students, agreed to reconsider the metaphysical speculations of Averroes and St. Thomas. The Platonic answers to some of these problems, sentimental and at times mystical answers, had been sought out and recorded at Florence by Ficino and Pico della Mirandola; but though Pomponazzi knew Plato, [3] it is clear that Platonism was uncongenial to the normal disposition of his thought. Against the Platonic humanism of Florence, the men of Padua set an Aristotelian humanism, which depended, unlike medieval Aristotelianism,

[3] In the *De Immortalitate Animae* (Leyden, 1534), Pomponazzi makes frequent trips to Plato, but he seeks him out mainly for contrast or secondary support; in the *De Naturalium Effectuum Causis sive de Incantationibus* (Basel, 1567), he quotes Plato almost as often as Aristotle and twice as frequently as he does St. Thomas.

on the non-logical texts, newly translated and annotated, and, in the case of Paolo Veneto and Vernia, adjusted to the system of Averroes. Though Pomponazzi can speak disparagingly of Averroes whenever it is a question of Aristotelian truth or Aquinian theology, he is, as Randall wisely observes, a Thomist who was almost an Averroist. "He consistently uses Thomas against the unity of Averroes' position, and Averroes against the separability and immortality of St. Thomas. The naturalism, and he would have said, the Aristotelianism of each he employs against the Platonism of the other." [4] But Pomponazzi was ground between the millstones of the "double truth," [5] and is fully aware of the predicament of the rationalist.

The philosopher is truly a Prometheus, who while he seeks God's secrets is chewed by perpetual cares and notions. He neither hungers nor thirsts; he does not sleep, eat, or spit; he is mocked by all and, finally held both foolish and impious, is persecuted by the inquisitors and made a vulgar spectacle. This is the philosopher's reward and salary; hence he is made

[4] *The Renaissance Philosophy of Man* (Chicago, 1948), pp. 257–79. For works relating to Pomponazzi or his milieu: see E. Renan, *Averroès et l'Averroisme* (Paris, 1882), pp. 322–416; K. Werner, *Scholastik des späteren Mittelalters* (Vienna, 1881–87), IV, 1, 141–48; Pietro Ragnisco, "Nicoletto Vernia, Studi Storico sulla Filosofia Padovana nella Seconda Mèta del Secolo XV," *Atti del Reale Istituto Veneto di Scienze, Lettere et Arti*, XXXVIII (1890–91), 241–308, 617–79; Fiorentino, pp. 3–79; Busson, *Les Sources* (1922), pp. 43–52; E. Cassirer, *Individuum und Kosmos* (Leipzig-Berlin, 1927), pp. 85–87, 108–15, 143–49; A. H. Douglas, *The Philosophy and Psychology of Pietro Pomponazzi* (Cambridge, 1910); M. de Andrea, "Fede e Ragione nel Pensiero del Pomponazzi," *Rivista di Filosofia Neoscolastica*, XXXVIII (1949), 278–97; R. Hönigswald, *Denker der Italienischen Renaissance* (Basel, 1938), pp. 61–90; G. Saitta *Il Pensiero Italiano*, II, 248–324; E. Weil, "Die Philosophie des Pietro Pomponazzi," *Archiv für Geschichte der Philosophie*, XLI (1932), 127–76; Ernst Breit, *Die Engel und Dämonlehre des Pomponatius und des Cäsalpinus* (Bonn, 1912).

[5] W. Betzendorfer, *Die Lehre von der Zweifachen Wahrheit bei Petrus Pomponazzi* (Tübingen, 1919).

the butt of poets as Socrates supplied topic and matter for Aristophanes and all philosophers for witty Lucian.[6]

In spite of this lament on the fate of philosophers, Pomponazzi found a noble explanation of man, whom he defined as of a nature "not simple but multiple, not certain but ambiguous, a mean between mortal and immortal." [7]

Pomponazzi printed his *De Immortalitate Animae* in 1516; and, when this book was attacked,[8] his *Apologia* (1518) [9]

[6] *De Fato, de Libero Arbitrio et de Praedestine*, ed. R. Lemay (Verona, 1957), p. 262.

[7] "Hominem scilicet non simplicis sed multiplicis, non certae sed ancipitis naturae esse, mediumque inter mortalia et immortalia collocari." *De Immortalitate Animae*, p. 5. A modern edition of this work by Gianfranco Morra was printed at Bologna in 1954; a facsimile and English rendering by W. H. Hay was published at Haverford, Pa., in 1938.

[8] P. O. Kristeller, "Two Unpublished Questions on the Soul of Pietro Pomponazzi," *Medievalia et Humanistica*, VIII (1955), 76–84; the same scholar's "The Theory of Immortality in Marsilio Ficino," *JHI*, I (1940), 299–319, admirably presents the counterdoctrine of Florence. The minor works of Pomponazzi are listed by Morra in his edition (pp. 17–19); his commentary on Aristotle's *De Anima* was edited by L. Ferri and printed at Rome in 1877.

[9] This work was written after the *De Immortalitate Animae* was burned at Venice and its author charged with heresy, a judgment in which Pope Leo X did not concur. He is thought, however, to have encouraged the subsequent controversy between Pomponazzi and Nifo. In the *Apologia*, Pomponazzi took up the arguments of his opponents point by point; he paid particular attention to those of Gasparo Contarini's *De Immortalitate Animae adversus Petrum Pomponatium*, which was written in 1517 and attempts to demolish fifteen arguments of Aristotle and Averroes: see *Opera* (Paris, 1571), pp. 179–231. Probably the best attack on Pomponazzi's views is found in A. Sirmond, *De Immortalitate Animae Demonstratio Physico et Aristotelica adversus Pomponatium et Asseclas* (Paris, 1635), which is analyzed by L. Blanchet in "L'Attitude Religieuse des Jesuits et les Sources du Pari de Pascal," *Revue de Metaphysique et de Moral*, XXVI (1919), 477–516, 617–47. For some seventeenth-century comments on Pomponazzi see J. de Silhon, *De l'Immortalité de l'Âme* (Paris, 1634), pp. 47–48; C. Cotin, *Traité de l'Âme Immortelle* (Paris, 1655), pp. 143–145; J. B. du Hamel, *De Mente Humana* (Paris, 1677), pp. 535–37, Pierre Huet, *Alnetaneae Quaestiones* (Paris, 1690), p. 49; and N. Malebranche, *De la Recherche de la Vérité*, ed. G. Lyon (Paris, 1925), p. 97.

and *Defensorium* (1519).[10] Two other of his works, *De Naturalium Effectuum Causis sive de Incantationibus* and *De Fato*, were widely read in manuscript but remained unpublished until the mid-century. The three philosophical treatises represent Pomponazzi's sincere attempt to supply the Christian world with a rational theology, but they succeeded mainly in arousing the resentment of orthodox theologians of all creeds. In them he attempts but fails to demonstrate the natural truth of the Christian doctrines of Providence, free will, and human immortality. Although he is aware of his hopeless task, Pomponazzi attempts, as he skates on the edge of rationalism, to redeem himself by bowing to the two greater champions of theology, tradition, and revelation.[11] The masters of apologetics refused his apologies; and his former student, Paolo Giovio, the humanist journalist and gossiper, after praising his professor with one pen writes with another of his doctrines which led "to the corruption of young men and the destruction of Christian discipline."[12]

Giovio's condemnation of Pomponazzi for his rational investigation of the doctrine of immortality was almost anticipated by Pomponazzi. He explains in the preface to the *De Immortalitate Animae* that he wrote the book at the request of an old student, Brother Hieronymous of Ragusa, who came to visit him and to remind him that once he had said the proofs of St. Thomas on immortality were inconsistent with Aristotle's disquisitions on the soul. He now asked his former professor what he, "leaving aside revelation and miracles, and remaining entirely within natural limits," thought about the matter and what Aristotle said on the subject.

[10] In this book, Pomponazzi replied to Agostino Nifo's *De Immortalitate Humanae Animae adversus Petrum Pomponacium*, (Venice, 1518).
[11] See *De Immortalitate Animae*, chap. XV.
[12] *Elogia Doctorum Virorum* (Antwerp, 1557), p. 154.

And I, when I saw that all there were filled with the same great desire—and there were many present—then I said to him: "Dear son, and you others, it is not a small thing you ask, indeed, for it is a most profound task upon which almost all famous philosophers have labored. However, since you ask only what I think, which is something I can answer, it is easy to make this known, and I gladly comply. Whether things are as I think, you must take counsel with more skilled men. Under the guidance of God, I proceed to the matter." [13]

After he has cleared away the opinions of Averroes, Themistius, and Plato, expounding their doctrines in one chapter and rejecting them in the next, Pomponazzi comes to St. Thomas, whose concepts of the unity of the intellect and the sensitive soul he presents most respectfully. "Concerning the truth of this position I have no doubts, since the canonical Scriptures, which are preferable to any reasoning and to human experience because they were given by God, hallow this doctrine." [14] Pomponazzi must first face three arguments for immateriality, which must be dissolved or established. Cardinal among these propositions was the assumed ability of the intellect to receive the forms of material things.[15] To this concept Pomponazzi responds that the vegetative soul does function "materialiter" (but this is not always true of the sensitive soul),[16] that it is not necessary for the soul to be independent of matter to apprehend it, and that it is only as the mind is receptive of sensible objects is it capable of thought. A second argument was based on the ability of the mind to abstract and to understand immateriality. Pomponazzi disposes of this notion by pointing out that all general concepts are drawn from particulars, or, in other words, from sense perceptions. The last argument, that the soul's ability to inspect itself proves its im-

[13] P. 5.   [14] P. 35.   [15] P. 32.   [16] P. 36.

mortality, is easy to turn aside. The human mind, says Pomponazzi, is incapable of perfect self-knowledge, of what might be called direct or intuitive knowledge of self. This is a power possessed only by higher beings. Man knows himself only through particular experience; he knows himself only in that he knows something else.[17] The soul is, then, mortal by nature and immortal only in the sense that it is endowed with intelligence and will, which are capable of knowing discursively, not intuitively, the universal.[18] Here Pomponazzi takes issue with St. Thomas and states that the soul is generated, not created; hence, the fluttering little creature is intermediate between the higher intelligences and the animals below. It is unable to think without images and cannot exercise its functions without a body. At best, it is a "halfway" creature, comprehending the universal but knowing it only in terms of the particular.[19] This conclusion provides Pomponazzi with a psychical motto: the soul is unqualifiedly material and relatively immaterial. "Simpliciter materiale et secundum quid immateriale." [20]

If the soul is mortal from a philosopher's point of view, ordinary man has some immediate problems.[21] It could be said that, having lost his immortality, man is without ultimate end and immediate happiness. For Pomponazzi, this is pure nonsense. Everything has an end that suits its nature. Happiness really depends on the degree of individual receptivity and the intensity of experience. He finds equally unphilosophical the contention that without heavenly rewards men would abandon their unselfish ideals on which the safety of the commonwealth depends. The valor of soulless animals shows the falsity of this notion; moreover, Pomponazzi writes, patriotic valor is actually self-interest. One helps himself in helping others. Reward and punishment, then, cling to virtue

---

[17] Pp. 75–78.   [18] Pp. 56–59.   [19] Pp. 67–70.   [20] Pp. 75–76.
[21] See chaps. XIII and XIV.

and vice as intrinsic qualities. In the same vein, Pomponazzi swiftly rejects ghostly apparition as a proof of immortality. Hauntings are simply charnal-house vapors shaped by ignorant imagination. Demonic prophecy and oracles, likewise, do not demonstrate a hereafter; they are more likely the ravings of the sick or the mad than divine tongues speaking.

Pomponazzi has to face the statistics of the public pollster, who was first invented by theologians. The results of the *consensus gentium* showed that with the exception of "dastardly" Epicurus, "infamous" Aristippus, "mad" Lucretius, "atheistic" Diagoras, and the "Epicurean beast" Sardanapalus, most men and all religions believed the soul immortal. Pomponazzi first opposes this electoral landslide by remembering an extensive number of decent and pious ancients who had practically no confidence in the post-mortem existence of the individual soul. Then he looked at the faceless majority and wrote, "It is likely that the whole world is deceived in this common idea of immortality, for if we assume that there are three major religions—Christ's, Moses', and Mohammed's—either all of them are false and the whole world is cheated or two are wrong and the greater part of mankind is deceived." [22] This easy arithmetical calculation shocked the literate Christian world and secured Pomponazzi's election of the society of atheists; it also got him mentioned as the author of the *De Tribus Impostoribus*, the atheists' bill of rights, which was probably written about two centuries after he was dead. Pomponazzi's religion was truly pragmatic; and, as a consequence, holding that most men are without virtue and kept honest only through fear of punishment, he took the altruistic side of the Machiavellian notion, writing that "the governor, seeing the inclination of men to

[22] P. 123. "Supposito quod sint tantum tres leges, scilicet Christi, Moysis, et Mahumethi: Aut igitur omnes sunt falsae, et sic totus mundus est deceptus, aut saltem duae earum, et sic maior pars est decepta."

evil and wishing the good of all, decreed that the soul is immortal." [23] The fact that the theory of immortality is legislated, and not revealed, does not make Pomponazzi a hedonist; pleasure is all right, but unless one would prefer to herd with Circe's flock, virtue is man's true end.[24]

In the last chapter of the *De Immortalitate Animae*, Pomponazzi, who may have invented fideism, draws back from philosophy and assumes the robes of Christian skepticism. The doctrine of immortality, as that of the eternity of the world, is a neutral doctrine which cannot be approved or abandoned. In matters of this nature, God alone has certainty. There is no question that man, who is not God and who is faced with living properly, needs further assurance. If his soul is immortal, he should despise temporal matters and seek eternal rewards; if this is not the case, he ought to suck life dry of pleasure. Thanks, however, to the Incarnation and its attendant Grace, man has been made sure, and these doctrines are now articles of faith, established by revelation and Scripture. Philosophical objections as well as philosophical proofs are foreign to the problem; hence philosophers are always wrangling and coming to no determination; whereas Christians, who can march to proper conclusions by infallible logic, are always in full agreement. After spreading out this safety net, Pomponazzi leaves this theological trapeze with philosophical grace. The grace of this backflip did not exactly save him.[25] In his *Apologia*, he remembers the Lenten sermons preached in Mantua by Ambrose of Naples, who attacked him for impiety and heresy be-

---

[23] P. 124.   [24] P. 141.

[25] Pierre Viret has Christians like Pomponazzi in mind when he complains in his *Exposition* (p. 896) that there are not two truths but only one. Girolamo Dandini calls it a scandal that a Christian would say the soul was immortal in the eyes of faith, but mortal philosophically. *De Corpore Animato* (Paris, 1611), col. 1832.

cause he did not believe in immortality or the resurrection of the body. Pomponazzi insisted that he stood ready to die for the doctrine of immortality because it was revealed by God and not found "through the light of reason." Unfortunately, his bad luck on this philosophical excursion did not keep him from similar outings.

In the *De Immortalitate Animae*, Pomponazzi glides over the question of Providence; in the *De Fato*, he surrounds it with a philosophical fence and studies it as an intellectual surveyor might. As a good Christian he believes in authoritative texts, and he finds one in Alexander Aphrodisias, a revered commentator on Aristotle, who had written that Nature and Fate were the same. "Ut idem fatum et natura sint." [26] With similar good reason, the same philosopher had doubted the freedom of the will. "We may seem to have a choice," he says, "but in making a decision, we are always influenced by its opposites." If this is true, Pomponazzi concludes, all actions are necessitated [27] and volition does not exist. There is also the very mortal fact that men, who are second causes, cannot move without a mover; hence, as individuals, they cannot be said to have free will.[28] One might also inquire whether or not it is reasonable to assume that the creatures of an all-ruling and omnipotent God have liberty. Or granting God to be omniscient, we may wonder whether man's knowledge derives immediately from the object or the event and not from the fact that God gives to all things what they are.[29] These are questions that the philosopher must escort from the seminary and examine later in the academy.

If we assume, as Alexander does, that Providence is the subject of necessity, writes Pomponazzi, then all human actions, virtuous and vicious alike, are out of human con-

[26] P. 13.   [27] Pp. 53–54.   [28] Pp. 59–60.   [29] P. 68.

trol; [30] therefore, neither merit nor disgrace can be attached to anything done by man.[31] "Non ex meritis sed ex ipso fato." If we are pious or otherwise, we can only be praised or blamed in that we are Fate's children.[32] There are, of course, occasions when we think that we are the subjects of accidental causes because the sequence of orderly cause and effect appears to be broken; but this is an illusion, demonstrating our inability to recognize true causes.[33] The iron cord of causation greatly disturbs Pomponazzi; he would like to believe that man can ascertain the causes of events and accept responsibility for them, but he knows this belief to be philosophical nonsense. The sense of nonsense arises from his equally strong conviction that no one can distinguish between natural and voluntary causes. Our inability to discriminate is the heart of the orthodox doctrine of free will. We waver in all our choices, and this uncertainty is for us intellectual liberty, but really it is only a manifestation of human perplexity. Hence, if Providence is necessity and man has no choice, man is also without responsibility.[34]

Though matters seem to be beyond the control of man, it is clear from experience that man goes more readily toward good than evil, and this might seem to be God's will; but second thought informs us the world is good and, in a universal sense, so is man. What we call "good" and "evil" are really proofs of a universal diversity that proclaims the existence of a divinity. Observing our fellows, we find some to be like gods, some like domestic animals, some like snakes and lions, and some as inert as stones. All of this simply fits together to make the great argument from variety; in no sense does it suggest a defective divinity. In this fashion Pomponazzi turns his back on the problem of evil, but he hardly makes his orthodox readers cheerful.[35]

---

[30] Pp. 69–73.   [31] Pp. 78–80.   [32] P. 81.   [33] P. 100.
[34] Pp. 103–7.   [35] Pp. 126–29.

It has been observed that the Aristotelian of the *De Immortalitate Animae* has become in the *De Fato* a kind of Neo-Stoic. The steel scepter of necessity rules all; and though in particular events this rule may seem a tyranny eventuating in the unjust and inequitable, this is not the case when events are universally valued. So all things work together for good, but Pomponazzi is not St. Paul. Man is the instrument of this great Fate and, moreover, he is a determined instrument. He thinks he makes choices, and to others he often appears to make them, but actually he is in the grip of circumstance.[36] Once again Pomponazzi knows he has walked out of the Church, but he admits he finds his deductions more reasonable than the rationalizations of the Scholastics.[37] But the time has come for him to buckle on the armor of the Christian warrior.

"If we wish to speak about Necessity in natural terms, no course seems to me more certain than this that we lean on the wisdom of God, which makes us absolutely certain and clears us of all error." [38] Let us then accept the Christian position on free will as a premise of philosophy. To establish this proposal, Pomponazzi is forced to posit a separation of will and intellect, which makes it possible for the unnecessitated will to make independent choices. Under ideal circumstances, he thinks, it will never make an evil decision; but, once again, experience shows how often the contrary is true. All that Pomponazzi can garner from this fact is that the will is sometimes the victim of an illusion which makes the worse seem the better reason.[39] He is well aware at this point that he is talking neither logic nor philosophy and tries to avoid the deadfall by inventing three classes of voluntary action: that which is willing and pleasing; that which is non-willing and displeasing; and that which is pure non-willing, a suspension of act. The last class can be further

[36] P. 196.   [37] P. 208.   [38] P. 221.   [39] Pp. 254–59.

qualified into good acts, suspending what ought to be suspended, and bad acts, suspending what ought to be achieved.[40] With this we have made with Pomponazzi a turn of the moral roundabout. It was, however, his way of showing that the Christian God, unlike the philosophers' God, is not the cause of evil.

It is now plain that in philosophy, or within the limits of the natural reason, the soul is not immortal; and, Providence and Fate being synonyms, the will is not free, and moral judgments are, consequently, absurd. With these problems settled, Pomponazzi turned to an inspection of the empirical universe, and his findings furnish the text of the *De Incantationibus*. This book was written in response to the inquiries of a Paduan physician who had witnessed cures effected by words and charms ("verbis et carminibus"). The physician wondered how an Aristotelian who did not believe in demons or miracles would explain the cures.[41] The fact that his correspondent could testify personally to these miracles is of great importance to Pomponazzi, who put his trust in the bright noun *experience* and constantly uses expressions like "Let us depend on experience" or "We know from frequent experience." [42] Not all experience, he insisted, is the same; thus man, using the superb Aristotelian tool of dialectics, must practice discrimination. Many events, seemingly beyond credit, are supported by high authority; hence, the sound philosopher must not accept them as extranatural but seek a rational explanation for each happening. Pomponazzi is aware that some of these events are fictions invented for fraudulent reasons,[43] or, in the case of certain biblical narratives, literal covers of spiritual truth.[44] When

[40] P. 279.
[41] *De Incantationibus*, p. 1. One man was cured of burns, another of a sword cut, and the third of erysipelas.
[42] P. 170.   [43] Pp. 113–15; see also pp. 43, 146, 297.
[44] Pp. 268–70.

we are sure the event occurred, we should look for its cause in the orderly processes of Nature.

The purpose of the *De Incantationibus* is the scrutinization of all happenings normally ascribed to the services of angels or the agency of demons. In the *De Immortalitate Animae*,[45] Pomponazzi had cast doubt on the ministrations of these creatures; in this book, he repeats his uncertainty again and again.[46] A reasonable son of Aristotle, he writes, can no more believe in the intervention in human affairs of these spiritual beings than he can subscribe to immortality.[47] To wonder at the marvelous is, in Pomponazzi's estimation, a characteristic of the ignorant who lack the intellectual power to entertain high concepts of either God or Nature. His previous observations and conclusions aid him now. If God is the Prime Mover and the world is ruled by a fatal necessity,[48] then miracles *qua* miracles are completely unthinkable. Hence all miracles must be looked into from the vantage point of reason, because Nature acts from time to time in a manner that men would call either angelic or daemonic.[49]

In spite of his exceptional emphasis on reason, Pomponazzi could not escape his intellectual environment. He lived in an age that believed in occult powers. Like most of his contemporaries, he assumed that animals, vegetables, and minerals had secret virtues which produced natural results. There were stones and plants which made rain and others which caused drought.[50] Animals foretold coming events; precious stones warned their owners; statues sweated to disclose some secret.[51] One should observe bird flight to anticipate good or evil.[52] The charms that induce or banish love may possibly do just that, and, like Burton, Pomponazzi found them no stranger than the natural causes of the sweet passion.[53] He

---

[45] P. 128.   [46] Pp. 131, 198, 230.   [47] Pp. 298–300.   [48] Pp. 200–1.
[49] Pp. 318–27.   [50] P. 24.   [51] Pp. 144–46.   [52] P. 170.
[53] Pp. 178, 181, 189–91.

thought, too, that reports on aery armies [54] and specters [55] should be seriously scrutinized, that it was absurd not to seek for natural explanations of unnatural events.[56] Actually, he found most of these happenings perfectly natural; they seem miraculous because they happen less often than other things. "Non secundum communem naturae cursum, sed in longissimis periodis." [57]

In keeping with his conviction that creatures have secret but natural powers, and in accord with the accepted cosmology of his age, Pomponazzi nominates the stars as the real servants of necessity. The astral bodies see to it that nothing unnatural occurs in Nature, for they are not only the efficient causes of things, but also in the disposition of creatures, the material causes, too.[58] Pomponazzi is least an Averroist —he knows the imputations of Averroes against astrology [59] —when he defends the stellar influences against those who doubt them. His indignation rises when anyone makes fun of the stars, "the most efficacious of Intelligences." [60] These forces are for him so potent and so universal that he finds it impossible to understand those who prefer to them the alleged powers of angels and demons,[61] whose virtues, if any, are only locally effective.[62] Behind the backdrop of Nature are the heavenly bodies, governing the great universal machine and enforcing natural laws. When Pomponazzi explains unnatural events by pointing to the ineluctable powers of the planets, he is not talking as a judicial astrologer but more like a modern scientist who hopes by his hypothesis to bring strange occurrences into a natural order. It seems highly absurd to him that prayerful men, who subscribe to

[54] Pp. 159–60.
[55] Pp. 161–69. Pomponazzi does not believe in real apparitions, though he seems to believe in necromancy, "ex artificio, sive hominum ingenio." He admits that if one could prove the immortality of the soul, the dead might be called forth.
[56] P. 115.   [57] P. 204.   [58] P. 210.   [59] Pp. 266–67.
[60] P. 120.   [61] P. 303.   [62] P. 306.

the doctrine of a special Providence, are always asking for divine intervention; for him there is only an absolute and unalterable Providence based on the stars.[63] *Star* is for Pomponazzi the philosophical and theological equivalent of *God, gods, Nature,* and *Fate;* and the whole process, as witnessed by man, is one of cause and effect.[64] He illustrates this causal sequence by describing how stellar influence will make a raven flee its accustomed nest and so warn men of impending disaster.[65] But men will still turn to prayer in order to forfend trouble or seek benefits.

If one asked Pomponazzi about the value of prayer, he would probably say that it resided to some degree in the peculiar personal powers, an "ex dono coeli," of the one who prays.[66] On second thought, he might abandon this quasi-astrological thesis and propose that, though the will of God is not changed by prayer, the act is an intrinsic part of its own fulfillment and in complete accord with the divinely predestined arrangement of events.[67] One must not think of prayer as necessary to its seeming result; it is by no means a determinate cause of whatever happens, but rather a necessary moment in a chain of events.[68] Here, as in the case of Providence or of immortality, Pomponazzi is halted again by theology in his philosophical speculation. Prayers, even unanswered ones, are part of the divine plan; they are good for man, especially when he prays for something of benefit to all men.[69] His comments on this aspect of the order of piety, though essentially noble, lead toward an astrological and revolutionary disquisition on religion itself.

The stars, Pomponazzi writes, that gave their forces to the name of Jupiter still hold their place in the sky and provide the same prepotency to the names of Jesus and the saints.[70] The identical stars, as a matter of fact, are responsible

[63] Pp. 157–60.   [64] Pp. 168–70.   [65] P. 169.   [66] Pp. 271–72.
[67] Pp. 244–45.   [68] P. 244.   [69] Pp. 248–50.   [70] Pp. 286–93.

for the prodigies that attended the births of Alexander and Christ.[71] All of these heroes were especially endowed by the stars and had as a birth gift from them a particular *deitas*. These leaders also were enabled to bestow their inherent powers on their chosen successors. He does not know how this was done; but he thinks that just as a piece of iron may become a magnet by being touched by a magnet, so Jesus transferred his special powers to Peter and John.[72] These men are also what he calls "wards" of the skies, because there is little doubt in his mind that the stars watch over important men more carefully than over unimportant ones. They also pay more attention to nations than to individuals. One must, however, remember with tolerance that the stars serve all religions and all religious leaders. Moses, Christ, Mohammed, and even the pagan priests are equally blessed by the heavenly bodies that serve the will of Fate. As a result of this service, religions rise, reach an apogee, and decline.[73] This statement was remembered and held against Pomponazzi as a sure sign of his atheism, but he went beyond it.

The Christian religion—he does not write as specifically as this—has endured for a long time, and men are inclined to think that it began with the beginning of things and will continue forever. "Quare existimatur sic semper fuisse, et in aeternum duratura." [74] But no religion is any more permanent than a political philosophy. Some religions are, indeed, far nobler and consequently more lasting than others; but in the due course of time, all religions change, decay, and wither away.[75] There is, Pomponazzi thinks, an undulation, a rise and fall, in the history of all human institutions; therefore, Christianity, resembling in its origins and evolution its spiritual predecessors, must eventually bow to this law. All

[71] P. 169.   [72] P. 284.   [73] Pp. 291–94.   [74] P. 286.
[75] Pp. 292–93.

religions pass through changes and cycles. "There will not be one which has not been; there has not been one that shall not be." [76] At what point on the wheel of eternal recurrence is Christianity? There is no doubt, Pomponazzi decides, that the Christian Church is dying.[77] It is not surprising to discover that the book in which all of this is said so trenchantly was brought into port by the ecclesiastical patrols and kept innocuously in the haven of the *Index Expurgatorius*. However, it sailed about a good bit before it was docked by the clergy and vexed good men like the famous witch hunter, Martin del Rio.

I am certainly amazed that Pomponazzi's *De Incantationibus* was so long tolerated by the Church and is now just recently and with full merit condemned in the *Index*. In truth, Anthony of Mirandola was right when he wrote that Pomponazzi showed himself neither a good philosopher nor, what is much worse, a good Christian when he ascribes all miracles to the influence of the stars and proposes that all religions and laws together with their propounders depend on them. This is, indeed, straightforward impiety.[78]

II

In his *De Libris Propriis*, Girolamo Cardano [79] informs us that he has written books in the fields of dialectics, geometry, arithmetic, music, astrology, optics, agriculture, architecture, geography, medicine, natural philosophy, magic, the inter-

---

[76] P. 290.   [77] P. 286.
[78] *Disquisitionum Magicarum Libri Sex* (Mainz, 1624), p. 10.
[79] For Cardano see J. Crossley, *The Life and Times of Cardano* (London, 1836); H. Morley, *The Life of G. Cardano of Milan* (London, 1854); A. Bellini, *Gerolamo Cardano e il Suo Tempo* (Milan, 1947); James Eckman, *Jerome Cardan* (Baltimore, 1946); and Saitta, *Il Pensiero Italiano*, II, 202–26.

pretation of dreams, politics, theology, and ethics.[80] Today, this statement, might be regarded as immodest even if it were made by an academic; but we have only to turn to a few of Cardano's major books—*De Sapientia* (1554), *De Subtilitate* (1550), and *De Rerum Varietate* (1557)—to discover how very much he knew of ancient wisdom, of cosmology, and of the natural sciences. By inclination a polymath but by profession a physician, he liked to think of his craft as a branch of philosophy, because "it is not deceptive and does not base itself on opinions but on reason which is the eternal law of nature." [81] Some of this confidence comes out in his *Contradicentium Medicorum Liber,* where he complains that the theories of Galen still dominate medicine and that his colleagues depend more on their rhetorical elegance than on experience. "I have had the custom of observing everything, for I hold that nothing happens by chance in nature. As a result of this notion, I am richer in scientific discoveries than I am in denari." [82] We can imagine, too, that comments of this nature did not make Cardano richer in medical friendships.

It must, however, be admitted that in spite of his learning and his often able ideas—he was, for example, one of the first to argue that not everything was made for man and that flies could have been made for themselves [83]—he was often confused and contradictory. This is, of course, one of the penalties paid by the voluminous philosopher, but Cardano was also one of the earliest of autobiographers. He wrote two books about himself, the *De Vita Propria* and the *De Consolatione,* in which he revealed his habits, thoughts, and experiences with a frankness that may have charmed some readers but armed the hunters of atheists. The contents of these books almost justify J. C. Scaliger's observation that

---

[80] *Opera Omnia,* ed. J. Spon (Lyons, 1663), I, 142.
[81] I, 8.   [82] VI, 795–96.   [83] III, 549–50.

Cardano was "a learned man with a child's mind"; but Scaliger, who set down a thousand other objections to Cardano in his pettifogging *Exotericarum Exercitationum Liber XV de Subtilitate*, did this learned child no favor when he devoted a large section of this work to Cardano's views on immortality.[84] Scaliger's readers would probably not remember the multitude of defects he found in Cardano's book, but his accusation of atheism had wings and nested in men's minds; and though Cardano printed a mild and kindly reply, *Actio in Calumniatorem* (1560), Scaliger's implications were of the sort that denial only verified.

For most humanists, the tomb was the strongest bulwark against envious malice; yet even when Cardano was dead, Scaliger did not soften his attack but complained of Cardano's "impious vanity" and pointed to his horoscope of Christ as its token.[85] It is impossible to understand this hatred; but Scaliger was joined in it by Del Rio, who had attacked demons and philosophers and who now warned Christendom against "those snakes in the grass," the *De Subtilitate* and the *De Rerum Varietate*.[86] Marin Mersenne also struck his solid blow by nominating the dead Cardano as author of the *De Tribus Impostoribus* and by discovering from a debate between a pagan, Christian, Jew, and Mohammedan reported in the *De Subtilitate* a further proof of its author's atheism.[87] "He does not give the victory to the Christian or grant more merit to his arguments than to those of others." [88] Out of such small matters, slips of the pen, the seventeenth century

---

[84] (Frankfort, 1612), pp. 918–97.

[85] I, 14. For the horoscope of Christ see V, 221–22. Cardano thinks that Christ was born six years after a great conjunction in Aries; and though he has God decorate the heavens for the occasion, it can be hardly said that Cardano attributes Christ's career to the stars.

[86] P. 8.   [87] III, 551–52.

[88] *Quaestiones*, cols. 15–16, 1829–30. For Mersenne on astrologers see R. Lenoble, *Mersenne ou la Naissance du Mécanisme* (Paris, 1943), pp. 109–34.

could make fervent anti-Christians. The French historian, De Thou, describes the death of Cardano in his annals and signalizes him as the astrologer who drew up and interpreted the horoscope of Jesus Christ. Our indulgence is begged for this impiety because it is clear that Cardano was "very mad." [89] Eccentric, odd, a genius—these are the usual adjectives. But an atheist, according to the Christian orthodox, always dies badly, so Cardano lost his mind. It is on the grounds of eccentricity or mindlessness that later foes of atheism sometimes offered pardon to this curious Italian scholar.

The philosophical indiscretions of Cardano brought his imprisonment in 1570 by the Inquisition; but he says nothing about this in his *De Vita Propria*, which presents us with an account of a man of superstitious religiosity. Offered an appointment in Denmark during a period of poverty, Cardano declined it because, as he tells us, he feared he might be forced to abjure his Catholic faith.[90] In another part of his autobiography, he describes his daily thanks to God for blessings and for admonitory corrections; and he thinks of his book on the immortality of the soul, a book that branded him with godless infamy, as a solid witness to his personal piety and religious devotion. To this childlike evaluation, he adds innocently, "It is also not out of accord with Plato, Aristotle, Plotinus, or reason." "Platoni, et Aristoteli, atque Plotino consentanea, et rationi et institutioni me dixisse reor." [91] This is the sort of naïve addendum, the saying-too-muchness, that revealed to sagaciously pious men like Voetius the grave spiritual maculations on Cardano's mind. But no matter what one can say in Cardano's behalf, one must admit that his remarks on the nature of the supernatural are, indeed, confusing.

[89] *Historia Sui Temporis* (Orleans, 1626), III, 136.
[90] I, 4.   [91] I, 15.

Though clearly believing in extranatural events which he experienced, Cardano, like Pomponazzi, sometimes ascribes the supernatural experiences of others to hallucination or to natural causes either carelessly observed or improperly understood.[92] It is not for him to deny the existence of demons, but he considers most stories of demonic possession as the clear products of hysterical imaginations.[93] As a consequence of this belief, he explains the story of the demonic possession of the children in a Roman orphanage as a case of mass hysteria.[94] When a certain Margaretta of the Porta Nuova thought she heard the devil speaking, Cardano put her hallucination down as a ventriloquist's practical joke.[95] His own experiences were otherwise. He made a great deal of the admonitory and instructional dreams that came to him, and his *Synesium Somniorum Libri IV* is largely devoted to relating and interpreting his dreams and those of others. Cardano was also inclined to see mystery or portentousness in events most men of his age regarded as ordinary happenings.[96] He writes in the *De Vita Propria* about ghostly knocking on his walls, about the shaking of the bedchamber at his mother's death,[97] and about the cornice that fell as soon as he decided not to walk beneath it.[98] Voices spoke to him from the air, and a light buzzing possessed his body.[99] His flesh breathed forth a sulphuric odor,[100] and he was always fleeing malefic forces.[101] He wrote all of his books in Latin, but he had learned the language by miracle; for, having purchased the writings of Apuleius because he admired the binding, he found on opening the book, without learning a single declension, that Latin was his language. One is not

[92] III, 292.
[93] III, 325–27. In the *De Vita Propria* (I, 25), he tells about the time he was asked to subscribe to a petition in behalf of a possessed woman whose advocates attempted to convince him that demons did not exist. "All these men got was a bad reputation with me."
[94] III, 281.   [95] III, 299.   [96] X, 462–64.   [97] I, 36–37.
[98] I, 18–20.   [99] X, 469; III, 305.   [100] I, 28.   [101] I, 3, 17.

surprised that he can ask in amazement: "Who was he who sold me that copy of Apuleius when I was less than twenty and then vanished? I, who had up to that time been but once in grammar school and had no Latin, foolishly bought the book for its gilding, and the next day I found myself as proficient in Latin as now I am." [102]

It is also not unusual, in an age when it was impious to doubt the influence of the stars and equally impious to predict the future by them, that a man of Cardano's strong love of the occult would give quantities of time and ink to the grave science of astrology. In his *De Libris Propriis*, he defines astrology as the science enabling man to understand the marriage of Heaven and Earth, [103] but he made it a marriage of convenience. The theologians said the stars moved and shed their influence for the benefit of the earth, but Cardano, no teleologist, held that the skies moved themselves for their own conservation. The heavens were, he thought, too noble to be servants; nonetheless, he wrote a half-dozen books, besides his great commentary on Ptolemy, to explain the influence of celestial motion on the actions of men and the phenomena of this world. In the *Duodecim Geniturarum*, he parades the personal qualities he owed to the stars and discovers that all the great moments of his life occurred when the moon, a planet he saw whenever he looked into the sky, was in one exact position. [104] Pomponazzi might have criticized some of these astrological notions of Cardano, but he would probably have accepted his disciple's theories about the influence of stars on religion.

When Cardano reread the history of the influence of the heavens, he discovered that Judaism emerged in the East when Saturn, a cold and dry planet, dominated the sky of

---

[102] I, 38. The question of miracles bothers Cardano (III, 294–97), who admits that a true one is rare.
[103] I, 144.   [104] V, 523–27.

Palestine. Christianity, on the other hand, owes its being to a benign and favorable conjunction of Jupiter and Mercury. The brutal cult of Mohammed evolved under a dominant conjunction of the sun and Mars; consequently, it is a religion without mercy, impious and cruel. Paganism—to go back to the beginning of things—is the product of a conjunction of Mars and the moon; hence it is violent and lunatic. By keeping his head high and his eyes on the stars, Cardano explains why Christianity and Mohammedanism have caught on in the parts of the world they dominate; [105] in fact, when he found there was a conjunction of Mars and Mercury with Jupiter in Aries in 1533, he no longer had any trouble understanding Henry VIII and the English schism.[106]

The books of Cardano are filled with pious utterance and religious veneration, but his real feelings are hard to ascertain. In the *De Sapientia,* he discusses theological matters on both pagan and Christian levels, but he slips from one plane to another so quickly that one is pressed to know whether he is now a Christian or a pagan. Religion, he states with a coolness of prose that would make Machiavelli shiver, is of the highest importance to those who govern; in fact, there has been no successful state without one. A false religion, consequently, is better than none.[107] In the same volume, he advises kings against allowing too much power to the church because, religion having great authority among the plebeians, an unbridled priesthood can be politically dangerous.[108] The doctrine of immortality also has for him a political utility. No sensible person, he states, will take the risk of saying whether there is an afterlife or not, but it is his impression that people who believe in immortality are happier than those who do not.[109] If civil contentment and a theory of post-mortem existence are concomitants, then there should be a

---

[105] V, 188–90.   [106] V, 210–11.   [107] I, 498.   [108] I, 540.
[109] I, 498.

government bureau for the propagation of the theory. On all these ticklish questions, he advises, the wise man keeps his true opinions to himself and approves openly what the public believes. "Sed tamen omnes sapientes, etiam si id non credant, vulgo plaudant." [110]

We may get the impression from Ciceronian remarks of this nature that Cardano is not so much a child as a cynic. Actually, he was a Christian skeptic with no great confidence in men's reason or emotions. "We know," he wrote, "that we are in the world, but now who is going to dare to say how we got here or why?" [111] Any knowledge we acquire during our short stay in this world is, he thinks, very, very finite, because finite is what we are. [112] We must not think from these comments that we are in the lecture hall of an anti-intellectual; Cardano never really doubts the importance of human reason. He wants man simply to correct his reason by experience, for experience is "of all proofs the most potent. [113] Authority, the idol of priest-dominated common people, is the weakest of evidences. Actually, Cardano was himself something of an authoritarian, but he also praised those "who abandon Aristotle and Galen for the sake of truth." [114] Belief is another matter. He always walks with care and talks behind his hand about belief, saying in the *Politices* that faith is easy when man is finally united with God; [115] but this is riding a long journey to avoid quicksand, and we are, perhaps, nearer the heart of the matter when he defines "faith," in the *De Rerum Varietate*,[116] as "the sleep of the mind" and states that the more a man thinks, the less he is likely to have faith. This book put Cardano in the prison of the Inquisition, so one can imagine what the clergy thought about this theological observation.

---

[110] I, 550.   [111] X, 3.   [112] X, 4.   [113] I, 501.   [114] III, 113.
[115] X, 67.
[116] III, 159. "Et ut quies spiritui somnus, ita illi (mens) fides. . . . Cessat enim in utroque rationalis animae opus: ob id qui plus ratione valent minus habent fidei."

Cardano must certainly have given his orthodox readers further pain when he informed them that matter—"not an evil but simply a lesser good"—is the basis of all creation.[117] Matter is eternal, and its eternity is proved by corruption, because matter never decays into nothing but into something other than it was. Wood burns into ash; water vaporizes to mist; other things putrify into worms or flies. Under form there is always something, and this something endures and gives value to form.[118] All bodies are contained in space, which is eternal, immobile, and unchangeable but itself contained in the universe. Space has no importance beyond this.[119] Matter, however, does not crowd space to immobility because heat—the instrument of motion through which the principle of form (*Anima Mundi*) acts on matter—causes one thing to change into another in a constant cycle of life and death.[120] Motion is imparted to matter by this caloric principle "through Nature." When he uses that famous word *Nature*, Cardano means nothing more than the assembly of things which constitute experience, a living and moving synthesis of space, matter, and intelligence—three entities which combine to produce existence.[121] At the center of this complex, Cardano, with special philosophic courtesy, places God, whom he carefully declines to define. "If I knew who he was, I would be God; for no one knows God or what he is unless he is God." [122] God may be in all things, and Cardano seems to have thought of him as an energizing force; but "where God or the soul are, man may guess but never know." [123]

In the *De Vita Propria*, Cardano affirmed the equality of living things, but he quickly qualifies this common right by stating that man alone possesses *mens*.[124] In his judgment, only man is conscious of self; and though animals may have

---

[117] III, 350. [118] III, 359–60. [119] III, 387–88, 417–18.
[120] III, 357, 368; II, 294–95. [121] III, 671. [122] X, 12.
[123] I, 39–40. [124] II, 287.

sensitive souls, they are actually guided through existence by instinct. They probably do not even know who they are, whereas man knows both himself and things external to him.[125] Animation is for Cardano something different from *mens* and depends to a large degree on his notion of form. Forms, he concludes, are similar to souls;[126] hence, apparently insensible bodies, like snowflakes and hailstones, are animated and have motion.

On the real nature of *mens*, he is really never very clear. It is not divorced from the body, which mirrors it in movement. In the *De Rerum Varietate*,[127] he describes it as a substance that is eternal and immaterial and which comes from without as a part of the Intelligence or *Anima Mundi*. Then, putting on the garb of an Averroist, a costume in which he was probably comfortable, he argues that the differences between men do not prove separateness of intelligence. These differences could be the result of climate. More than likely, they are derived from the part of the *mens* an individual has, and depend on how he uses it. It is, says Cardano, not uncommon for some individuals to do perfectly natural things that seem miraculous to others. The spontaneous acquisition of Latin is probably an example. In the *De Consolatione*, as Saitta points out,[128] Cardano does support separateness, arguing that there are as many intellects as there are men. We must remember, however, that in this book he is comforting himself for the death of his beloved, but useless, son. His view in other tracts is somewhat different, and it is on these dark pages that the antiatheists seized.

The *De Animi Immortalitate* (1545) is the earliest of Cardano's philosophical books, and with it he takes part in the central controversy of Renaissance Aristotelianism that was inaugurated by Pomponazzi and his contemporaries. De Neufville is probably pointing at this controversy and even

[125] II, 549–51.   [126] II, 135–38.   [127] III, 159–60.   [128] II, 219.

at Cardano's book when he writes in 1556 that "neither the future union of our souls with God through the instrumentality of Christ, nor the return of individual souls to the Soul of All is correctly understood by these philosophers; I shall not mention Epicureans and Atheists, who dream, I know not what, about a new Soul of All animating the universe of which our souls are but rays or sparks." [129] These words recall the concluding paragraphs of the *De Animi Immortalitate*,[130] but this is not the only time Cardano fondled this idea. The notion turns up later in the *De Subtilitate*, and we are informed that particular souls are functions or attributes of the universal soul, which is to the totality of Nature what the particular soul is to the total man.[131] A dozen years after this, the *De Rerum Varietate* states that the spiritual principle man shares with Nature is both eternal and continuous; by eventually returning to this principle, the individual soul attains immortality.[132] The doctrine, here so staunchly expressed, seems to be ignored or even denied by the old man who wrote the *De Vita Propria*.

> But he who lives without this hope (immortality) is deprived of a double and true good . . . that is of both hope and reward. If it has been God's pleasure to make us in our mortality participants of immortality, it does not befit us to neglect his free gift nor to hold any other than a hopeful view of our condition.[133]

That customary *if*, which here and elsewhere Cardano uses to qualify statements verging on orthodox piety, introduces the second sentence.

---

[129] P., 29–30. He defends Aristotle against the Paduans, who have set up a false Aristotle, an atheist who denied immortality, free will, and Providence. Aristotle often mentioned God, and thus relieved men of the tyranny of Fate (pp. 170–92).

[130] II, 536. [131] II, 357–59. [132] III, 159. [133] I, 44.

"I shall consider," the *De Animi Immortalitate* begins,
"whether human souls are eternal and divine or whether they
perish with the body." If we assume the soul survives, we
must ask whether it survives as a separate entity or whether it
returns to a single, eternal, universal soul. Since Cardano is
both a learned and impartial man, he now reprints more than
fifty arguments against immortality. The soul seems to increase in vigor after childhood and decline with old age.
Most men act like animals, and animals are mortal. Souls
cannot be immortal because those of the dead are never seen.
If men have immortal souls, why are they so eager for
worldly fame? If death were truly a translation to eternal
life, would most men find it so bitter? Should there be so
many theories about something which is a fact? If souls are
immortal, why are some intelligent and others stupid? Should
not an immortal soul be housed in a body of fire or air and
not in one that is essentially earth? As a matter of fact, is
it not absurd to house an immortal soul in temporary flesh
and especially absurd in the case of infants who are aborted
or die shortly after birth? [134] To the horror of subsequent
writers, Cardano thus put doubts in the minds of feeble souls,
whom he supplied with fifty-four reasons against their personal immortality.

To offset his intellectual wickedness, Cardano now pre-
pares to reprint the arguments for the immortality of the
soul excogitated by Plato and other pagans; but before he
commences his anthology, he pauses to consider whether or
not a belief in immortality makes men better.

> I think not! We see in Cicero and Diogenes that the Epi-
> cureans were more upright and honest, and had more true
> goodness toward men than the Stoics or Platonists. It is as
> Galen says: men are good or bad by custom. But no one trusts

[134] II, 458–64.

them who do not make a profession of righteousness, and, therefore, they are obliged to observe morality more than others and prove themselves to the people lest men should think they act the way they talk. As a result, few men nowadays are as honest as pawnbrokers, who otherwise lead very bad lives. It should also be noticed that the Pharisees, who believed in the resurrection and immortality of the soul, never gave over persecuting Jesus Christ and that the Sadducees, another sect that rejected both ideas, attacked him very seldom, at most but once or twice, and in such a manner as caused him no trouble. Furthermore, if you compare the life of Pliny with that of Seneca, their lives, I say, and not their words, you will discover that Pliny, with his belief in the mortality of the soul, surpasses Seneca in his moral conduct as far as Seneca surpasses him in his discourses on religion and virtue. The Epicureans cultivated honesty; they cared for the children of their pupils and supported the families of dead friends. Everyone regarded them as honest men, even though they paid little attention to the worship of the gods in whose existence they did not believe. . . . Nor does it seem to me that belief in immortality makes men more courageous. Brutus was no more so than Cassius; and if the truth is told, Brutus' deeds were crueler than those of Cassius, for Cassius treated the Rhodians (wicked as they were) better than Brutus treated friendly cities.[135]

Having said this, Cardano pauses (and perhaps he should) to confess that the conflicting tenets of various religions so balance each other that all they achieve is an unseemly contention.[136] He proceeds to review and respond to the arguments of Aristotle and of such post-Aristotelians as Avicenna, Johannes Scotus, and Albertus Magnus.[137] By this course of philosophical contention, he arrives at Averroes, and here

[135] II, 464–65.   [136] II, 469.   [137] II, 485–505.

he sticks, happily contending that the soul of the individual human being is attached to the universal soul "as the aphid to the leaf." To the degree that it participates in the *Anima Mundi*, it is immortal; but it is also tied closely to the organs of the body and, in this respect, must suffer death. This, in a sense, is the best that Cardano can do to make men feel their godlikeness; but the philosopher here, as in the case of Pomponazzi, has his own problem. Maybe, as he says later in the *De Sapientia*, it is prudent to express a belief in immortality. "Ergo animum affirmare immortalem, non solum pium et prudens est, sed irreprehensibile, ac multorum honorum causa." [138] It is, after all, in a good cause. But how about Cardano? In the last pages of the *De Subtilitate*, where he is making one of his careful excursions into the nature of God and good and evil, he observes that hatred of death makes men love to beget children. "They are from us; they preserve our countenances; they restore us." [139]

III

Giulio Cesare Vanini,[140] born Lucilio Vanini in the Kingdom of Naples probably in 1585, died in the Place du Salin in Toulouse on February 9, 1619.[141] His final date is precise because he was eradicated by official fire, but his name was used for more than a century as a bogie to frighten the pious. No seventeenth- or eighteenth-century historian of atheism

[138] I, 568.   [139] III, 671.

[140] Vanini's *Amphitheatrum* and some dialogues of his *De Admirandis Naturae* were translated into French by M. X. Rousselot as *Oeuvres Philosophiques de Vanini* (Paris, 1842). The modern edition is *Le Opere*, ed. L. Corvaglia (Milan and Rome, 1933–34). For the life see A. Baudouin, "Histoire Critique de Jules César Vanini," *Revue Philosphique*, VIII (1879), 48–71, 157–78, 259–90, 387–410. See also Charbonnel, pp. 302–83; Fiorentino, pp. 425–71; and Saitta, *Il Pensiero Italiano*, II, 440–49.

[141] The *Mercure Français*, V (1620), 45–46, describes his death.

overlooks him; the compilers of even the shortest and most
intellectually impoverished attacks on disbelief know about
him, if they can name no other hobgoblin to the good. His
legend began to spread as the ashes of his pyre turned cold.
Garasse [142] and Mersenne [143] intone the opening notes of the
hymn of horror that added chorus upon chorus as the century grew old. The Age of Enlightenment, bothered by its
fathers' bad consciences, bickers over the guilt and fate of
the "martyr de l'athéisme." [144] Voltaire, up to his usual sophistries, compares the end of the witty Italian with that of
Socrates; and then, discounting the implied compliment, describes Vanini's concept of a sanitary God as "pas bien
philosophique, mais cela de la Théologie la plus approu-
vée." [145]

There was a sort of symbolic opening of Vanini's grave
and an inspection of his charred bones in 1709. At this time,
Johannes Schramm, writing in Küstrin on the Oder, recited
all of the poor man's theological errors in an unflattering
biography. For him, Vanini was the Huxley of Pomponazzi
and Cardano as, indeed, he was. Schramm complains that
Vanini saw to it that Cardano's horoscope of Christ and
his astrological commentary thereon were both widely

---

[142] *La Doctrine Curieuse des Beaux Esprits de Ce Temps* (Paris, 1624),
pp. 144 ff.

[143] *Quaestiones*, col. 671.

[144] G. Barthelemi de Grammont writes that some thought Vanini a
heretic, but he was an atheist and a seducer of young men. He ascribed
everything to Fate or Nature and infected the youths of Toulouse with
his ideas. When he was interrogated, he claimed that he venerated Christianity and made a speech on the power of God as seen in a straw. On
the way to his execution, however, he pointed out that whereas Christ
went to his death in fear and sweat, he was himself totally unperturbed.
He was, says Grammont, not so brave at the end; and though he said,
"Let us die like a philosopher," anyone hearing the oxlike sound he
made when his tongue was ripped out would know he died as a beast.
"Finisse ut brutum nemo negaverit." *Historiarum Galliae ab Excessu
Henrici IV Livri XVIII* (Toulouse, 1643), pp. 208–10.

[145] *Dictionnaire Philosophique*, in *Oeuvres Complètes* (Paris, 1878), XVIII,
470–72.

known. He accuses him of viciously popularizing the thesis of Caesalpino that man was spontaneously produced from putrefying matter and not divinely created by Jehovah from good, red dust.[146] Schramm's book appeared the year after Olearius, another German savant, took his theological doctorate at Jena with two theses: *De Vita et Fatis J. C. Vanini* and *De Vanini Scriptis et Opinionibus*, both evidence of his skill in disputatious research. The prior dissertation (Schramm's was on Pomponazzi) is an anthology of anti-Vaninian vituperation selected from the writings of the narrowest orthodox minds of Europe; the second is a summary, with certified objections, of Vanini's two dangerous volumes. Published in 1709, both parts of the thesis are exhaustive in both senses of the word, but the new doctor of theology's conclusion is sound enough. "We may safely assert that on the basis of authority Vanini was an atheist of the most extreme type." [147]

In 1712 a German scholar living in Leyden, Frederick Peter Arpe, published his *Apologia pro J. C. Vanino Neapolitano* at Amsterdam. Arpe begins indignantly by protesting that the ghost of Vanini had been stoned for a hundred years by antiatheists who had never looked into either one of his so-called blasphemous books. The epithet *atheist*, he complains, is carelessly tossed about without any reference to its true implications. It is an abusive term applied by one Christian to another. It has been awarded to pious and orthodox men such as Cardinals Bembo, Cajetan, and Perron; and, for no adequate reason, it is a crown of thorns bestowed on Pomponazzi, Cardano, Campanella, Giovio, Poliziano, Barbaro, Postel, Muret, Bodin, Descartes, Fludd, Thomas Browne, Puffendorf, and other Christians.[148] Arpe recites

---

[146] *De Vita et Scriptis Famosi Athei Julii Caesaria Vanini* (Küstrin, 1709), pp. 13–30.

[147] *Dissertatio Posterior: De Vanini Scriptis et Opinionibus* (Jena, 1709), p. 16.

[148] Pp. 23–27.

and rejects the accusations made against Vanini by personal enemies and gives him, in each instance, a *non probatur.*[149] Unfortunately, the *Apologia* did not sweeten Vanini's reputation. It achieved little more than to get Arpe also nominated for the authorship of the *De Tribus Impostoribus.* Durand, who wrote a *La Vie et les Sentiments de Lucilio Vanini,* published at Amsterdam in 1712 and later translated into English, says that Arpe was a learned man who loved a little game and undertook the defense of Vanini in jest. "I can assure you the book is not serious." [150] As these guns were being hauled away, Voltaire arrived with his rifle.

Vanini's first book had a mouth-filling but pious title. Suggesting to the reader the agonies of the Christian martyrs, it was called *Amphitheatrum Aeternae Providentiae Divino-Magicum, Christiano-Physicum, nec non Astrologo-Catholicum adversus Veteres Philosophos, Atheos, Epicureos, Peripateticos, et Stoicos* and was printed at Lyons in 1615. The preface immodestly relates the author's immense theological studies and growing disgust with all patented proofs of the presiding presence of Providence. Now that the "old plant of atheism is greening and man's morals are in decay," the obsolete arguments of "Tully's talkers," the "grandmotherly dreams" of the Platonists, proofs drawn from decayed Scholastic trash ("ex putridis scholasticorum quisquilis"), and even the demonstrations of St. Thomas are of little help. Vanini proposes to begin where his predecessors have left off.[151] We know at first reading that almost nothing Vanini says is very original, but his language is charmingly flamboyant and filled with delicious self-esteem. His arguments are from Cardano, Scaliger, Fracastoro, and Pomponazzi; but he is eloquent, and he has that quality possessed by no atheist hunter and feared by most self-important men—that is, wit.

---

[149] His method is to take up the eighteen indictments against Vanini and disprove them from his two books.

[150] P. 213.   [151] Pp. +4–8v.

In spite of the tone and the dubious arguments, the manuscript presented by a smiling Vanini got past the papal examiners, four of whom, Deville, Du Soleil, Daveine, and Seve, can be seen (to quote Milton) nodding and ducking to each other within the piazza of the preliminary material.[152]

Vanini's vast reading and immense intellectual effort, as he confesses, appear at once in the sequence of time-honored proofs of the existence of God with which his book begins. After God is proved to be, Vanini defines him elegantly, but, as Voltaire complains, not exactly philosophically.

> You ask me what is God; but if I knew, I should be God; for no one knows what God is except God. We may, however, know him to some degree in his works, as we know through the eclipse of a cloud the height of the sun. . . . Notice how bold our hand is to describe, though in vain, the first of beings. God is beginning and end although he has neither himself. Since God needs neither, he is author of both. He exists eternally out of time, subject neither to past nor to future. Having no place, he rules everywhere. Without situation, he is unmovable; without motion, swift; he is within all but not enclosed and without all but not excluded. Though in all things, he governs all. Without all things, he created all. He is good without quality, immense without quantity, universal without parts, unchangeable yet all-changing. God's will is his power; and when he exerts his will, he exerts his power. Naught in him is in potential and all is in act, because he is pure act, first, middlemost, and last. In short he is all, above all, beyond all, before all, after all, and he remains all.[153]

Though he can almost define God, Vanini admits that Providence is undefinable; [154] however, he holds it completely responsible for creation. He establishes its actuality by argu-

[152] Pp. ++2-3.   [153] Pp. 8-10.   [154] P. 12.

ments drawn from celestial motion, the fulfillment of prophecy, and miracles. In order to make the last point, Vanini is forced to attack the astrological theories of religion advanced by his great masters Pomponazzi and Cardano. In the light of his open veneration of these men, his opponents felt that he criticized these ideas in order to promulgate them.[155] To the same end, he probably relates and attacks the improper doctrines of Providence proposed by Diagoras, Cicero, Protagoras, Epicurus, Themistius, and Averroes.[156] Vanini had a penchant for fuller explanations; hence, he often expounds in his own way what these philosophers would have said had they had more time. This expansive method of supplementation, rather than interpretation, was not profitable to orthodoxy; it may be illustrated by Vanini's exposition of the so-called views on Providence expressed by Protagoras.

The Greek philosopher, standing before a world that seemed to him filled with wickedness, assumed that its divine supervisor, if one existed, was either blind or evil. This opinion Vanini illuminates in six time-worn philosophical sallies. First, God either knows the wickedness of men or not. If he knows, he is the author, because with God knowledge and action are one. On the other hand, if he does not know, he clearly does not know the world. Second, since evil always increases and God does nothing about it, he either neglects creation or can do nothing to halt evil. He is, then, either careless of evil and responsible for it or impotent and not God. Third, God either approves or disapproves of evil. If he approves, he is its author. If he disapproves, he is either powerless and cannot subdue it or unaware of it and not omniscient. It is possible, of course, that he is just nasty, disliking evil but doing nothing about it.

---

[155] Pp. 21–78. The names of these men appear frequently in his works; see *Amphitheatrum,* pp. 25, 39, 41, 151, 234, 328.
[156] Pp. 79–238.

Fourth, God should do good. Refusing to do this, he is both improvident and odious. Fifth, legally the causer has the same responsibility as the actor; hence, God, since he cannot permit it from good motives, is the author of evil. Sixth, God either desires to extinguish evil or not. If the second conclusion is true, the atheists are correct. The first conclusion relies on the dialectic rule that whoever desires an end desires the means to that end. The death of martyrs, said David, pleases God. Martyrdom requires a tyrant; hence, the impiety of tyrants must please God because through it men achieve martyrdom.[157] Vanini labors for many pages to demonstrate the wrongness of these arguments. In this effort he may succeed, but the arguments are easier to read than his exhaustive criticism of them.

The greater part of Vanini's book is concerned with expounding and exposing the errors of all that had been previously written about Providence; but, finally, he presents his own invincible views, and we are hardly overwhelmed. It cannot be shown, he announces as principle number one, that God is not everywhere. Then, if the Creator does not know each creature, he cannot be said to know himself; in fact, his mind is circumscribed, and ignorant of particulars, he does not know even as much as animals know.[158] But the main unorthodox argument against Providence, as Vanini sees it, is the presence of monsters in a world directed toward God. To circumvent this perplexing problem, Averroes and Alexander Aphrodisias contended that monsters had naught to do with a perfect process because, as results of material necessity, they had no part in an immaterial procedure. Aristotle turned the point by simply defining monsters as "sins" or "lies" of Nature; and Cardano ("vir nunquam satis laudatus") thought monsters came from errors in Nature, which resulted from a lack of stellar virtue.[159] Vanini had

[157] Pp. 90–124.   [158] Pp. 238–43.   [159] Pp. 260–66.

put his mind on this impious matter, so he had several Christian answers. Monsters are the products of unusual or inordinate copulation, of the force of the imagination either during coition or in pregnancy, of parents with similar physical defects, of too little or too much semen in both quality or quantity, of two kinds of semen, and of the influence of the stars.[160]

Vanini's proofs—his earlier series on immortality also bear this out [161]—are often clever and amusing, but in no sense highly convincing. In fact, although he described his titanic efforts in the library at the beginning of this book, he forgets his preface and concludes by begging the reader to gaze kindly on a work of no study written for the relaxation of the author's mind. "But if," he continues, "the reader should find (what I hardly believe) notions not in accord with the institutions, decrees, and dogmas of the Roman Church, we hope that he will pass them over as neither said nor set down." [162] The best commentary on the closing phases of gladiator Vanini's great fight in the arena of Providence is

[160] Pp. 273–81.

[161] Pp. 163–66. Vanini writes that "Several Christian doctors have refuted atheists on the point but so frivolously and ineptly that in reading the commentaries of these great theologians, one feels doubts rising in oneself. I confess openly that the immortality of the soul cannot be demonstrated by physical principles. It is an article of faith, for we believe in the resurrection of the body, and what would it be without the soul or what would the soul be without it? Christian and Catholic in both name and origin, if I had not been taught by the Church, the infallible dispensatrix of truth, I could scarcely believe in the immortality of the soul." He now states his proofs: I) The soul being a simple substance cannot decompose. II) The soul being a celestial substance cannot decay. III) If nothing cannot be made of nothing, something cannot disintegrate into nothing.

[162] Pp. 323–24. Before suggesting that the reader fail to notice matter repulsive to the Church, Vanini also encourages him to correct or rub out anything offensive to reason, "ut si quod rationi minus conveniens adverterit, emendet, deleat etiam et obliteret." The distinction made between the reader's reason and the Church's authority and tradition is touching. The book concludes with a not meritless hymn in praise of God and Providence.

probably supplied by a passage of dialogue in his second book. In this instance, he is questioned by his friend Alexander about the truthfulness of an anecdote in the *Amphitheatrum*. "There are," Julius Caesar responds, "many things written in that book in which I have no confidence." [163]

Printed with the desirable "Privilège du Roi" and dedicated to Bassompierre, who with Baron Panat, Redon, Abbé de Saint-Luc, and the soon-to-be-burned Fontanier, constituted, according to Mersenne, part of the atheist circle about Vanini, the *De Admirandis Naturae . . . Arcanis* also deceived the censors. On the reverse of the title, two clerics testify that this book by "Vaninus, Philosophus praestantissimus," contains nothing repugnant or contrary to the Catholic, Apostolic, and Roman religion. Once again it is impossible to believe that these busy licensers read much of the manuscript. Had they simply looked at the last page (the first is quite innocuous), they would have noticed the little Italian verse blooming amidst the cold Latin which caught the eye of Garasse and made him see Satan.

The last page—in a sense it contains Vanini's last words —discloses the two friends talking about the hard lot of men who struggle for knowledge and fame. Alexander's hope is that his name will outlast his body. "If the atheists are right," says Julius Caesar, "that would be good enough," but, given his choice, he would rather go to heaven, where the joys of the world will seem but a hair, or to purgatory, where the music of the *Dies Irae* is sweeter than Ciceronian rhetoric or Aristotelian discovery. "But if I went Hellward, what hope would I have?" Alexander, saddened by all this, is encouraged by Vanini to conduct his life in terms of the present. He brightens and remembers an old song: "Perduto e tutto il tempo/ Che in amar non si spende." Love of God? The text

---

[163] *De Admirandis Naturae Reginae Deaeque Mortalium Arcanis* (Paris, 1616), p. 428.

is not explicit, but the work ends with Alexander praising the day, now declining into sunset, as beautiful and happy.

The book so carelessly approved by the censors is composed of four sets of dialogues between Alexander and Julius Caesar. The first dialogues are about the planets and the elements; the second, about sublunar matters; the third sequence is about man; and the last, about the pagan church. The final eleven discussions are what atheist hunters called "Lucianic," but any talented orthodox reader would have smelled the fumes of sulphur before he got so far. The text is filled with those characteristic little utterances that betray the author's impiety. "If I had not been raised a Christian," says Vanini, "I would say that the sky is an animal moved by its own soul." [164] A few paragraphs later, he states that if he were a Christian, he would rather believe the world was eternal than that the mountains were formed by the Deluge.[165] These reiterated phrases—"if I were not a Christian," "if I were not instructed by the Church," or "if I were a believer"—that so often precede an attractive but highly non-Christian proposition are clear marks of Vanini's attitude. His courage in employing them is reckless. However, all one now needs to notice is that numerous sections prior to satanically transparent Part Four should have given Frater Edmundus Carradinus and Frère Claude le Petit, who authorized publication, serious doubts about the author's Christian intent.

The eyes of the clergy would certainly have noticed, had the clergy opened the manuscript, the section in Book Three where Caesalpino's theory of man's origin from decaying matter is carefully outlined. It is a conjecture favored by Alexander, because mice being so made, a large enough mass of rotting matter should vent oxen and horses. Atheists, Julius Caesar admits, think that man originated from the

[164] Pp. 20–21.   [165] Pp. 134–35.

putrefying carcasses of apes or hogs because anatomically he is so similar to these animals. "But does not," asks Alexander, "man's upright stature prove him divinely created?" To this Boswellian question, Vanini replies that some atheists say primitive man walked on all fours and had to learn erect loco-motion. "But were not," Alexander goes on, "men created to dominate the animals?" "Basilisks?" asks Julius Caesar, pointing out that man's true superiority over animals is very slight. Alexander blames man's lost animal empire on the fall of Adam, and Vanini responds to this excuse in a way that it would be timid to call ironic. "I should like to say the happy fall of Adam has brought us, by merit, so great a Redeemer that now we not only rule all things but also have angels for schoolmasters. But I suppose we should leave these matters to the learned old men of the Sorbonne and exercise our wits, if it pleases, in Philosophy." "Sed quaeso haec doctis Sorbonae senibus reliquamus, et nostra, si placet, in Philosophicis exerceamus ingenia." [166]

There are moments other than these to warn the wary. In Dialogue 48, Vanini discusses the advantage of bastardy and concludes with an impious wish that is worthy of Shake-speare's Edmund.

Would that (it is a dream of course) I had been procreated in an illegitimate bed. My parents would have worked to frame me with such vigor that I should have had elegance of form, a robust body, and a clear head. Because I was born to a married bed, I lack all these advantages. My father was bent under age, and all his youthful fire had departed when he gave himself over to matrimony. The powers of the seventy-year-old were flaccid, his spirits were exiled, his natural faculties were languid; he paid his debt to the marriage bed, as they say, by default. Not excited by reasons of valor did he enter the

[166] Pp. 232–35.

robust combat. As a result, I was born short of strength and vigor; and if you see me of aspiring mind, pleasing in manner, my body subject to few infirmities, it is because my father, though old, was of a bland and cheerful nature, and a girl in her teens (do philosophers laugh at Christian marriage?) undertook to warm that member frozen by age. Moreover, he waited for that sweet time of the year when Nature once more renews her strength and heated moderately by wine, he carried through the comedy of Venus again.[167]

His remarks are amusing and very Italian, but, nonetheless, not of the nature to make one confident of his virtues as a Christian philosopher.

The first dialogue in the very dubious last book is titled *De Deo*, exactly the sort of title for the first chapter of most books purporting to present a rational exposition of Christian doctrine. Vanini's chapter differs somewhat from those of others by stating that as God is greater than man, he cannot be man's end. Since God can himself have no end, man was, says Vanini, created that he might have constant felicity from God. Alexander, who is the object of this instruction, cannot believe the testimony of his ears. "Man," he exclaims, "is overwhelmed by so many great miseries that if it did not contradict the Christian belief (for which I would die), I should not hesitate to assume that if there are devils, they were punished by being sent into the world as men." [168] Wrapped in this one remark are agnostic doubt, fake piety, potential diabolism, and the famous heresy of Origen. The horns and tails are not well concealed. The instructive conversation now wends its way toward Doomsday, and the "Atheist of Amsterdam," a curious third person, enters the Vaninian *dramatis personae*.

[167] Pp. 321–22. He has some similar observations on the sexual advantages of marrying a relative (p. 326).
[168] Pp. 352–53.

The "Atheist of Amsterdam" is filled with impieties which always enrage Alexander and Julius Caesar, who never fail in their sacred indignation to repeat his utterances so closely that quotation marks are required. On this occasion, encountering Alexander, the "Atheist" began his comments by stating that all Christian martyrs were probably mentally ill. Then he made sport of the doctrine of the Antichrist, saying the story was fabulous but not so absurd as the 1600 years fearful Christians had awaited his coming. Dropping into a meditative silence, he suddenly burst forth with, "O marvelous wisdom of Christ!" For a moment Alexander hoped, he says, for his conversion, but the "Atheist" continued as if talking to himself.

> What admirable skill! He gave signs of it in the case of the woman taken in adultery and when the Scribes questioned him about the tribute owed Caesar. In this fable of the Antichrist, he surpassed himself, for all that he predicted about the coming of the Antichrist does nothing less than assure the perpetuation of Christianity. As a matter of fact, many men would have been tempted, as the prophets predicted, to proclaim themselves the Messiah, but Christ, the cleverest of all prophets, painted such a frightful portrait of the Antichrist that no one would want to assume the shame and infamy of such a person; hence, the Antichrist wanting, Christian doctrine is guaranteed everlasting endurance.[169]

The "Atheist" exits, and Julius Caesar explains the mystery of the Trinity so lucidly both he and Alexander are forced to admit his arguments would convert those philosophers "who laugh at the idea as an impossible hallucination." Alexander, however, has another question: "How did pre-Christain men learn about their gods?" The pagans, Julius Caesar informs him, were instructed by Nature and regarded other

[169] Pp. 356–57.

religions as "depending on works of illusion and falsehood
. . . works invented by princes to render their subjects
sheep or by priests to get both cash and honor." These
works, Alexander is told, are not confirmed by miracle, but
by accounts of miracle and by a Scripture that promises re-
compense for good and punishment for evil. "When? In a
future life!" In this way, Christian Vanini concludes, "they
kept the little field folk in slavery through fear of a false
supreme being, who sees all and has eternal rewards and
chastisements for all." [170]

Vanini's technique in these dialogues is hardly sly. Paganism is ostensibly under discussion, but the symbolic fish of
Christianity remains allegorically on the surface. The two
Christians speak of pagan visions, which they attribute to
sick imagination, and of pagan prophecy, which they describe as "priestly imposture." Julius Caesar draws seventeenth-century parallels by noticing that any lucky astologer
who makes a few sound guesses can thereby convince "the
little people" he is a heaven-commissioned prophet.[171] Com-
mon-sense mockery is similarly used to laugh away pagan
belief in inspiration and demonic possession; and the two
ardent Christians, strong in their condemnation of the
heathen, walk always just to this side of home truths.

Dialogue 7 starts off with stories about ancient statues
sweating, weeping, or bleeding; then Alexander (for he has
read the *De Natura Deorum*) recalls the *ex voto* pictures
found in pagan temples that represent divine rescues. Vanini,
good Christian, sees in them pure heathen nonsense.

> One does not represent in these votive paintings all those
> who perished, although they, too, had invoked the gods. Con-
> sider the facts. One finds himself in danger. He turns to the
> gods at once. He offers prayers and makes vows. If by pure

[170] Pp. 365–67.   [171] Pp. 368–91.

accident the affair goes according to his vows, he thinks he must give the gods thanks for his good luck. If he survived but his requests are not granted according to his vows, the priests were sure to point out that it was his fault. He was burdened with guilt and for this reason the gods did not answer his prayers. On the other hand, if it happens that a pious man becomes a victim, the priests tell of the pity of gods who chastise in this life those dear to them. It also goes without saying that when the vowmakers perish, there is nobody about to reproach the gods for indifference or hardness of heart.[172]

After this bit of exegesis on stupid pagan practices, the "Atheist of Amsterdam" appears once more.

When he first came on the stage, the "Atheist" was seen and interrogated by Alexander. It is now Vanini's turn, and he meets him in the dialogue on augury, where, "impelled by some sad and miserable destiny," this faceless stranger remarked blasphemously to pious Julius Caesar:

> According to the Bible, one would assume that the Devil was stronger than God. Against the will of God, Adam and Eve sinned and thus perished the human race. The Son of God, coming to remedy this fault, was condemned by his judges, incited by the Devil, to an ignominious death. So, according to the Bible, the satanic will is stronger than God's. Lo! God wants all men to be saved; but he saves only very few. On the contrary, the Devil wishes all men damned and their number is infinite. Out of the vast world, only those people who live in Italy, Spain, some districts of France, Germany, and Poland have any chance for salvation. If one deducts from these candidates for redemption Jews, secret heretics, atheists, blasphemers, simonists, adulterers, and sodomites who are not likely to inherit the Kingdom of Heaven,

[172] Pp. 411–12.

scarcely a squad remains compared to the millions who will be damned.[173]

To this most compelling objection of the "Atheist," Julius Caesar responded with a number of impressive arguments. He began by insisting that Satan was not the equal of God; then he said that God permitted Adam and Eve to fall so that the miracle of the Redemption might be revealed. He turned to the Bible to demonstrate how Satan, acting through the wife of Pontius Pilate, attempted to prevent Christ's crucifixion but was divinely thwarted. He next stated that Satan, who had won at the first tree, lost at the second. He recited the well-known verse of Scripture: "Many are called but few are chosen"; and, finally, he announced that the more souls are damned and go to hell, the more the labor and trouble of the devils are increased. Satisfied with this magnificent refutation of the "Atheist's" contention, Alexander congratulates Julius Caesar and describes him as "the world's leading antagonist of atheism."

Three more similarly pious dialogues complete Vanini's book against the pagans. Heathen miracles, such as Vespasian's healing of a blind man by anointing his eyes with the imperial spittle, or the handling of poisonous serpents by pagan priests, or the various non-Christian accounts of the resurrection of the dead, are pushed aside by the two Christians as fraudulent, the deceptions of pious imagination, hysterical manifestations, or improperly interpreted natural situations. The two carefully named conquerors of religious barbarism, Alexander and Julius Caesar, thus come to the end of their day and their talk and decide to relax with a game. The boy Tarsius, called by Julius Caesar, brings the tables and the pieces; and as he arranges them for play, he recites a little-known verse of Ovid.

[173] Pp. 419–21.

Parva sedit ternis instructa tabella lapillis
In qua vicisse est continuasse.

The men of the game are to be placed in orders of three, but to win, one must continue to advance his own. Even in leisure the Trinity is not forgotten and will win if it keeps ahead, provided, of course, it is one's personal Trinity.

No one can fail to see what a pious and orthodox age found objectionable in the writings of this Italian triumvirate. Pomponazzi's unreadiness to accept philosophical responsibility for the Christian doctrines of Providence, immortality and free will is hardly excused by his rhetorical genuflections to Christian revelation; and this is especially so when he suggests, even though he is certain of its Platonic reoccurrence, that the faith begotten by this revelation diminishes as its stars fade. Cardano, more prolix than Pomponazzi and a man of apparently wider interests and certainly of more tangled emotions, does no better than his fellow countryman when he also stares at the human soul and the doctrines men invent for its permanent perpetuation. The doubts and restrictions of both men are put into agreeable prose by Vanini and salted with wit. Erasmus could be witty about Christianity, but he could hide his jests in a corner. In his *Colloquy of the Shipwreck*, one of the sailors regrets that the Stella Maris, no sailor herself, had replaced as the seaman's saint the Lady Aphrodite, sea-born herself. "Ah, yes," says a fearful companion, "in place of the mother who was not a virgin, one has supplied a Virgin who was a mother." No one complained about this, but even theologians could understand Vanini's humor.

Three French Atheists:
Montaigne, Charron, Bodin

〜〜〜〜〜〜〜〜〜〜〜〜〜〜〜〜〜〜〜〜〜〜〜〜〜〜〜〜〜〜〜〜〜〜〜〜〜

I

THE EFFORTS of the philosophers of Italy to test Christian beliefs by the touchstone of reason resulted more in a growing distrust of reason than in an indifference to religious dogma. The proper use of reason in matters of theology recommended by St. Augustine, St. Thomas, and even lesser divines like Montaigne's client, Raimond de Sebonde, came to be regarded in certain orthodox quarters as dangerous or, at least, highly suspect. There have always been Christian thinkers who preferred the simple piety of the rustic kneeling before a crossroad shrine to the rational sophistications of a theological philosophy; these men knew that in its way fine ignorance was more learned than minds stored and furnished with centuries of theological thinking. To illustrate this point Malebranche invented a little drama in which one actor says that whereas his faith accepts certain religious principles, his reason holds back. The protagonist of this piece, a Christian named Theodore, then remarks that such a person is not likely to be helped by either faith or reason.[1] Aristarque, the first

---

[1] *Conversations Chrétiennes*, ed. L. Bridet (Paris, 1929), p. 7. In *A Treatise of the Four Degenerate Sons*, John Weemse complained earlier

speaker, talks for the philosopher, for Pomponazzi, Cardano, Vanini, and many others, but Theodore has the surest and greatest voice. The dialogue is a late dramatization of the continued questioning of the value of reason in religious discussion.

One of the first witnesses to this Renaissance contention about the real value of reason or philosophy in settling problems of supernatural importance is Ludovicus Vives, who attacks the fort of Aristotelianism in his *De Dialecta Corrupta*, arguing that because of the Scholastic method men deprive themselves of the right to test their ideas by experience.[2] Experience is also the measure of Valla's *De Vero Bono*, but in this debate, he can award the tactful prize medal to the Christian, who has hardly put down the opposition of the Stoic or the Epicurean. The Aristotelian method is likewise condemned by Pico della Mirandola in the final three sections of his *Examen Vanitatis Doctrinae Gentium*; and in the preface to the last part, he carefully divides all formal thinkers into dogmatists who affirm, academics who deny, and Pyrrhonists who doubt. The third contingent, until this time mainly unnoticed, is thus given a ticket of admission to modern thought. Melchior Canus, who was distressed by the Paduan philosophy, was at the same time disturbed by the steady disappearance of reason from theological discussion.[3] His contradictory regrets are stressed a decade later when the Jesuit

---

that "nothing will serve against the Atheist, but only to bring him to the bar of Reason, and God hath left this reason within him to convince him and make him inexcusable" (IV, 7–10). Abra de Raconis writes in his *Metaphysica* (Paris, 1624), p. 414, that "it is the misfortune of our age that questions once discussed to sharpen Christian minds must now be used to defend faith against atheists." In the preface to his translation of J. B. Morin's attempt to prove God's existence mathematically, Henry Care writes that atheists "pretend highly to Reason, and intimate they would be satisfied could they but meet with such Demonstrations as might be necessarily Conclusive to their Understandings and enforce their Assent." *The Darkness of Atheism Dispelled*, pp. B2–B2v.

[2] *Opera* (Basel, 1550), I, 383.   [3] P. 425.

philosopher, Benedict Pereira, complaining that Catholics have given up philosophy because of its errors, relates how much many of the Fathers had depended on this discipline.[4] A heathen philosopher, Sextus Empiricus, now rose from the dead to help the Christian antirationalists.

In 1562 Henri Estienne, having read Sextus' manuscript of the *Hypotypöseön* during convalescence, decided to give the Greek, who was "so amusing," Latin dress. He tells his friend Henricus Memmius, "a lover of clever Greek trifles," that the new book is not only filled with matter for philologians and historians of philosophy but has other merits as well. He hopes that by making the dogmatists mad, it will restore their sanity. A second text of Sextus, the *Adversus Mathematicos*, was translated in 1569 by Gentian Hervet; in Hervet's dedicatory letter to Charles, Cardinal Lorraine, we learn that the "new Academics" are the Calvinists, whose trust in reason could possibly be destroyed by the philosophic methods of Pyrrhonism.[5] While the Christian world was learning to hold its rational breath, a young Portuguese philosopher, who praised Socrates because he wrote nothing, worked out his own system of negation.

Francisco Sanchez wrote his *Quod Nihil Scitur* in 1576 and printed it five years later. It is by no means the first modern excursion into anti-intellectualism because it was preceded by similar works from the doubting pens of Henry Cornelius Agrippa, Omer Talon, and Guy de Brues. It was, however, the first systematic handling of the question of the validity

[4] *De Rerum Natura* (Paris, 1579), p. Aiii.
[5] Sextus Empiricus, *Opera*, ed. J. A. Fabricius (Leipzig, 1718), pp. B3–C1. Calvin relied on reason only when it was enlightened by Grace, but the attitude that bothered Roman Catholics is expressed by Mornay's "Préface au Lecteur," in his *De la Vérité de la Religion Chrétienne* (Paris, 1585), where it is admitted that reason is of no help with the mysteries of religion; nonetheless, it will lead man to know God exists and help him separate the lies of religion from its truth. See Richard Popkin, *The History of Scepticism from Erasmus to Descartes* (Assen, 1960), pp. 17–87, 112–30.

of reason and knowledge, and it begins with a very basic hypothesis: "I do not even know this—that I know nothing." The target of Sanchez' philosophic arrow is, as in the case of his equally ignorant predecessors, that unhappy bull's-eye, Aristotelianism. For Sanchez, the logic and dialectic of the great Greek are words, nothing except words, of which many are totally without meaning. Knowledge, he contends, requires a mind that is perfectly free. If knowledge does not spring spontaneously from this pure source, it is not likely to be forced by some Aristotelian pump. "Nullis coacta demonstrationibus." [6] Knowledge is, he writes, usually regarded as the heaping of detail in the brain; yet the piling up of images in the eye has never been regarded as vision. If science can be defined at all, it would be called "the perfect knowledge of the object." Where will we get such knowledge in this world where we cannot know the part, let alone the whole? Man pretends to wisdom, but he cannot comprehend essence; he proposes to understand the world, but he is ignorant of himself.

To understand a clock, Sanchez states, one must know the smallest detail of its mechanism. This is substantial knowledge. What we seem now to know are fragments of knowledge based on opinions and fables, making it plain why man's wisdom is "God's foolishness." [7] The one thing we know about the world is its variousness. Men are of diverse natures and talents, and each goes his rational or irrational way. The thousands of different human faces are emblematic of the multiplicity of men's customs, laws, and religions; but this

[6] *Opera Philosophica*, ed. Joaquim de Carvalho (Coimbra, 1955), p. 10. In his *Essai sur la Méthode de Francisco Sanchez* (Paris, 1904), pp. 72–96, Emilien Senchet tries to show that Sanchez had a real knowledge of the *Hypotypöseön;* with this view Carvalho agrees (pp. lvii–lix) within limits. For further discussion see Popkin, pp. 38–43. The *Quod Nihil Scitur* was attacked by Ulrich Wild in *Quod Aliquid Scitur* (Leipzig, 1664) and by Daniel Hartnack in *Sanchez Aliquid Sciens* (Stettin, 1665).

[7] P. 19.

fantastic state of diversity makes knowledge impossible. Moreover, man cannot learn what happens in this world or in worlds beyond this one; [8] and he, himself, has no fixity of character: he is not the man at noon he was the moment before. "De homine uno post horam non asseri posse eundem esse, qui ante horam." [9] The human condition is one of complete uncertainty, and Sanchez points to the everyday experiences of his readers, which they cannot explain. The senses, instruments of knowing, vary in effectiveness; the reason, which sorts and stores sensation, has basic defects. Even if both instruments of knowledge were perfect and all other obstacles were removed, the shortness of human life and the breadth of human misery would conspire to make knowledge uncertain. In a world where the best knowledge is simply relative, the attempts of man to comprehend are pathetically useless. He may get relative knowledge, but he will never know. In the end, the best man can hope for is a modest understanding of a few facts. Sanchez concludes his modest little book with "Quid?"—reminding one of Montaigne's famous "Que sais-je"—but he also admits that even a limited pursuit of knowledge is a chase humanly worth-while.

This haunting sense of the relativity of both experience and knowledge which arises from the Academic skepticism of Sanchez is partially responsible for the conversion of Montaigne from the agitated perplexity of Christian Stoicism to the calm perplexity of Christian Pyrrhonism. [10] The author of the significantly named *Les Essais* is often at odds with

[8] Pp. 20–24.   [9] P. 26.

[10] The literature on the subject is vast, but one could consult: Arend Henning, *Der Skepticismus Montaigne's und seine geschichtliche Stellung* (Jena, 1879); Ivan Georgov, *Montaigne als Vertreter des Relativismus in der Moral* (Leipzig, 1889); F. Strowski, *Montaigne* (Paris, 1906), pp. 72–82, 146–52; Maturin Dréano, *La Pensée Religieuse de Montaigne* (Paris, 1936); Busson, *Les Sources* (1957), pp. 361–516; Popkin, pp. 44–65; H. Janssen, *Montaigne Fideiste* (Utrecht, 1930); and Donald Frame, *Montaigne's Discovery of Man* (New York, 1955), pp. 49–96.

himself, but he most plainly saw in the doubting doctrine of
Sextus Empiricus a more tolerant and humane disbelief than
the rigorous denials of the Academics permitted. The painted
quotations from Sextus and the Bible which adorned the walls
of his library are mainly sad texts describing the unhappy
conditions of man, slave either to his doubt or to his ignorance. To improve this perplexity, one neither accepts nor
rejects.[11]

> The ignorance that knows itself, judges itself, and which
> condemns itself, is not a complete ignorance; to be this, it must
> be ignorant of itself; hence the fashion of the Pyrrhonist pro-
> fession is to waver, doubt, and inquire, not to make themselves
> sure of or responsible for anything. . . . Now this position
> of their judgment, upright and inflexible, receiving all objects
> without application or agreement, led them to their Ataraxy,
> which is a peaceful condition of life, temperate and exempt
> from the agitations we receive through the impression of the
> opinion and knowledge that we think we have of things.[12]

This statement, from the "Apology for Raimond de Sebonde," was probably written down after that day in 1576
when Montaigne resigned from the Stoa and had his new
motto, " Ἐπέχω," struck on a copper jeton with the device
of a balance in equilibrium. Stoicism is a disease of young
men, and Montaigne had been recovering from it for some
time.

There are other symptoms of the break with Seneca, but
the one that has always struck Montaigne's modern readers
most forcibly is his growing awareness, as he learns more and

[11] Jean Plattard, *Montaigne et Son Temps* (Paris, 1933), p. 183. Montaigne's "atheist notions" were under attack for the next century: see
Alan M. Boase, *The Fortunes of Montaigne* (London, 1935) and Pierre
Villey, *Montaigne devant la Postérité* (Paris, 1935).
[12] *Les Essais*, ed. H. Motheau and D. Jouaust (Paris, 1886–89), III, 383–84;
see III, 25: "Philosopher c'est douter."

more, of the relativity of all knowledge. Sanchez, who wrote his book in the year of Montaigne's philosophical decision, had reached the same notion, and it had colored the face of his world. When Montaigne wrote on "The Education of Children," he accepted this relative world as the "mirror where it is necessary for us to regard ourselves so that we may know ourselves according to the right bias." In this mirror, Montaigne concludes, his "young scholar" will discover the "many humors, sects, judgments, opinions, laws, and customs" that should teach him to judge the validity of his own beliefs and enable him to recognize the imperfections and weaknesses of his own understanding as well—"no easy apprenticeship." [13] The increasing awareness of a universe which is a haze of firmly held, but widely differing, beliefs stands behind Montaigne's recommendation that the best part of wisdom is to regard all sides of any question,[14] a recommendation he illustrates by presenting the conflicting views and opinions of philosophers.[15] For Montaigne, truth becomes little more than opinion nailed to the cross of custom; and in an essay on this subject, he says flatly that "matters received with absolute and undoubting opinion have no other support than the white hairs and wrinkled face of ancient usage." [16] To the subsequent horror of Malebranche, he devoted all of "A Custom of the Isle of Cea" to the conflicting opinions about suicide as an honorable exit from a foul situation; but this hardly meant he endorsed self-murder. He is, likewise, not amazed to discover that truth is influenced by patriotism, that for most men it is the national attitude, not the *consensus gentium*, which establishes truth. "Là [the native land] est toujours la parfaite religion, la parfaite police, parfait et accompli usage de toutes choses." [17] Like Sanchez, he stood watch in hand and noticed how men as individuals were al-

[13] II, 42. [14] I, 183. [15] II, 267–71; IV, 188–91. [16] I, 164.
[17] II, 131, 149–50, 269.

ways in a state of intellectual flux;[18] this observation made him question the intelligence of men who claimed to know answers. In "Of Experience," printed in 1588, he describes "l'affirmation et l'opiniâtreté" as the ineluctable marks of "bêtise et d'ignorance."[19] Almost a decade later, in a marginal note to an early essay, he calls "conscience" a kind of custom: "chacun ayant en vénération interne les opinions et moeurs approuvées et reçues autour de lui, ne s'en peut déprendre sans remords, ne s'y appliquer sans applaudissement."[20]

One of the finest products of Montaigne's persistent belief in the relativism of human customs and notions is the rambling "Apology for Raimond de Sebonde," which was read in its own age and since with various emphases. The discourse begins with the familiar story of the presentation of a copy of Sebonde's *Theologia Naturalis* to Montaigne's father by Pierre Bunel. The latter had served time as a Protestant and knew from first hand how "this distemper would easily run into an execrable atheism," because people without judgment are likely to give up all religion when some articles of their faith "are brought in doubt." Aware of the Protestant confidence in right reason, Bunel perceived in Sebonde's "hearty and bold design" (for he undertook through "human and natural reason" to support Christianity "against atheists") a

[18] III, 4: "Ce que nous avons à cette heure proposé, nous le changeons tantôt." See also I, 50; II, 268, 279–80; III, 2–4; VI, 102.

[19] "Reason has so many shapes that we do not know which one to accept. Experience has no fewer. The consequence that we must draw from the comparison of events is uncertain, because they are always different. There is no quality so universal in this image of things as diversity and variety" (VII, 2). "Never did two men make the same judgment of the same thing, and it is impossible to find two opinions exactly alike, not only in several men, but in the same man at different hours" (VII, 6). He points out that the mind's eternal wheeling and juggling with diversity and variety is responsible for the difficulty men have in framing moral laws. Eventually, he comes to the conclusion that man's moral relativism is so profound that he has to seek his standards from animals (VII, 288–89; II, 75–77, 148–49).

[20] I, 161–62.

proper antidote for the poison of the Reformation.[21] Montaigne, who translated the book for the confusion of Huguenots, claims at the beginning of the "Apology" to be troubled by two objections commonly offered against it.

The first objection is that "Christians are to blame to repose upon human reasons their belief." This is the new Roman position; and Montaigne, denying any personal skill in theology, writes that revelation was required when the vast intellectual efforts of ancient philosophers failed to get them a proper comprehension of God. This is, of course, no ground for the abandonment of reason; but a Christian should make the embellishment, extension, and amplification of faith his proper study. He must realize, though, that he cannot arrive at spiritual ends by his own effort. "If it enter not into us by an extraordinary infusing, if it only enter, not only by arguments of reason, but, moreover, by human ways, it is not in us in true dignity and splendor, and yet, I fear, we only have it in this way." [22] So much for the first objection. The second, which will require the remainder of Montaigne's effort, is that the arguments of Sebonde are "weak and unfit to sustain his propositions." [23]

Before he comments on the second, common objection against Sebonde's excursion in natural theology, Montaigne states that "signs" such as hope, trust, ceremonies, penance, and martyrs were "common" to all religions and should not

[21] III, 171–73.
[22] III, 174–75. In his preface, Sebonde describes the two books given man by God. The Book of Creatures, given in the beginning, is made up of words in which each letter is a creature "written by the finger of God." The Scriptures, or second book, can be falsified and misinterpreted and can best be read by clerks; but the Book of Creatures is sound; even heretics cannot misread it. One must, however, be illuminated by God, and for want of this light, the pagan philosophers missed the true wisdom in this book. *Theologia Naturalis sive Liber Creaturarum* (Frankfort, 1635). Sebonde urges men to hold to what suits them even if they do not understand it (p. 112).
[23] III, 187.

be held as something special in Christianity.[24] It is also plain that he does not consider atheism, which he describes as "dénaturé et monstrueux," as worse than any other fantastic religious notion—Calvinism, for example. It, too, is merely a "superficial impression" that arises from the "disorder of an unhinged understanding." When Montaigne looks at the Book of Creatures, he, like Sebonde and many men before him, sees in it the marks of the "grand architecte"; [25] hence, he can assume that rational arguments, "faith coming to tint and illustrate them," [26] are sound. He realizes that one man is inclined to alter the statements of another (and this may have happened to Sebonde) to suit his own prejudices. "To an atheist all writings tend to atheism, and he infects innocent texts with his poison." [27] Christians, Montaigne confesses, are very kindly in meeting atheists on their own rational grounds when they could take a great advantage by bringing forward the invincible force of authority. Sebonde has, consequently, followed the decorous pattern of Christian attack. Are there better arguments than he found? "Considérons donc pour cette heure l'homme seul." [28]

This portion of the "Apology" is succeeded by the well-known excursus in which Montaigne, reversing the method of Sebonde, compared man with animals to prove that man has no advantages some or all animals do not own and that even man's highly vaunted reason is probably only a kind of animal trait. Animals, contrary to man's notions about himself, may have both religion and pious customs, because elephants are known to pray and ants have been observed interring their dead.[29] In other words, creatures, "subject to man," are almost his equals. In addition, they have some advantages. They have, for instance, not caught the infection of thinking. "The plague of man is the opinion of wisdom;

[24] III, 177.   [25] III, 183–84.   [26] III, 186.   [27] III, 187.
[28] III, 189.   [29] III, 222.

and for this reason it is that ignorance is so recommended to us by our religion as proper to faith and obedience." [30] In the due course of time, the essayist added a Pascalean note for the final edition: "Il nous faut abêtir pour nous assagir, et nous éblouir pour nous guider." [31]

Some years later Montaigne would buy a copy of the *Learned Ignorance* of Cusanus at Venice, but now he follows the text of Sebonde when he talks of Christian truth.

> The participation that we have in the knowledge of truth, such as it is, is not acquired by our own power. God has informed us by the witnesses he has chosen out of the common people, simple and ignorant men, to instruct us in his admirable secrets. Our faith is not of our own acquiring; it is a pure gift from the liberality of another. It is not by thinking or understanding that we have received our religion; it is by the authority and command of a stranger. The weakness of our judgment aids us more than its strength, and our blindness helps more than clear-sightedness. It is by the mediation of our ignorance rather than of our knowledge that we know aught of divine wisdom. It is not strange if our natural and earthly means could not conceive supernatural and heavenly knowledge. . . . If I ask, finally, whether it be in the power of man to find out what he seeks, and if that search wherein he has been busy for so many centuries has enriched him with some new power or solid truth, I believe he will confess to me, if he speaks conscientiously, that all he has from the long pursuit of knowledge is an awareness of his vileness and weakness. The ignorance naturally ours is thus by long study confirmed and made sure.[32]

This text eventually leads Montaigne to the camp of those who have learned "to judge their ignorance" and whose "mot sacramental" is "je soutiens, je ne bouge." [33]

[30] III, 259. [31] III, 267. [32] III, 278–79. [33] III, 287.

Montaigne adorns the skeptical tenets of the Pyrrhonists (those of the Academics having been declared nefarious) with the green wreaths of Christian approval. Through a series of pages, he describes their method of inquisitive discussion—he will eventually show the follies of all other schools of philosophy [34]—and commends it as the finest preparation for revelation. Illiterates and ignoramuses were gathered from Palestine to hear the actual words of Christ; similarly ready, Pyrrhonic man, naked in mind, confessing his weakness, humble, obedient, and hating heresy, will be like a blank page for God to write upon as he pleases. "C'est une carte blanche préparée à prendre du doigt de Dieu telles formes qu'il lui plaira y graver." [35] Later, after he has reiterated how many of man's speculations have come to nothing, Montaigne observes that his "poor, naked forked animal" would have been better off had philosophers "let him alone in his natural estate to receive the appearance of things as they present themselves to us through our senses." [36] It is plain enough that even when the philosophers, relying alone on their reason, speak of some noble subject such as immortality, they can find only weak arguments to support it; because "all things produced by our reasoning or understanding, true or false, are subject to disagreement and uncertainty." [37] As a consequence, Montaigne advises men to put aside "this infinite confusion of opinions and this universal debate about the knowledge of things." The best men by birth, talents, and education cannot even agree that there is a sky above us.[38]

To illustrate his doctrine, Montaigne turns once more to the relativity of knowledge. For centuries men thought the earth was the center of the universe, but now Copernicus, agreeing with the older views of Cleanthes and Nicetas, says

[34] III, 290–IV, 48.   [35] III, 290.   [36] IV, 53.   [37] IV, 73.
[38] IV, 91.

the earth moves. In due time, remarks the dubious essayist, there will be another cosmic theory. Medicine, like astronomy, has also a venerable history, but a "nouveau venu," Paracelsus, announces that the whole "order of ancient rules" has only been successful in making men die. Other noble and respected theories, like those about winds, have blown away. Jacques Peletier, for instance, has demonstrated in Montaigne's house that Euclid's first proposition can be upset. The geography of Ptolemy has vanished with his cosmology. These observations permit Montaigne to write another long and heavily illustrated account of relativism in morals, laws, customs, and rites.[39] One may steal in Sparta; in some countries infanticide, patricide, and free use of women are morally approved. "In short, there is nothing so extreme that the custom of some nation or other permits it." [40] But Montaigne is never satisfied with description. If he were called upon to explain this undulating sea of variety, in which doubting man strives to swim with ignorant hands, he could offer his theory of sensation, which he shares with Sanchez.

First, Montaigne inquires whether or not man has enough senses to obtain full and accurate knowledge of the world? Perhaps, like a man born without sight who knows no difference, he lacks some organ of sensation he knows not of. Granted, however, this is not the case, are the senses accurate? Can we not perform experiments which show how our senses may be deceived and lead us into illusion if not into temptation? [41] Montaigne anticipates at this point both Calderon and Descartes and remarks that "they who have compared our life to a dream were probably righter than they knew." [42] He now piles doubt upon objection, objection on doubt, until man can say only "to me it seems so." Actually, we are all, as he puts it, in the position of those who, "since they never knew Socrates, cannot, when they see his picture, say it is

[39] IV, 105–37.   [40] IV, 124.   [41] IV, 138–50.   [42] IV, 152.

like him." [43] After the thread is wound off and we are at the bare Pyrrhonic bottom, we are forced to admit that man can rise to nothing through the unaided power of his reason. "He will rise if God will lend him his hand; he will rise if abandoning and renouncing his own means, he will let himself be lifted and sustained by Divine Grace. There is no other way." [44]

On this note the "Apology" ends, and this ultimate tone supports those who have claimed Montaigne for the yellow tents of the fideists. Reason can offer us very little spiritual information, they say, so one should wait, and, perhaps, in time God will help by raising the level of our wisdom and explaining the nature of being. This portrait of Montaigne is probably better than the ungenerous one which exhibits him as unsportingly throwing the dust of skepticism in the eyes of Protestants. It is unquestionably better than the one delineating him as a masked agnostic who accepted the state church because it provided for his personal comfort and his political convenience. The painting of Montaigne as the sardonic mocker is washed from the wall by the essays themselves; in fact, Montaigne goes out of his way to attack "ce moqueur ancien," the elder Pliny, for his bitter opinions on man's restful mortality.[45] True enough, Montaigne objects, as an intelligent Christian, to the superstitious and indecent beliefs and practices of vulgar Christians. He thought it improper to subject God "to the vain and feeble appearances of our understanding," [46] or to promise oneself a heaven "with all sorts of worldly conveniences and pleasures." [47] He cannot tolerate those people who judge a religion by its worldly success, men who are "record keepers of the designs of God." [48] He had, likewise, a most jaundiced eye for many reported miracles and for the supernatural luggage in most

[43] IV, 160.   [44] IV, 166.   [45] IV, 31.   [46] IV, 23.
[47] IV, 13–15.   [48] II, 148–49.

saints' legends. But these solid objections make him an intelligent Christian, not an agnostic disguised nor a Christian
for convenience' sake. Montaigne simply agrees, as he admits,
with St. Augustine that "it is better to lean towards doubt
than assurance in things hard to prove and dangerous to
believe." [49]

II

Three years before his death, Montaigne met Pierre Charron, who became his great disciple.[50] Though Charron was
a priest with a reputation as a preacher, he became, perhaps
more than Montaigne, the special target of the antiatheists.
Greatly admired by Gassendi, Naudé, and Patin—the last
described *De la Sagesse* as a "livre divin" [51]—he was violently
attacked by Garasse and held in deep suspicion by Mersenne.[52] When one remembers that he composed a typical
book against all doubters (and especially against Mornay),
the *Les Trois Vérités contre les Athées, Idolâtres, Juifs,
Mahométans, Hérétiques, et Schismatiques*, one is amazed
that these charges could come from the Roman side.

The first part of this book, directed partly against Mornay's
De la Vérité, strikes against atheists, who deny the existence
of God, Academics and Pyrrhonists, who live by doubt, and
deists.[53] We are introduced into the area of unknowing by

[49] VI, 262.
[50] Henri Barckhausen, "Pierre Charron," in Paul Bonnefon, *Montaigne
et Ses Amis* (Paris, 1898), II, 213–311. The standard study is Jean-Baptist
Sabrié, *De l'Humanisme au Rationalisme: Pierre Charron (1541–1603),
l'Homme, l'Oeuvre, l'Influence* (Paris, 1913), pp. 1–254.
[51] *Lettres*, I, 252, 267; Patin later (III, 510) describes him as "un divin
homme."
[52] Sabrié, pp. 454–88. See also Heinrich Teipel, *Zur Frage des Skeptizismus
bei Pierre Charron* (Eberfeld, 1912). Robert Lenoble thinks that his stress-
ing of variety à la Montaigne aroused Mersenne's fears (pp. 542–44).
[53] *Les Trois Vérités*, pp. 7–12.

being told that God is so infinite we cannot know him. As finite creatures, we do not understand limited phenomena, such as the pull of the magnet on iron or that of the moon on the tides; not knowing these things, we can hardly hope to learn to know God. "If one will consider the disproportion between a single drop of water and the sea with its rivers, will this drop tell aught about the sea and its waters?" There are, however, three modes by which we can come to some intimation of God's nature: we can know him as a negative of imperfections, through his creatures, and through all perfections. The best way of knowing God is, however, through perfect ignorance.[54] Charron follows his master and faces the consequences of a double ignorance: God cannot be known; man lacks the power to know. With these premises announced, he proposes to meet the atheists on the plains of reason and prove God's existence.

Charron does not offer very original theological proofs; the Greeks had done that. But he points out that the existence of a finite world, which moves, is various, harmonious, good, and with an end in view, requires the existence of a creator.[55] To these common enough proofs, he adds the one based on the conscience, which exists in all men even though they worship other gods. These demonstrations of God's being are further supported with proofs drawn from demonology, prophecy, and the prevalence of miracles.[56] The claims of Providence are proudly advanced,[57] and the contrary arguments of Sextus Empiricus against God's existence are dashed to pieces.[58] Charron now gets Calvin in his gun sights, and this change of quarry permits him to discharge his doubts against the value of the human mind. There is, he insists, no religious reality outside the Gothic walls of the Roman Church; moreover, this "inner light," so highly regarded by

[54] Pp. 19–20.   [55] Pp. 28–35.   [56] Pp. 40–45.   [57] Pp. 49–51.
[58] Pp. 60–61.

the Protestants as a bright form of illumination, is really a private and very eccentric lamp, not likely to help in the dark. It is clear to Charron that Protestants, by stepping away from authoritative tradition, have really moved into the shadows of religious skepticism.

Les Trois Vérités would probably have gained for Charron neither blame nor fame; the work that won him renown and got him charged with theological doubt is *De la Sagesse*, a book prefaced by a carefully explained allegorical plate that shows Sagesse, a nude girl crowned with laurel and olive, standing on a symbolic cube and gazing at her reflection in a mirror extended by "a hand of God." Chained to the cube are four fully dressed women, personifying Passion, Opinion, Superstition, and the False Science, against which Sagesse protests. "La science, vertu ou preud'hommie artificielle, acquise, pédantesque, serf des lois et coutumes."

De la Sagesse tells the reader at its beginning that man's first duty is to study himself because this is the only way to arrive at a knowledge of God. "Par la connaissance de soi l'homme monte et arrive plutôt et mieux à la connaissance de Dieu." [59] All knowledge, however, comes to man through his senses; they are his first masters, and they are the beginning and end of all; [60] but the senses are not altogether trustworthy. Beasts may have other notions than man, "and who is to be believed? An infant sees, hears, and tastes other than a man; a man than an old man. . . . In this great diversity and contradictoriness, what shall we hold for certain?" [61] There is then, Charron observes, something above the sense; certain seeds sown in the soul that are not always properly tilled and cultivated. Man, unlike animals, does not depend

---

[59] *Traité de la Sagesse* (Paris, 1783), p. 3.   [60] P. 96.

[61] Pp. 101–2. Charron has previously differentiated between men and animals (pp. 67–84) by observing that animals have the advantage of health and bodily vigor, moderation, repose, exemption from vices, superstition, avarice, ambition, etc.

entirely on his sense. "It would be shameful if this so high and divine faculty should beg its goods of things so low and vile as the senses." [62] *Sagesse* is, therefore, the inhabitant of the soul.

In the second part of his book, Charron makes a strong distinction between "science" and "sagesse." Science is simply a heap of information gathered from what one has seen, heard, or read; it is a small and sterile good, unnecessary and really without use, since many people live quite successful existences without it. At its worst, it is proud, presumptuous, arrogant, opinionated, indiscreet, and quarrelsome. *Sagesse* "is worth more than all the science in the world" because it is the rein of the soul managed by judgment. It is "un bien nécessaire et universellement utile à toutes choses; elle gouverne et règle tout; il n'y a rien qui se puisse cacher ou dérober de sa juridiction et connaissance." [63] In other words, *sagesse* is like the sapience of God; something above human reason but not denied to men. It is the proper adornment of what Charron would call "Preud'hommie."

"Preud'hommie," as the allegorical prefatory plate showed, is both real and artificial. The latter, product of submission to customs, religions, laws, "troubled by scruples and doubts," is totally worldly. Produced by many various factors, it is wavering and completely unstable, utterly different from true "Preud'hommie," which lives by Nature's laws; "that is to say, the universal equity and reason which glows in each of us." To follow this glowing light is to follow the richest and noblest creature in us, for we are by nature good, and when we stray, we are led by some badly conceived notion of profit or pleasure. To live contentedly and happily does not require courtliness, learning, or cleverness. One need follow Nature and nothing more. All sages, Charron states, have advised this, for under the tutelage of Nature the seeds

[62] Pp. 121–22.   [63] Pp. 625–28.

of virtue, probity, and justice, which are in man, are shown how to grow and bear fruit.[64] But man has been so diverted by customs, ceremonies, and opinions from following Nature that he is forced to observe animals to find the true image of Nature now lost in him.[65] Man has a natural certainty, but it is founded on a philosophic relativism. This relativism bothers Charron as much as it did Montaigne. To illustrate the fragility of human truth, Montaigne's *exempla* come handily to Charron's aid. "In our time the principles and rules of antiquity about astronomy, medicine, geometry, and the nature and movement of winds have been completely overturned." This uncertainty of man's knowledge suggests that one human opinion or so-called conclusion is as good as another. "Man has no principles not divinely revealed; all else are only dreams and smoke." [66] This axiom forces Charron to contemplate the diversity in all human matters, a topic to which he frequently returns.[67]

The diversity of the world's laws and customs and the strangeness of many of them are curious. There is no opinion so odd, says Charron, echoing once again the grave words of Montaigne, that it is not established in some place by law or custom. "I shall be content to mention only a few examples to show how difficult it is to believe anything. I shall not talk about diversity in religion because religion is subject to enormous strangenesses and immense impostures." "De plus grandes étrangetés, et impostures plus grossières." [68]

It is good of Charron to state that he will not consider religion at this point, because he had finished a long chapter on the subject just a few pages earlier. The religion Charron discusses in the famous fifth chapter of his second book is not in his judgment religion at all, but superstition. It occupies a place in his system with "science" and with "preud'-

---

[64] Pp. 317–22.   [65] P. 326.   [66] P. 65.   [67] Pp. 145–46, 206–18.
[68] P. 387.

hommie artificielle." It is "frightfully diverse" because there seems to be nothing in the world—no matter how high or low—that has not at some moment been deified. All religions, Charron writes, agree in principles; they have miracles, prodigies, oracles, saints, prophets, festivals, and articles of faith necessary to salvation. They all begin modestly, but they grow and add authority. They all teach that God may be appeased or persuaded by "prayers, presents, vows, promises, feasts, and incense." They all believe that giving ourselves pain is the best way to move God, and so the world is filled with "compagnies et confréries" devoted to this end.

Each religion has some differences which make it feel it is better and truer than the others, but actually they all depend on their predecessors. The Jewish religion was based on the Egyptian and other gentile religions; Christianity sprang from Judaism; Mohammedanism is the child of both Christianity and Judaism. The human mind, capable only of middle flights, cannot really understand religion, for all religions "are strange and horrible to the common sense." For this reason there are numerous non-religious people. The trouble is that people examine religion with their own judgment, when it is necessary to be simple, obedient, and good-natured to receive religion properly.[69]

Religious people, says Charron, sometimes say religion, in that it is contrary to common sense, cannot be received by natural or human means but must be celestially revealed. The history of religion proves the contrary. Religions are transmitted and developed through natural human means. "The nation, the country, the locale," he writes, remembering Montaigne's similar remark, "give the religion . . . we are circumcised, baptized Jews, Mohammedans, Christians before we know we are men." [70] This conclusion, he feels, is established because people often turn against the religion of

[69] Pp. 341–46.   [70] P. 347.

their parents or their land; this revulsion would not occur "were religions divinely planted." One must—and here is the rub—distinguish between religion and superstition. One characteristic of the superstitiously religious man is that he cannot let men who think differently live in peace. The God he imagines is a difficult God, one hard to appease, who examines all men's deeds in the manner of an unusually severe judge. The superstitious man is always trembling with fear because he is always afraid he has either done wrong or failed to do right. He is also given to flattering God, importuning him with prayers, offerings, and vows. To prove his doctrinal points, he invents miracles and "interprets purely natural events as expressly sent by God." Altogether, the superstitious man reminds the sensible priest Charron of a badly advised husband who neglects his honest and modest wife to run after a tricked-out quean, being deceived by her "mignotises et artifices." [71]

There is no question that men are naturally given to superstitions, and Charron cannot deny that it is an inclination encouraged by the "great and powerful" who find superstition a good means of controlling and leading the simple citizenry by the nose. He finds true religion not hard to identify and distinguish from superstition. True religion has little in the way of exterior trapping. It impels the soul to admire and contemplate the grandeur and majesty of the First Cause "sans grande déclaration ou détermination d'icelle, ou prescription de son service." As a result of the union of admiration and meditation, "they know," Charron writes, "the goodness, perfection, and infiniteness of the all-comprehensible and unknowable, as the Pythagoreans and the most worthy philosophers teach." [72] This is not really an impious or atheistic remark, but these are hardly words to find proper accommodation in the mouth of a Christian priest. Some his-

[71] Pp. 349–50.   [72] Pp. 352–53.

torians of thought have been inclined to see in Charron a kind of philosophical mystic following his own road to God. This may not be true, but it is plain enough that he was no atheist. Actually, he was moving in the same direction as Silhon,[73] Gibieuf, Berulle, and Suarez, the Catholic masters who directed the attention of Descartes, and perhaps that of Herbert of Cherbury, to the doctrine of innate ideas. Provided that they were not too limitedly defined, these inborn notions

[73] In his first work, *Les Deux Vérités* (Paris, 1626), Silhon states that certain ideas are accepted by the mind as soon as they are comprehended (pp. 16–17), and one of these is God's existence (p. 21). In the *De l'Immortalité de l'Âme*, he holds that the knowledge of God is innate. Philosophers get it from the light of reason; common people, from tradition and authority and "par l'impressions infusées par la nature, et entretenues par les choses de dehors, et les traces des mains de Dieu qui sont semées dans le monde" (p. 106). Pyrrhonists contend that sensation is subject to error and thus weaken the basis of Christianity, which depends on sensational certainty for proof of miracles (pp. 109–25). God, he thinks, provided us with exact senses, if we use them properly. In *De la Certitude des Connaissances Humaines* (Paris, 1661), he writes that Montaigne's doubts make all things Christian doubtful (pp. 1–6); there is good in Montaigne, but there are also "des germes de libertinage" (p. 9). He urges his readers to trust the senses because God would not make them defective any more than a watchmaker would make a clock that does not keep time (pp. 25–30). With his views one may compare those of P. de Villemandy's *Scepticismus Debellatus* (Leyden, 1697).

De Villemandy, one of many seventeenth-century antiskeptics, complains that learned people become skeptics and that skeptics become atheists (p. 5). Ancient skeptics, he says, attempted to dismiss all knowledge; the moderns, Descartes and Gassendi, attack only physical and natural concepts, but they have disciples who bring doubts into all areas. Men now, he continues, discuss whether or not polygamy, divorce, adultery, and incest are right; whether the Bible is authentic or not; and whether there is a true religion (pp. 7–14). He lists Beauregard, Gassendi, Machiavelli, Hobbes, and Spinoza as the victims of skepticism, which is the ultimate refuge of those who are running from their consciences and the justice of God (pp. 21–32). Truth depends on diversity of mind, differences of men, multiplicity of senses in all men or variations of sense in the individual, the diversity and multiplicity of objects, dissimilarity in quantities, and rareness or frequency of observation (pp. 32–36). He concludes that truth is the mind's center of gravity. It does not move toward falsehood but toward some truth; in fact, the more truthful a proposition is, the more quickly the mind accepts it. To be a skeptic, then, is to renounce the history of the human mind.

avoided the unhappy relativism proclaimed by Sanchez and Montaigne and spoiled one of the finest weapons of skepticism by providing the mind with tools for the measurement of sensation. Relativism, which was to mother comparative studies of religion, had, however, come to stay. One may turn to Jean Bodin, an economist, historian, and philosopher, slightly older than Montaigne, to learn more about it.

III

In his essay, "The Defence of Seneca and Plutarch," Montaigne describes Jean Bodin as "a good author of our times, and a writer of much greater judgment than the crowd of current hacks." When Montaigne made this statement, Bodin had written *Les Six Livres de la République* and the *Methodus ad Facilem Historiarum Cognitionem;* he had also issued his very stout attack on witchcraft, the *Démonomanie*, which Montaigne assuredly had not read when he praised Bodin's judgment. The humanist, who expressed his grave distress over the burning of witches, would hardly praise the wisdom of a fellow jurist who wrote such a superstitious book. Charron, like Montaigne, had read the *République* and the later *Naturae Theatrum;* [74] but the *Heptaplomeres*, Bodin's most learnedly impressive work, extant only in manuscript until Guhrauer's 1841 edition, was unknown to both. One wonders what they would have made of it. It is the product of the same intellectual season that turned their thoughts to relativism, but it goes far beyond limits known to them, for it is really the first attempt at what is later called "higher criticism."

Bodin is assumed to have finished this book in 1593, when he was sixty-three. Withheld from the press, it was, never-

[74] Sabrié, pp. 262–67.

theless, well known to men of the next two hundred years.[75] They read it; they copied it; they refuted it. Pierre Huet attacked it in his *Demonstratio Evangelica* (1679); Johannes Deicmann replied to it in his *De Naturalismo cum Aliorum, Tum Maxime, Jo. Bodini* (1683), and describes Bodin as both a Protestant and an indifferentist.[76] Huet is probably the first of Bodin's critics to report him a secret convert to the synagogue, a rumor (accepted by Bayle) which was current before Huet's book was printed.[77] There were, indeed, doubts about the nature of Bodin's religious beliefs as early as 1593,[78] when a lack of pious fire was noticed by readers of the *République*. The doubts of the orthodox about Jean Bodin's convictions were removed after manuscripts of the

[75] Most manuscripts are annotated "H.E.J.B.A.S.A.AE. LXIII," which is read "Hic est" or "Haec ego" Johannes Bodinus Andegavinus "scripsi anno" or "suae anno" aetate LXIII; see Henri Baudrillart, *J. Bodin et Son Temps* (Paris, 1853), pp. 190–221. There were numerous publications about Bodin as a political thinker in the nineteenth century; the modern accounts of the *Heptaplomeres* are found in Charbonnel, pp. 622–27, Busson, *Les Sources* (1957), pp. 540–60, and Roger Chauviré, *Jean Bodin* (Paris, 1914). Chauviré also published a summary and partial text of a French-manuscript translation of the *Heptaplomeres*, the *Colloque de Jean Bodin des Secrets Cachez des Choses Sublimes entre Sept Scavans Qui Sont de Differens Sentimens.*

[76] Chauviré, *Colloque*, pp. 4–22. Deicmann's book (Kilon, 1683) continues the speculation about Bodin and repeats Patin's report that the *Heptaplomeres* is an account of a real discussion. He also tells about the extant manuscripts and their origins. He does not think Bodin so bad as Vanini, Hobbes, or Spinoza, but he objects very much to the discussion on the fourth day of the historic evolution of religion. I expect from his account that he had only a partial manuscript.

[77] Deicmann (p. 12) says Bodin died a Jew, as does Patin on two occasions (II, 480; III, 679).

[78] A. Possevinus, *Judicium de Nuae . . . Scriptis* (Lyons, 1593), p. 41. Actually, the discussion of Bodin's real beliefs still continues. Pierre Mesnard, in "La Pensée Religieuse de Bodin," *Revue de Seizième Siècle*, XVI (1929), 77–121, argues on the evidence of the letter to Bautru (reprinted by Chauviré in *Jean Bodin*, pp. 521–24) that Bodin was a deist when he wrote the epistle in which Plato and Christ are tacitly compared as servants of the Divine. Febvre (p. 118) holds, as he had in an article of 1934, that Bodin and Postel were both in search of some universal belief that could be used as a substitute for a Catholicism, which they felt was ruined.

Heptaplomeres were in free circulation. By then he was safely dead, but, thereafter, he stands shoulder to shoulder with other French atheists before the firing squad of the faithful.

The *Heptaplomeres,* following the manner of Plato, is a conversation among seven carefully characterized exponents of the cults of Europe: Paulus Coronaeus, a Roman Catholic; Antonius Curtius, a Calvinist; Fredericus Podamicus, a Lutheran; Octavius Fagnola, a Mohammedan convert; Solomon Barcassius, a Jew; Diego Toralba, a naturalist; and Hieronymus Senamus, an indifferentist.[79] Though numerous philosophical and theological subjects enter into the talks between these interlocutors, who have come to Venice from Turkey, Spain, Belgium, France, Rome, and Tübingen, an attempt is made by Bodin to give the *Heptaplomeres* a dramatic and a literary emphasis. We know, for instance, that the author is one of the speakers. He addresses the whole work to "N. T." and relates how he came to Venice and was asked to the house of Coronaeus, which was splendid in its collections of plants and minerals; but he never reveals which one of the speakers he is. We are, as a consequence, led into the midst of a real fiction, and we are not dramatically surprised when the host, at the end of a grand dinner, says, "Gentlemen, did we talk enough yesterday about the immortality of the soul?" [80]

The literary nature of this impressive series of discourses is enhanced by frequent quotations from poets. The rather short first book contains verses from Horace, Homer, Virgil, a so-called epitaphic poem, "Ego Isis Sum Aegypti Regina/ A Mercurio Erudita," fragments of sailor songs in four lan-

---

[79] One should at this point recall Geoffrey Valée and his account of the different sects in his *Le Fleo de la Foy;* see F. Lachevre, *Mélanges* (Paris, 1920), for a reprint of the book and a biography.

[80] *Colloquium Heptaplomeres de Rerum Sublimium Arcanis Abditis,* ed. L. Noack (Giessen, 1857), pp. 1–3.

guages, and the full text of "L'Esprit, si Dieu le Mande/ Souffle Tempêtueux." Toward the end of the book, an original poem in praise of the "Thrice great Father of the Waves" is placed in the mouth of Mohammedan Octavius, who has been describing his attempt to smuggle a mummy out of Egypt and the storm which, as a consequence of this act, almost sank his boat. This Octavius is a dramatist as well as a poet; it is his "Turkish Tragedy" that the narrator is reading at the beginning of Books Four and Five when he is summoned to dinner and the next colloquy. This play about the murder of King Suleiman by his sons furnishes the subject for a discussion of the nature of musical, poetical, and mathematical numbers.[81] Besides Octavius, others of these men are accomplished Latin poets. The disciple of naturalism, Toralba, writes a fine iambic, "Avare Piscator"; [82] the two Protestants present poems [83] of their making, and Fredericus even attempts a Sapphic. Toward the end of the *Heptaplomeres*, the literary Mohammedan reads another of his compositions, a somewhat pessimistic piece beginning, "Humani generis querelas/ Coelestis pater audiit gravate/ Excusantis originem malorum." [84] The gravest poet is, of course, Solomon, who furnishes his associates with three of his original verses.[85] But Bodin did not intend the *Heptaplomeres* to be a work of literature; its purpose is more serious than sheer delight. The first part of the book considers matters essential to any solemn consideration of the supernatural; the second part is concerned with a discussion of the best religion and an examination of the nature of Christianity.

The first three books of the *Heptaplomeres* treat of many topics that follow one another by a kind of theological or historical association, but the principal subjects discussed from all sides are the nature of miracle, Providence and the eternity

---

[81] Pp. 112–14.   [82] P. 52.   [83] Pp. 100, 114.   [84] P. 307.
[85] Pp. 147, 199, 311.

of the world, the existence and qualities of demons and angels, the corporeity or incorporeity of God, the obscurity of Scripture, the nature of allegory, the problem of evil, and the resurrection of the dead. In the course of these discussions, the personal qualities of the representatives of religious attitudes become clear. Toralba, for instance, is urged by Coronaeus to offer a scientific explanation of modern miracles; to this he replies that there are certain things he can learn by reason, but he prefers to go slowly on this subject. He does not hesitate to admit the immodesty of many rationalists.[86] He believes in the creation of the world,[87] the incorporeity of God,[88] and a strong distinction between physics and metaphysics.[89] He cannot, however, stomach the notion of the resurrection in one day of all the dead and their immediate ascension to heaven in flesh and bone. It is, he remarks, at least 74,697,600 miles to the fixed stars, and, moving at the phenomenal rate of fifty miles a day, it would take about 80,000 years to get that far.[90] This whole discussion had been brought about by Coronaeus' conviction that all the cadavers would get up and by Senamus' observation that he could believe anything but this. He is, in fact, not surprised that the Athenians laughed at St. Paul when he proposed a universal resurrection. To Toralba there is no mystery in this laughter, since he does not always adhere to his earlier, more pious view that "in matters difficult and remote from common sense we ought not to seek out the exquisite subtility of arguments but accept that which has been wisely ascertained about the mysteries of God." [91]

Whereas Toralba maintains, in spite of the fact he is often the center of combined Catholic and Protestant attack, a moderately rationalistic position, Senamus, the indifferentist, pushes much harder against orthodox positions. When

[86] P. 19.   [87] Pp. 24–25.   [88] Pp. 38, 46.   [89] P. 41.
[90] Pp. 106–7.   [91] P. 82.

the men of faith point to the Great Chain of Being as evidence
of Providence, he objects that without the necessity of causal
sequence all knowledge is destroyed.[92] He is the only speaker
who presents arguments for the corporeity of God; he does
so in order to show his companions how foolish it is to talk
about this power, which "no one living has seen." [93] Throughout a long passage in which the others recall the appearance
of flights of birds or shoals of fish to warn or nourish men
and relate other disturbances in the natural course of things,
he continually argues for a natural explanation.[94] He points
to the vast number of angels and demons required to do all the
good and bad things they are said to do.[95] When the subject
of evil comes up, and it is simply defined as the absence of
good, Senamus remarks, "If evil is naught, then he who does
evil, does nothing. But he who does nothing gets no punishment; hence, he who does evil should not be punished." [96]
Later, he inquires why God permits devils to assail men and
quotes St. Augustine's remark to the effect that God inclines
men to evil.[97] Hearing this, Coronaeus promptly changes the
subject to the nature of angels.

Throughout the first three books, it is clear that Paulus
Coronaeus, the Venetian host, is a man of simple faith, who
accepts without question what Rome accepts. As a result, he
always has the word "confidimus" at the end of his tongue.
The representatives of Protestantism are more learned than
he, but they all betray some of the doctrinal peculiarities and
prejudices of their sects. Fredericus, who is a professional
mathematician, objects, for instance, to allegorical interpre-
tations of Scripture; he is twitted by Octavius about the
literal worth of the story of Eve and her encounter with the
symbolic serpent and about the literal meaning of the famous
text from Corinthians: "Littera occidit, spiritus vivificat." [98]

[92] Pp. 24–25.   [93] Pp. 42, 45.   [94] Pp. 56–67.   [95] Pp. 69, 91–101.
[96] P. 87.   [97] P. 90.   [98] P. 76.

The Jew, Solomon, a man made tolerant by learning, listens like a schoolmaster to the others and then supplies them with illumination from Leo Hebraeus or Rambam. The major objections to Christian doctrine do not come, as one would normally expect, from him or Octavius, but from Toralba and Senamus. Neither of these men is an atheist; each simply has a sense of God which differs from that of the others. Senamus quotes Psalm 64:2 against his fellows and then turns, for he is a learned Semiticist, to Rabbi Moses in an effort to gloss the praise of silence. "One praises God in silence because who and what he is can be explained by no word or grasped by no understanding." [99] With the characters of the speakers established and the ground cleared of general topics, Bodin now directs his puppets to talk about "true religion," the Bible, the Incarnation, and the history of Christianity.

Though Book Four begins with a literary discussion followed by a choral hymn, Senamus promptly gets matters under way by objecting to Coronaeus' recommendation of the "true religion"; no one knows what it is, and an eclectic faith is, under those circumstances, the only wise faith. Fredericus, surprised, inquires whether there is anyone who doubts the truth of Christianity. "Only all of Asia, most of Africa, and a great part of Europe," responds Octavius,[100] reminding us of a man who had read Pomponazzi and Vanini. All the world, Coronaeus tolerantly remarks, is convinced it is better to have the wrong religion than none. "Illud omnibus persuasum esse opinor, multo praestabilius esse falsam, quam nullam habere religionem." [101] Senamus agrees with this remark because he objects to the leaders of new religions who feel they must destroy old ones. In this way "man's necessary fear of the divine is decreased." [102] Toralba enters the discussion with his theory that religion depends on knowledge, opinion, or faith. If it depends on knowledge, it is infallible;

[99] P. 43.   [100] P. 125.   [101] P. 124.   [102] Pp. 126–27.

but no one has been able to supply religion with such a basis, though many have tried. So theologians insist on faith, which is nothing but agreement and is based largely on our confidence in some religious author or teacher.

It is clear that a true religion must be certified. Some of the interlocutors will not accept Coronaeus' proof by authority; others will not accept the Scriptures, even when they are interpreted by "wisemen." Senamus thinks God must be the author of the true faith, but how does one know? "Hoc opus, hic labor est." Curtius defines it as the doctrine and rites proved by the authority of the Church, the truth of Scripture, antiquity, divine oracles, heavenly manifestations, and good arguments. This reminds Senamus of Apollo's answer to the question, "Which is the best religion?" "The oldest." "Which is the oldest?" "The best." Solomon argues that Judaism is oldest, but wins no converts. Octavius does even worse than the Jew when he speaks out for Mohammed. Toralba, who held that the best religion was the oldest,[103] eventually explains what he meant by defining natural religion, which is the pure and simple adoration of a single God, the faith of the Golden Age. In that sweet time, he says, Nature filled men with necessary virtues, and their acts have since been approved by all philosophers. The religion of Nature demands that one subscribe to no rites, avoiding by this wise provision the quarrels between sects. "Hanc enim religionem omnium antiquissimam ac optimam esse confido."[104] Toralba has, it is clear, learned to use Coronaeus' favorite verb, *confidere*.

Book Five and the fifth day of debate opens with Senamus enumerating ten categories of religious practitioners,

---

[103] Pp. 129–33.

[104] P. 172. Solomon and Octavius claim he is talking about their religions, but he had done this before when he said to Solomon (p. 143) that if a man was innately aware of natural law and religion, the rites established by Moses were unnecessary.

ranging from those who worship God without hope of profit
or without legal or social pressure to those who live like animals and have no conception of a higher power.[105] Toralba
holds that in the search for God, divine inspiration is an essential force and guide; [106] whereas Senamus believes virtue
would be quite enough.[107] Each speaker now makes a confession of his own beliefs; and Toralba once again takes a
stand for natural religion by observing that Abel, Enoch,
and Job managed without the Mosaic laws and that Moses
did not require the Christian dispensation.

> I do not reject these holy books that are so famous, but I
> would not govern myself by their authority. I cannot do so,
> but I would not if I could. I am always controlled by reason.
> I am, however, often in dispute with the Epicureans, who re-
> gard these books as fabulous, and I do not wish to oppose them
> with the authority of books. I would rather bring them to
> accept my views by powerful arguments.[108]

Each one of the orthodox—Coronaeus, Curtius, and Fredericus—proclaims his confidence in his revealed faith; Senamus accepts all beliefs and observes that even the atheist testi-
fies in his negative way to the existence of God. As a consequence, Senamus worships in every church.[109]

The Christians put Solomon on the defensive by attacking
Jews for their rejection of Christ. Solomon is, however, so
much wiser and more erudite than they are that they have
little chance against him. He gives a sorry account of the
transmission of Old Testament texts; and when Fredericus
asserts the same cannot be said of New Testament texts,
Solomon agrees. "No," he says, "they are in really worse
condition since they have passed through so many hands."
He describes the textual variations between the three hun-

---

[105] P. 180.   [106] P. 186.   [107] Pp. 189–90.   [108] Pp. 190, 193.
[109] P. 192.

dred manuscripts of the New Testament and expatiates, to the horror of the Christians, on the spurious first chapters of Luke. "It is impossible," he says, for a philosopher to believe "virgins can conceive and give birth." [110] Toralba remarks that since they have talked earlier about demons cohabiting with women, he sees no serious problem here; but Octavius observes that this is one of the reasons why his faith rejects the divinity of Christ.[111] The whole New Testament, Solomon insists, should be rejected; and, the Christians objecting, he and Octavius point out in it dozens of textual faults, anachronisms, and historical discrepancies.[112] The discussion circles to the death and resurrection of Christ.

Solomon, who has previously complained that the so-called Messiah was not God if he could be tempted by Satan but could not be visited by the Holy Spirit until he was thirty, now says that Christ's death was unbecoming a God and that the seven brothers, whose death in the flames is related by Josephus, ended more bravely. Toralba tries to save the situation by suggesting that Christ feigned his suffering, and Octavius brings about a momentary union between Catholic and Protestants when he states that a man named Simon, according to the Koran, took Christ's place on the cross. The nature of Christ's resurrection is as vexing as his death. Octavius, quoting Celsus, says the whole tale is borrowed from the legend of Cleomedes. Senamus then asks his fatal question about the body of Christ. "If he was born from the womb without tearing the vulva, as the Christians say; if, as John writes in his eighth chapter, Christ vanished when his enemies sought to stone him; if, the doors of the house locked, he was suddenly seated among his disciples, because, like Gyges, he could be invisible when he wished; and if he walked on the sea and kept his feet dry, he must have been either a specter or had a body of vapor." The Jew Solomon, who cannot

[110] Pp. 204–15.   [111] Pp. 216–17.   [112] Pp. 219–30.

accept Christ as the Messiah, responds that surely he had
flesh; in fact, it was his display of fleshly weakness which
makes it impossible to accept him as God. Curtius, the Calvinist, observes that what Solomon calls "fleshly weakness"
is the proof of Christ's double nature. Octavius now quotes
Scripture to prove Christ never said he was God, and Fredericus quotes it to prove Christ was God.[113]

The sixth day is Friday, the interlocutors are fasting, and
their major topics of debate are the double nature of Christ
and the question of original sin. Toralba simply cannot
swallow the notion of the double nature. Man is the subject
of physics; God belongs to metaphysics; the two philosophies
cannot be discussed at the same time. God has no natural attributes; he cannot be a finite man and an infinite divinity at
one and the same time. He expresses his extreme disgust with
the Christian hypothesis that after "an infinite time during
which God was incorporeal" he suddenly "dropped down
from heaven into the narrow womb of a little woman, where
he remained for nine months; then dressed in bone, flesh, and
blood was born through her uterus. . . ." He is graveled by
the whole concept. "You could believe it," says Fredericus,
"if you had Grace." [114]

After a discussion of the authenticity of Christ's miracles
in an age which abounded in miracle workers and magicians,
Toralba's remarks once again turn the discussion back to the
double nature of Christ. Unorthodox questions come forth.
Could an infinite and eternal God create another infinite and
eternal God? Could Christ, at once man and God, create himself? [115] The third person of the Trinity poses even more
difficult problems. Toralba points out that the Holy Spirit is
said to be produced through a union of the Father and the
Son; in this case, the first and second persons are fathers and
the second and third persons are brothers! All theories which

[113] Pp. 232–36.   [114] Pp. 248–50.   [115] Pp. 258–59.

postulate infinity creating infinity strike him as absurd.[116] Solomon agrees with his objections. "There is nothing about the Trinity in either the divine law or the Prophets." [117] Octavius, convert to the Turks, states that Christians were monotheists until the time of Constantine; Christ was not made a god until the Council of Constantinople; and the Holy Spirit was not declared divine until 430 A.D.[118] The Christians object, saying the decrees of councils simply authorized accepted Church views. The knotty problem they have been considering comes, however, from the sheer necessity of the Incarnation, and they now focus their attention on this doctrine.

Senamus, the indifferentist, says that if God really wanted to cleanse men of sin, could he not have done it by an act of the divine will? However, instead of doing it easily, God created a coequal, coeternal son fifteen centuries after the Fall, put him in a woman's womb, from which he emerged (leaving her a virgin), so he could die an agonizing death. "Id enim frustra pluribus tentatur, quod paucioribus confici possit." [119] "Christians and ignoramuses believe this," says Toralba, "but no one is ever going to persuade a philosopher to accept it." [120] All current sects, he continues, insist on Christ's humanity and omnipresence; they are, consequently, forced to imagine his body in many places at once or, more horrible still, confusedly mixed. "Pedes in cerebro, manus in visceribus." The whole argument gets absolutely nowhere because the three Christians stand ready to accept the doctrine of the double nature of Christ, whereas the others find it totally absurd. Since there seems to be no rational solution to this matter, they turn to the doctrine of original sin.

Solomon, who is a great authority on allegory, cannot believe Adam's sin consisted in eating the forbidden fruit. Adam let his mind wander from his right occupation, the contem-

---

[116] Pp. 274–75.   [117] P. 277.   [118] P. 283.   [119] P. 284.
[120] P. 285.

plation of God, to sensual matters. The problem is, however, a question of the inheritance of guilt. Adam committed this sin, but the penalty descends, according to theologians, to his children. This whole doctrine is distasteful to Solomon. "All philosophers and theologians are forced by their common experience to agree that the virtues of parents do not descend to their children." If virtues are not transmitted, it would be contrary to logic to think that vice would be. There is no such thing, then, as original sin.[121] In order to offset this argument, Coronaeus and Fredericus present a list of authorities who accept and support the doctrine. Curtius, in his turn, thinks he has overthrown the opposition when he points out that a son inherits his father's legal obligations. "But not," says Octavius, "his prison sentence." The non-Christians unite in agreeing with Solomon's theory that each man is his own Adam, "and whatever happened to Adam will happen to all who abandon themselves to the charms and pleasures of the senses." [122]

After this rather exciting moment, the speakers of the *Heptaplomeres* present relativistic accounts of the problems of Grace and salvation, the adoration of saints, the nature of the Eucharist, purgatory, and indulgences. The non-Christians oppose and object; the Christians, while quibbling among themselves, attack the rationalism of their opponents with arguments derived from authoritative revelation. In the end Senamus and Octavius, seeing no solution to the variety of men's beliefs, vote for religious tolerance. Senamus goes back to his earlier position: "I willingly enter the temples of Christians, Mohammedans, and Jews—those of Lutherans and

[121] Pp. 296–99.
[122] P. 306. "Quisque sibi est Adamus et quaecunque Adamo contigerunt, eadem contingunt in omnibus, qui sensuum illecebris ac voluptatis praeter modum lascivientis cupiditate ac suavitate delectantur, et qui in illa sensuum suavitate bonorum extremum, in doloribus vero et aerumnis adeundis malorum finem posuerunt."

Zwinglians—so that I can avoid the charge of atheism and of being one who disturbs the peace of the republic." [123] There is, he continues, one God, creator and master of all, and all men should pray to him to lead them to truth. Fredericus takes an amazingly liberal position. "We cannot prescribe a religion because no man can be forced to believe against his will." With this view, Curtius agrees, and at Coronaeus' command they conclude their religious discussion by the harmonious singing of the canticle, "Ecce, quam bonum et quam jucundum cohabitare fratres in unum." No one's views were changed, writes Bodin, and they never discussed religion again. "Tametsi suam quisque religionem summa vitae sanctitate tueretur." [124]

Bodin, learned man of religion, is plainly not an atheist. His Coronaeus states, as did Cardano, that any superstition is more tolerable than atheism,[125] echoing in this remark some lines from the *République*, where it is held that a tyranny is better than anarchy and "aussi la plus forte superstition du monde n'est pas à beaucoup près si détestable que l'athéisme."[126] Like Pomponazzi, like Montaigne, like his own character Toralba, he lives by reason, even when reason convinces him there are demons and witches. In his last printed book, the *Naturae Theatrum*,[127] he supports individual reason against massive authority; but he stresses this attitude throughout all of the *Heptaplomeres*. He does not scorn the convictions of the orthodox; but they, in turn, must not scorn the contrary views of learned rationalists, who live according to reason, or what Toralba calls the "divine light," which shines in every mind "to see, to sense, to judge what is right, what is wrong, what is true, what is false." [128]

---

[123] P. 354; see also p. 192.   [124] P. 358.
[125] P. 182. "Superstitio, quantacumque sit, quovis atheismo tolerabilior est."
[126] *Les Six Livres de la République* (Paris, 1579), p. 456.
[127] (Lyons, 1596), pp. 446, 512.   [128] P. 273; see also pp. 190, 257.

Chapter Four

Rational Theology
against Atheism

~~~~~~

I

THE INGLORIOUS defection of most Renaissance atheists, we are told by their correctors, begins satanically with intellectual pride. As many men before them, they, too, sought for a rational system of theology that proved the essential, but not mysterious, principles of Christianity. Their initial intent may have been piously innocent, but reason is a jealous god, and they often ended by abandoning religion. This unhappy outcome is not logically unpredictable; hence, we are surprised when so many of their critics follow the untheological method of the philosophers in order to convince the rational. Wiser men of religion, firm in their convictions, refused to surrender the fortress of revelation, which was impregnable in its invisibility; but Christian advocates, regardless of sectarian badges, marched outside the solid walls of dogma to fight on the windy plains of reason. At the beginning of the seventeenth century, Bishop Fotherby attempts to overwhelm atheists "with the testimony of Heathen-writers and not of holy Scripture";[1] many years later, William Bates uses "common principles which they [atheists] cannot disa-

[1] Pp. 13–14.

vow." [2] The same strategy is used by scores of other men who must have known that God's existence did not depend on human logic. All of them pretend that man can go to belief by reason, but reason should have told them the opposite was true.

St. Paul rejected the taunts of the philosophers with his well-known comments on the wisdom of this world, but his pessimistic views were sometimes modified by his successors. Justin believed so firmly in the reasonableness of Christianity [3] that he thought divine reason informed Socrates [4] and other gentile philosophers who expressed honorable notions.[5] Origen adopts the same tone against Celsus; [6] and Clement of Alexandria, finding philosophy weak in vision [7] and action,[8] proclaimed it, nonetheless, as the proper preparation for Christian theologians.[9] The study of philosophy, he hoped, predisposed the Greeks for conversion to Christianity.[10] The Latin churchmen agreed that naked reason showed the pagans the existence of a providential God; [11] but they could not believe that reason, wanting revelation, could comprehend the magnitude [12] and perfection [13] of God or the nature of Christian mysteries.[14] A natural man, they said, knows God no better than a blind man knows light.[15] More than a thousand years of similar discussions culminate in the accommodations granted to reason by St. Thomas, who opens the

---

[2] Pp. A5v–A6. The best modern accounts of this topic are found in Herschel Baker's *The Wars of Truth* (Cambridge, Mass., 1952) and Howard Schultz's *Milton and Forbidden Knowledge* (New York, 1955).
[3] *PG*, VI, 466.   [4] *PG*, VI, 335.   [5] *PG*, VI, 338, 355, 358, 415, 458.
[6] *PG*, XI, 975–86, 1011.   [7] *PG*, IX, 281–84.   [8] *PG*, VIII, 795.
[9] *PG*, VIII, 727, 795, 982.   [10] *PG*, VIII, 718–19.
[11] Tertullian, *PL*, I, 515–17; II, 687, 795–96; Lactantius, *PL*, VI, 121, 129–31, 153; VII, 113; St. Augustine, *PL*, XXXIII, 389; XXXIV, 361, 604, 1056.
[12] Tertullian, *PL*, I, 806, 809–10.
[13] St. Anselm, *PL*, CLVIII, 210, 608–9; Rupertus, *PL*, CLXVII, 1249.
[14] St. Hilarius, *PL*, X, 53, 107, 230; St. Ambrose, *PL*, XVII, 511; St. Jerome, *PL*, XXX, 561, 700.
[15] St. Gregory, *PL*, LXXVI, 403.

great *Summa* by explaining how reason is insufficient to salvation and expends the third and fourth chapters of the second *Summa* assigning theological boundaries to reason's great offspring, natural theology. St. Thomas' careful distinctions between the objects of rational inquiry and his sequestration of unrestricted reason were hardly written down before Duns Scotus qualified them further and Ockham made them impossible. Christian reason, bleeding and shaken but fully aware of the rules, still went out against unbelievers except in those happy areas where Augustinianism prevailed. For an understanding of this surer state, we turn to John Calvin.

That man knows God at all, Calvin maintains, is an act of divine Grace, because a donkey can learn harmony as readily as the human mind can learn the nature of God.[16] Calvin thus avoids all ontological argument untouched by "the calling of God" for fear that rational man will make God in his own image.[17] He is, consequently, prejudiced against all teleological proofs, not because he doubts the genuineness of the text of the Book of Nature, but rather the ability of degenerate man to read.[18] The eye of reason is far, far less sensitive than the ear of faith. "All knowledge of God is naturally presented to all men as in a mirror . . . but they know him by the teaching of the Gospels." [19] It is not surprising that Francis Bacon, who wished to save nature from theology, agreed with Calvin, who saved revelation from reason. For theology, Bacon said, "is grounded only upon the word and oracle of God and not upon the light of Nature"; [20] then, putting words in Dr. Thomas Browne's mouth, he adds, "in divinity many things must be left abrupt and concluded with this: 'O al-

---

[16] Comment on Eph. 3:19; I Cor. 1:20; Rom. 1:20; John 1:9; Acts 17:23; and *Inst.* I, 14, 3.
[17] *Inst.* I, 11, 8–9; III, 2, 1; Comment on John 5:22, 6:27, 11:41.
[18] *Inst.* I, 2, 1; I, 5, 11; I, 6, 3; Comment on Rom. 1:20.
[19] Comment on Pss. 19:4.
[20] *Advancement of Learning,* in *The Works* (London, 1778), I, 123.

titudo sapientiae et scientiae Dei.' " [21] The frequent balancing of the evidence of reason against the facts of revelation in order to find some agreement was an obsession of Renaissance men.

Coeffeteau, a Catholic philosopher, admits that reasoning leads to doubt and that every atheist was first a philosopher.[22] Athens is not Jerusalem; Plato is not Solomon; the *Iliad* is not the Evangels, says Polycarpe de la Riviere; so "let us sacrifice our sense and judgment on the altar of faith." [23] In this sweeping of the porch, Aristotle, who had almost survived Talon and Ramus, went too. Balzac, once a friend of libertines, puts the babble of the Academy behind him to wait no more in the lower courts of Aristotle,[24] and the final defeat of the great Greek is reported by Jean de Launoy in 1653.[25] Reason, however, does not go with Aristotle. It is, says one distinguished Catholic, beneath, not against, revelation.[26] Jean Boucher, who invents a debate with the deist Typhon, says again and again that no difficulties can occur if philosophers think in terms of first causes.[27] In France, the Protestant attitude is only slightly different from that of the Romans. We begin with reason, according to De Gravelle, and progress to revelation.[28] The grave Huguenot, Amyraut, thinks God does not expect us to abandon reason for religion. Reason, which enables Mornay to separate true and false doctrine and which Amyraut will cheerfully use to disprove transubstantiation, leads man to God and is truth's touchstone.[29] Between Protestant and Catholic stands the Roman

[21] I, 126–27.
[22] *Premier Essai des Questions Théologiques* (Paris, 1607), pp. 20–21, 46.
[23] *Angélique* (Lyons, 1626), pp. E4–F.
[24] *Socrate Chrestien*, in *Oeuvres* (Paris, 1665), II, 213.
[25] *De Varia Aristotelis in Academia Parisiensi Fortuna* (Paris, 1653), pp. 100–60.
[26] N. Caussin, *La Cour Sainte* (Paris, 1624), p. 5.   [27] Pp. 1–9.
[28] *Abregé de Philosophie* (Paris, 1601), pp. B3–6.
[29] *De l'Elevation*, pp. 20–27. On pp. 42–65 he lists the doctrines known to reason and on pp. 66–95 those above reason.

Calvinist Pascal, the pure mathematician who thought with his heart.

Pascal, inventor of "the thinking reed," agreed with Montaigne [30] that "truth this side of the Pyrenees" was error on the other; [31] hence, he defended the knowing heart. Nature is only the image of God and contains nothing that will convince hardened atheists. Man is incapable of knowing what God is or, even, whether or not he exists. "Reason will settle nothing here; an infinite chaos is in our way." [32] It is the heart which knows God and not the reason. "This is faith: God made evident, not to the reason, but to the heart." [33] What Pascal has to say is not too different from what Calvin said except that he has humanity and poetry, and Calvin would have objected to the first of these attributes. On the other hand, Calvin would have considered Hooker, who defended the uses of reason against the British scripturalists, [34] as a blind man seeking darkness. Hooker's lesser disciples (Andrewes, who smells in the too great insistence on rational theology the sin of the Manichees and of the Renaissance "quaeristae," [35] and Donne, who reads the *Liber Creaturarum* but notices that its frontispiece is man) might agree with Bacon's objections to a theology drawn from Nature and with his complaint that a scientific divinity weakened religion and diluted its values. Thus, in place of the old double truth recommended by Pomponazzi, one now has a double reason which is beneath revelation but authenticates and ex-

[30] *Entretien avec de Saci sur Epíctète et Montaigne*, ed. M. Guyau (Paris, 1875), pp. 27–28, 36–40.

[31] *Pensées*, ed. L. Brunschvicg (Paris, 1904), II, 216.

[32] II, 145–46. It is a rather old notion that God's existence is hard to know; in fact, the so-called atheist, Claude Beauregard, says "nothing is more difficult to prove, but easier to accept, than God's existence and the soul's immortality." *Circulus Pisanus* (Padua, 1661), pp. 171–76.

[33] II, 201.

[34] Hooker, I, 227–34, 365–78, and the answer to Travers, III, 594–95.

[35] *A Pattern of Catechistical Doctrine*, in *Minor Works* (Oxford, 1846), pp. 19–20.

pounds it. It "makes clear the evidence," as Thorndike re-marks, "but does not produce it." [36]

The world known to Dean Donne is not the inverted palimpsest at which Calvin's natural man squinted. Every man who comes into life is possessed of "Natural Reason" and can see in the "Theater of Nature and in the glass of Creatures" such evidence of God's existence that "the atheist who can see cannot deny." [37] One of his regrets is that athe-ists lack the faith of natural men.[38] God exists in many vol-umes, but abridgments are everywhere: "Every worm in the grave"; "every weed upon the grave." Man may even hear God in his pulse; know him even in his thoughts. He may see "that all, this all, and all the parts thereof are *opus*, a work made, and *opus ejus*, his work, made by God." [39] Donne does not doubt the value of the world's testimony to its maker, but it would be incorrect to think he heard it incautiously.

Natural man, we are informed, does not deny God's ex-istence because the soul brings this knowledge with it; [40] consequently, "natural man hath as full a library in his bosom as the Christian." [41] Not all the proper books are at hand, however; so natural man wanders into superstition. Many ancients also wandered into a quasi-Christian state; they were "as good as a Plato or a Socrates, who had no more but those natural faculties," [42] and were commended even by St. Augus-tine.[43] This is all to the good, but the kindness of those church-men who accorded them salvation is of no great avail. The Catholic Campanella described the philosopher-pagans as chil-dren,[44] and Milton's Christ speaks the Puritan mind about

---

[36] *Of the Principles of Christian Truth*, in *Works* (Oxford, 1845–56), II, 16–19.

[37] *LXXX Sermons* (London, 1640), pp. 227, 527, 620.   [38] Pp. 484, 486.

[39] *Fifty Sermons* (London, 1649), pp. 273–74; *LXXX Sermons*, p. 620

[40] *LXXX Sermons*, p. 484.   [41] Pp. 477–78.   [42] Pp. 483, 644.

[43] Pp. 68–69.

[44] *De Gentilismo non Retinendo*, in *Atheismus Triumphatus*, pp. 5–6.

them in *Paradise Regained*. Donne, who moves more comfortably between the two sects, agrees that the possible salvation of Trismegistus, Numa, Plato, or Socrates is "spiritual prodigality." [45] The way is not through Nature or reason but through revelation.[46]

To arrive only at the outer edge of Christian truth is, for Donne, tantalizingly insufficient. Some pagans had shapeless notions of immortality; they had all that was needed, but "they knew no Holy Ghost." Since they had no keeper of the inner archives, the "first planters" of Christianity found them poor prospects for conversion. "They would believe it in the nine Muses, and would not believe it by the Holy Ghost. They would be saved poetically and fantastically, not reasonably and spiritually. By copies and not by originals, by counterfeit things at first deduced by their authors out of our Scriptures, and yet not by the Word of God himself." [47] The text of Nature is of no use without the rubrics of Grace; but though it is in itself misleading, God sometimes employs it. When he entices a man to him, he sometimes uses the "dark and weak way, the way of Nature and the Book of Creatures" or he may use "the powerful way, the way of miracles;" but "these and all between them are uneffectual without the Word." [48]

Reason is for Donne what it was for Hooker. It is important but far beneath revelation. Roman Catholics, unaware of this, are continually mingling philosophy and theology; [49] and everyone knows what strange speculations arise from the abandonment of "the solid foundations of religion." [50] Men, as a consequence, are inclined to make "philosophy and reason speak against Religion." They talk of the "double truth" and are unaware that, unless truth is distorted, "whatsoever

[45] P. 261.
[46] Pp. 763, 314. On the salvation of virtuous pagans see L. Caperan, *Le Problème du Salut des Infidèles* (Toulouse, 1934).
[47] Pp. 370–71. [48] Pp. 315, 428–29. [49] P. 744. [50] P. 63.

is true in philosophy is true in divinity too." [51] One philosopher, whose name Donne refrains from mentioning, is proud to discover he does not even know he knows nothing; [52] but all philosophers rest on the phrase "nil admirari," when what is needed is "O altitudo." Admiration and wonder stand between faith and reason "and have an eye to both." [53]

The poet Donne had explained to Lady Bedford that "reason is our soul's left hand, faith her right," and he elaborated this text when he wept his measure of iambs for Prince Henry. On that solemn occasion, he told his dead prince that reason comprehends the natural world; but faith is required for beliefs such as "God's essence, place and providence,/ Where, how, when, what souls do, departed hence." Donne's reason, "rectified reason," is that "true sound, divine reason," which Hooker thinks can deduce correctly the inferences of Scripture. Knowing there is one God, this reason can convince us of the truth of basic doctrines,[54] but it cannot prove a virgin could have a child or a man could rise from the dead. It will tell us there is a God to be worshiped according to his will, and point to the will in Scripture. "And when our reason hath carried us so far as to accept these scriptures for the Word of God, then all the particular articles, a virgin's son and a mortal god will follow evidently enough." [55] Reason leads men to a revelation agreeable to faith; because faith and reason are "contiguous, they flow not from one another, but they touch one another; they are not of a piece, but they enwrap one another." [56]

[51] *Six and Twenty Sermons* (London, 1660), p. 91.
[52] *LXXX Sermons,* p. 818.   [53] P. 194.
[54] *Six and Twenty,* pp. 77–78.
[55] *LXXX Sermons,* p. 611. Elsewhere (p. 23) we are invited to accept the virgin birth for the same reason that we accept the burning bush: "whatsoever God in his Word says was done let us believe it to be done; how it was done, as we know that God knows, so we are content not to inquire more than it hath been his pleasure to communicate to us."
[56] P. 178. Donne realizes (*Six and Twenty,* p. 390) that the Bible and

Man, Donne remarked in the *Second Anniversary*, wears himself out searching for "unconcerning things, matters of fact"; yet, "Why grass is green, or why our blood is red,/ Are mysteries which none have reached unto." An analogue to this illustration is John Hales' observation that man spends sweat and lamp fuel on his studies and has not discovered why grass is green and not purple or scarlet. Dull wits of this sort should take God at his word and believe him "above, against our reason." [57] Hales advises weak persons to marvel and believe while others reason and dispute; [58] but he, like Hooker, exalts reason within its reasonable limits. It has been "a common disease of Christians from the beginning" to seek knowledge "of which we have no light, neither from Reason nor Revelation." This curiosity results in dissension and faction, [59] but this unhappy consequence is no excuse for intellectual servility. To abandon reason, leaving that "piece of the Lord's pasture" untilled and unsown, may result in following deceived teachers. [60] With this view, Chillingworth could agree, knowing God does not accept of the "Sacrifice of Fools" [61] nor require a Roman Scholasticism which produces cobwebs "fitter to catch flies than souls." [62] One must be led by reason, writes the great advocate of the Protestants, not following every shepherd "or every flock that should chance to go before." [63] However, reason, for both men, needs allies.

Ethnic philosophers, by scorning the world and worldliness, writes Hales, almost reached Christian opinions; [64] hence,

---

the Book of Creatures will be removed at death, when "in an instant I shall know more than they all could reveal unto me."

[57] *Golden Remains* (London, 1673), I, 56–57. This edition is divided into unnumbered parts. See also J. H. Elson, *John Hales of Eton* (New York, 1948).

[58] II, 48.   [59] IV, 4.   [60] I, 41.

[61] *The Religion of the Protestants a Safe Way to Salvation*, in *The Works* (London, 1704), pp. 73–74.

[62] P. C1.   [63] P. B1.   [64] Hales, II, 235.

the moral precepts found in some of their philosophies, inspired with "Natural Wisdom and Moral discretion," have the certainty "which they have when we read them in the oracles of God and the same uncertainty . . . in regard of some particulars, when they be spoken by Solomon which they have when they are uttered by Plato or Euripides." [65] Natural man, like Old Testament man, has Christian knowledge without Christian profit; and so the pious pagans may have their punishment reduced but cannot be redeemed.[66] Natural virtues are, consequently, worthy but worthless, and natural theology can only beget unresolvable doubts.[67] One must approve philosophy and reason, but the Christian revelation must be the highest guide. "Christ is our Aristotle, he hath written us a Spiritual Logic." [68]

The Catholics, Chillingworth maintains, though they call their opponents "atheists," are not themselves unlike atheists and skeptics in their distrust of reason.[69] This distrust is justifiable if men choose to reason from "principles of Nature," from prejudice, popular errors, and chance. However, if this is "right Reason grounded on Divine Revelation and Common Notions, written by God in the hearts of all men, and deducing, according to the never failing rules of Logic, consequent deductions from them," he who follows it "follows always God." [70] One must necessarily distinguish between human and divine reason. Unreasonable men demand certain proof "above that of sense or science"; whereas God, reasonable in all things, wants men only to "believe the conclusion as much as the premises deserve." [71] The gauge of reason is the Bible, "the Religion of the Protestants." Its "influence and efficacy" are assumed before understanding can assent.[72]

---

[65] II, 189.   [66] II, 210–11.   [67] II, 12.   [68] II, 225.
[69] *Religion of the Protestants*, p. B2v.   [70] Pp. B3v–B4.
[71] Pp. 27–28.   [72] P. 53.

Once God has spoken, Chillingworth can submit because he knows no rational demonstration more convincing than "God hath said so." [73] Early in his *Meditations*, Descartes had wondered whether or not God might deceive him; but this stony question made no ripple on Chillingworth's rational surface or on that of Jeremy Taylor, who, likewise, never permitted reason to question "the clear sense of Scripture" [74] because "whatsoever God hath said is true." [75]

Taylor knows two types of Christians: those "who stick" at irrational articles of faith, and those who say reason is "of little or no use in religion." If it is a matter of Christian mysteries, he aligns himself with the second group, where "the poor humble man" is safer than those of fine discourse and sharp argument.[76] He will not "go beyond religion." [77] But Taylor is no Calvinist; he is simply a tired disciple of Hooker. He will, consequently, not disown reason. He will not "require revelation to prove that nine and nine makes eighteen" [78] or, Roman Catholics to the contrary, to validate the Anglican creed.[79] He knows what is above reason is not opposed to reason; [80] so he warns men against explicating what they cannot understand.[81] Religious truth is "clear and plain"; [82] but should one be bothered by some doctrine like resurrection, one should remember it is less difficult to understand than the creation. Man is surrounded by the resurrected, and Taylor writes, employing Thomas Browne's famous but troublesome illustration, it is "imitable by art, which can out of ashes raise a flower." [83]

---

[73] Pp. 290–91.
[74] *Ductor Dubitantium*, in *The Works*, eds. A. Taylor, R. Heber, and C. P. Eden (London, 1883), IX, 74. See T. G. Steffan, *Jeremy Taylor's Criticism of Abstract Speculation* ("University of Texas Studies in English"; Austin, 1941), pp. 96–108.
[75] IX, 56–57.   [76] IX, 55–56, 78.   [77] IX, 57.   [78] IX, 60.
[79] *Liberty of Prophesying*, V, 498–99; IX, 59.   [80] IX, 70.
[81] IX, 73; V, 361–62.   [82] IX, 77.   [83] IX, 72.

Although he finds in "true natural religion" the Christian essentials and even the first four commandments,[84] Taylor cannot agree with Clement of Alexandria that the Greeks were saved by their moral philosophy.[85] *Noesis* first informs man about the God,[86] who writes in the tables of man's reason and heart; [87] but to this knowledge man adds information from proper first principles and from "secular experiences and conversations with the world." In spite of these occasional and guarded endorsements of the rational way, Taylor knows reason is "a box of quicksilver" that led skeptics, who saw atheists defying the common knowledge of nations, "to think there was no truth in the reasoning of men." [88] Whereas reason has limited virtues, a pure religion that is revealed, not cogitated, is best.

> Thomas Aquinas did a little change the scene and blended Aristotle so with school divinity that something of the purity was lost while much of our religion was exacted and conducted by the rules of a mistaken philosophy. But if their speculations had been right, Christianity would at first have entered without reproof as being the most sublime speculations; and it would also have continued pure if it had been still drawn from the fountains of our Saviour through the limbecks of the evangelists and apostles, without the mixture of the salt waters of that philosophy which every physician and witty man now-a-days thinks he hath reason and observation enough easily to reprove.[89]

Taylor's disenchantment with a reasonable religion that pointed toward deism, atheism, and skepticism was not shared by his latitudinarian contemporaries, Isaac Barrow and John Tillotson. The former corrected men whose intellectual

[84] *Holy Living, Holy Dying*, III, 171.   [85] V, 437.   [86] IX, 59–62.
[87] IX, 74–75.   [88] IX, 293–94.   [89] IX, 54–55.

arrogance forbade them to admit anything "too high" for their wit; [90] but he associates reason with virtue,[91] and in his "Sermon on Faith" describes the reasonableness of his faith.[92] Tillotson, who insists that mysteries are mysteries [93] and urges men to assent to things their own reasons could not discover,[94] observes that the Scriptures do not reveal the existence of God, a fact man must learn from "things," from his "notion and idea," from "universal consent," and from "the visible frame of the world." [95] Reason is the judge of revelation; [96] and unless "it be first naturally known that God is a God of truth," how can anyone believe "his Word?" [97] Natural reason enabled the first churchmen to defeat the pagan philosophers, and only the Romans (Bellarmine) and the enthusiasts (Behmen) oppose it. Chillingworth, "the glory of this age and nation," acquired a black and odious character in his worthy attempt "to make the Christian religion reasonable," according to Tillotson; "but if this be Socinianism for a man to inquire into the grounds and reasons of the Christian religion and to give a satisfactory account why he believes it, I know no way but that all considerate inquisitive men, that are above fancy and enthusiasm, must be either Socinians or atheists." [98]

The Anglicans used reason against Rome's authoritarianism and Geneva's Biblicism; the atheist is for them a minor foe because their spiritual effort is otherwise engaged. Nonetheless, they half open the door to a rational theology as a preparation to Christianity, as a faith in itself, and as an introduction to the scientific study of the universe. The same process can be observed among that Anglican sect, the Cam-

[90] *The Works*, ed. J. Hamilton (London, 1861), II, 79.
[91] I, 139.   [92] II, 88, 199.
[93] *The Works*, ed. Thomas Birch (London, 1820), III, 331–32.
[94] IV, 226–27.   [95] IX, 193.   [96] IV, 41–43.   [97] III, 236.
[98] IX, 270.

bridge Platonists, who were vigorous in their opposition to rational non-believers, although they themselves advocated reasonable belief.

II

Benjamin Whichcote defines atheists as those who "never use reason in that that is the peculiar and proper act of reason but only to keep sense company." The atheist suppresses his "innate sense of God," abandoning doctrines regarded by men as essential to the safety of the universe.[99] God is knowable in the creatures and especially in man himself.[100] We know we have being, but we also know we are finite and not our own authors; we know, therefore, that God exists and speaks to us through our reason. [101] "To go against reason is to go against God." [102] Since man's mind moves naturally toward God, [103] he should find God as soon as he can reason.[104] Therefore, the reasonable man chooses a reasonable religion, and "right religion . . . is watched by right reason." [105] The Puritan notion of individual revelation is unacceptable because it requires that revelation be certified by revelation and not by reason.[106] Even Scripture "must be taken in a rational sense," [107] although its authority is su-

[99] *The Works* (Aberdeen, 1751), III, 237–40. See S. P. Lamprecht, "Innate Ideas in the Cambridge Platonists," *Philosophical Review*, XXXV (1926), 553–73. For general accounts of the Cambridge Platonists: see F. J. Powicke, *The Cambridge Platonists* (London, 1926); J. H. Muirhead, *The Platonic Tradition in Anglo-Saxon Philosophy* (London, 1931), pp. 25–107; Ernst Cassirer, *Die platonische Renaissance in England und die Schule von Cambridge* (Leipzig, 1932); W. C. de Pauley, *The Candle of the Lord* (London, 1937); J. de Boer, *The Theory of Knowledge of the Cambridge Platonists* (Madras, 1931); and G. P. H. Pawson, *The Cambridge Platonists* (London, 1930).
[100] III, 196.   [101] III, 241–42.
[102] *Moral and Religious Aphorisms*, ed. W. R. Inge (London, 1930), p. 11.
[103] *The Works*, IV, 144.   [104] I, 37.   [105] *Aphorisms*, pp. 41, 52.
[106] P. 51.   [107] P. 99.

preme. "Where you do not have a text of Scripture for what you do, be rational in what you do." [108] These are Whichcote's *obiter dicta;* but the men of Cambridge were more of a club than a church and did not always agree.

Convinced that God is known to man not by "the labour and sweat of the brain," but "by an heavenly warmth in our hearts," John Smith is perhaps closer to Pascal, or to an emotional Descartes, than to Whichcote. Like Bacon, he is at odds with the Neo-Scholastics, who invent a "divinity of systems and models" that is at best "a poor wane light." [109] He has the anthropomorphic fear that the God adored by most men is "a picture of their complexions," [110] but he also knows God has put his "impress" on the souls of all rational creatures. [111] This is simply a way of discussing common notions, a theory invoked by both error and superstition; [112] but Smith is convinced the idea of God imprinted in man is more evident than a Euclidean demonstration. [113] The inward "perpetual memorial" to the Creator is repeated in the universe.

Aristotle, Smith charges, defaced the "sacred monuments of the ancient metaphysical theology," and his seventeenth-century disciples continue to do so. They separate metaphysical truths from those of Nature and thus destroy the phil-

---

[108] P. 90. "Reason," says Whichcote (p. 13), "discovers what is natural and receives what is supernatural." The discussion is, of course, extensive: see Cheffontaines, pp. A5, 1–2v; Dove, pp. 17–22; Geoffrey Goodman, *The Fall of Man* (London, 1616), pp. 7–10; Faber, pp. 155–61, 208–12; Pierre de Moulin, *A Treatise of the Knowledge of God,* trans. R. Codington (London, 1634), pp. 41–42; C. Wolseley, *The Unreasonableness of Atheism Made Manifest* (London, 1669), pp. 37–54; J. Abbadie, *Traité de la Vérité de la Religion Chrétienne* (Rotterdam, 1684), pp. 1–19; and George Rust, *A Discourse of Reason* (London, 1683), pp. 27, 37–41. A very complete defence of reason is Robert Ferguson's *The Interest of Reason in Religion* (London, 1675), which is the final seventeenth-century answer of the Protestants to Sebonde.
[109] *Select Discourses* (London, 1660), p. 3.
[110] Pp. 6, 8.   [111] P. 124.   [112] P. 64.   [113] Pp. 14–15.

osophical divinity by which men lived for ages.[114] The world contains "the prints and footsteps" and sometimes "the face and image" of God. This distinction, borrowed by Smith from the hated Scholastics, permits him to state that philosophy, "which professed it most," is not as effective as "true Religion" in teaching men to pass from the sensible to the intellectual.[115] The means of passage is the visible world, always "whispering out notions of a Deity." But "some interpreter within" is required to understand the whispers,[116] and this is reason. Reason is the power which makes our souls known to us;[117] it sits "on the throne and governs all the powers of the soul."[118] In the glass of understanding, we see the image of Divinity, misted over by the "gross dew" of our "imaginative powers." When mortality is "swallowed up of life,"[119] the soul will "behold itself in the midst of that Glorious Unbounded Being, who is indivisibly everywhere."[120]

To the presence of this indivisible being, Smith writes, the superstitious and the atheistic are blind. The former fear a "cruel and tyrannical" God; atheists, more stout and surly by nature, hate God for the same fearful reasons. The atheists known to Smith are the atomists, Epicurus and Lucretius. Even Aristotle had to find a Prime Mover; but Epicurus overlooks a required "external weight or spring" that moves the atoms, fictions in themselves too weak "to support that massy bulk of absurdities." Smith, like Bacon, says that atheism lurks on the border between knowledge and ignorance; in this negative wasteland, the "natural instinct of God," present in the "dullest sort of vulgar men," is clouded over, and true wisdom has not yet been obtained. Rather than be ignorant, atheists throw away the serenity of vulgar men. They depend on chance and fortune, on the humors

[114] Pp. 434–35.   [115] Pp. 430–31.   [116] P. 125.   [117] Pp. 126–27.
[118] P. 388.   [119] P. 21.   [120] P. 434.

and passions of mankind, and see not their "own misery always staring." [121]

Reason, though it never provided Smith's nervous associate Henry More with completely convincing arguments,[122] enabled him to prove God's existence and exalt Christianity as a reasonable religion.[123] "Headstrong melancholy and blind enthusiasm" alone exclude reason from the discovery of divine truth.[124] Agreeing with Plutarch and John Smith that superstition is the mother of atheism,[125] More believes the idea of God is innate [126] because he subscribes to St. Anselm's discredited proof that idea implies reality.[127] Knowing that man can believe in matter but not in God,[128] More asks him to suppose God's existence and God's desire to make himself known, not indecorously and "dazzling" to man's five wits, but to man's inwardness as "a natural idea." [129] But the sight of God is not limited to the chambers of the mind; one should look through the windows at the world.

The lamp of God is externally nourished in man; [130] so More invites the atheist to walk with him through "the wide Theater of this outward world." [131] Here More finds not only all the conventional refutations of atomism in seventeenth-century costume, but also some new actors in the role of design, "the perpetual parallelism of the earth's axis," the laws of gravity, and Boyle's second and thirty-second experiments with the air pump.[132] The immaterial principle present in these modern discoveries indicates the existence of God. But the manifestation of final causes cannot be

---

[121] Pp. 41–55. See also T. Mayo, *Epicurus in England* (Dallas, 1934).

[122] *Antidote against Atheism*, in *A Collection of Several Philosophical Writings* (London, 1662), p. 10. See also H. C. Jentsch, *Henry More in Cambridge* (Göttingen, 1935).

[123] Preface, p. vi.   [124] *Conjectura Cabalistica*, in *A Collection*, p. 2.

[125] *Antidote*, pp. 9–10.   [126] Pp. 21–23.   [127] P. 22.   [128] P. 25.

[129] Pp. 26–28.

[130] *The Grand Mystery of Godliness* (London, 1660), p. 408.

[131] *Antidote*, pp. 37–38.   [132] Pp. 43–47.

avoided. Mines and forests supply industrious man with raw material.[133] Plants cure him and are marked with hieroglyphs so he will know their virtues.[134] Animals feed and clothe him; and should he cringe at their slaughter, he should remember he saves them "the tedious melancholy and sadness of old age." [135] More follows the familiar canal of teleology through all of nature to man, to the magic of his organs, the purpose of his passions, and his "strong propension to Religion." [136] The first two books of the *Antidote against Atheism* are devoted to these ancient demonstrations, and More complained that "obstinate and refractory" atheists still require ocular proofs and always question the veracity of those who testify to miracles or relate experiences with witches, incubi, fairies, and ghosts. The last book is, consequently, an anthology of occult tales, including the charming one of the Pied Piper of Hamlin. Here are the documents about spirits visible, but unbelievers still refuse assent. This obstinate disbelief disturbs the kindly and peaceful man. "For assuredly that saying is not more true in politics, 'No Bishop, no King' than this is in metaphysics, 'No spirit, no God.' " [137]

In 1678 a massive fragment, the erudite and repetitive *The True Intellectual System of the Universe* of Ralph Cudworth, was printed as the Cambridge men's ultimate attack against the ineluctable phantom of atheism that haunted each reasonable man. Actually, it is the first attempt to write in English an account of what Smith called "the ancient metaphysical theology," but this was, of course, not its author's conscious intent. The book proposes to examine the pernicious and infective doctrines of Anaximander, Democritus, Strato, and Zeno, but these are but masks for Cudworth's real opponents. Hobbes, though never honored by name, is as omnipresent as the God he is alleged to deny. He is the "Democritic atheist,"

[133] Pp. 47–51.   [134] P. 56.   [135] P. 63.   [136] Pp. 78–81, 83.
[137] P. 142.

a professed theist with "a tang of mechanic atheism"; and more often, he is "a modern writer," a phrase that almost applies to Cudworth. In his preface, Cudworth admits he cannot convince practical atheists, so he will attend to those of a speculative disposition. With the sly faces of these men before him, he adds that he will not use a priori proof by inferences "from principles altogether undeniable" [138] which are contained in the mind "by undeniable principles of reason," enabling one to show "that the thing is, though not why it is." [139]

Seventeenth-century materialism, which nullified eternal, unchanging morality and justice and tied rational man to the bed of mechanistic necessity, is the center of Cudworth's learned rage. The exponents of "corporealism" [140] were atheists who tendered arguments against "animalish, sentient, and conscious nature," destroying in this way Christian dogma at its roots. The concept of God was for them "a bundle of incomprehensibles, unconceivables, and impossibles" that was produced by human fear and amazement.[141] To this Lucretian illusion, they added the *ex nihilo nihil* impiety of Aristotle or the pantheistic doctrine that God created eternally from his own matter. Some of them were basic dualists but

---

[138] Cudworth, *Intellectual System*, ed. John Harrison (London, 1845), I, xliv–v. Cudworth also criticizes a "late eminent philosopher" who held that philosophical certainty depended on the existence of an "essentially good" God who would not let us be deceived in our clear ideas. Cudworth points out, as others before him, the circularity of this argument, which leads to an undivine God whose power swallows his wisdom (III, 31–35). See J. A. Passmore, *Ralph Cudworth* (Cambridge, 1951).

[139] III, 30.

[140] I, 202–3, 297. Cudworth constantly complains that the vulgar (*sic*) get theists and atheists confused and, consequently, miss the gross impieties implied in the philosophies of Diagoras, Theodorus, Euhemerus, Protagoras, and others (I, 190–91). His list of the seventeen atheist objections to the principles of rational theology had been mentioned before: see Pollot, pp. 6, 98–99, 104, 131; Mersenne, *Quaestiones*, cols. 233–38; Faber, pp. 1–8; M. Claussen, *Atheus Convictus* (Kilon, 1672), pp. 26–30; and Wagner, pp. 47–54.

[141] I, 108.

permitted an *ex nihilo* emanation of "forms and souls of animals in their successive generations." In an anti-Christian manner, they maintained that God could not create substance "which was not before" because all which is, "will be, and can be, was from eternity self-existent." But it was God, not matter, who needed Platonic succor.

The atheist, Cudworth fears, is against the idea that God can be at the same time both incorporeal and infinitely extended or that he has extension "otherwise than body." If the Christian understanding of God is right, say non-believers, God must be either space or vacuum. They thus, remarks the exasperated Cudworth, associate entity and extension. But the Greek skeptics who are responsible for these notions do not stop with physical observations. The Christian concept of the spiritual, they say, is the invention of "deceiving and deceived literati, scholastics, philosophers, and theologers enchanting men's understanding," and was spun out of the gossamer of insubstantial and eternal essences.[142] Body only is eternal, and all phenomena are body. Sense and understanding and the highly esteemed reason are creatures of "matter and motion." Some of these atheists approximate a theism by animating the universe or producing a general soul "from the fortuitous motion of matter." Some assume a quality of understanding in matter itself. Most of them conclude, unfortunately, that spiritual qualities emerge only from brains and blood in "animal configurations." [143]

Cudworth's atheists think the immortality and unchange-

[142] I, 110–17.
[143] I, 117–24. The assault on atomism is universal, and one of the commonest arguments is the inability of dead atoms to combine by sheer chance into all sorts of handsome things. The argument of the alphabet of gold letters that, when shaken from a bag, spells out some lines of Ennius, first used in Cicero's *De Natura Deorum*, is repeated again and again: see Ellis, p. 97, and John Ray, *The Wisdom of God Manifested in the Creation* (London, 1691), pp. 18–19.

ableness of the Christian God are attributes only of matter and space and that the prototype of this God is the Prime Mover borrowed by St. Thomas from Aristotle and foisted on the Christian church.[144] A similar paralogism is the Christian doctrine of a "first" or "antecedent mind." Ideas, the atheists assert, arise from causes, and an automatic cause is as stimulating as an intelligent cause. Knowledge is junior to things, and there must be things before the mind can know them.

The atheists, according to Cudworth, also focus the hot rays of their reason on Christian theodicy. If the Creator is intelligent, why is creation so rich in trouble? God is apparently impotent to cure his blundering creation, or enjoys the torments of his creatures, or is ignorant of human grief, or indifferent to it. If, as the Christians insist, this God lives in a state of foolish happiness, he may not care to be troubled with "infinite negosity," with perpetual "tumult and hurly-burly." These modern, Athenian atheists ask other embarrassing questions. They inquire about the time and purpose of creation. They wonder whether God needed to improve his condition, supply his deficiencies, or find companions whose adulation bathed his pride. To the belief that God created the world for men, atheists object, "What hurt would it have been to any of us never to have been made?" [145]

Many of the folios of Cudworth's erudite report on seventeenth-century rationalism are used to choke the ordinary arguments of the godless mechanists against a rational theology based on natural observation, a theology which provided for many antiatheists a spiritual *antipasto* to the feast of revelation. When Nature failed to come, Grace, it was felt, had no table companion. In the course of his dusty

[144] I, 125–32.
[145] I, 133; see also Dove, p. 62; Boucher, pp. 277–81; Faber, pp. 238–44.

suffocation of the ancient rationalists and atheists, Cudworth announced his own saving doctrine of "plastic nature." [146] His theory was not too different in many ways from that of the non-believing Strato of Lampsacus, and it was a great comfort to materialism. In other words, the Cambridge Hercules, in saving himself and others, not only strangled a series of pythons long yellowed in their pickle, but also hatched, as his age would say, a lively bosom snake of his own.

The Calvinists, who were the hard center of British dissent, did not share the confidence of the Anglicans in reason, even in "right reason." One finds occasional definitions of reason as "a light in the soul that is a relic of that light which was in Adam," [147] but Richard Sibbes is more Puritanically typical when he subjects this "beam of God" to the light of Grace.[148] There is also a great deal of Puritan talk about "lamps" and "candles," but these are not symbols of reason or con-

---

[146] Cudworth attempted to save teleology, which was questioned by Descartes (*The Works*, trans. E. S. Haldane [Cambridge, 1931], I, 173, 271; II, 175, 223), by inventing a doctrine that steers between the idea of a creation without the "direction of any mind" and the doctrine that God forms "every gnat and fly, insect and mite" with his hand (I, 218). Plastic Nature is not "a god or goddess, but a low and imperfect creature" (I, 250), totally incorporeal, a lower faculty of some soul, or "a lower substantial life by itself" (I, 255). Cudworth is himself not really sure, but he finally gets a definition of a force depending on a higher intellect but functioning unconsciously (I, 271). This force, not unknown to Plato, Aristotle, and Strato, enabled Cudworth to attack the materialism of the Neo-Epicureans and the vorticism of Descartes. One would expect the advent of this new physical force to erase the formerly necessary argument from design; but Cudworth repeats it at length (II, 608 ff.) and even brings in the tired, old "architect," who saw to it that all was made "fit for habitation and other human uses." See W. B. Hunter, "The Seventeenth Century Doctrine of Plastic Nature," *Harvard Theological Review*, XLIII (1950), 197–213.

[147] Walter Craddock, *Gospel Liberty* (London, 1648), p. 117. See B. Blandshard, "Early Thought on Inner Light," *Byways in Quaker History*, ed. H. H. Brinton (Wallingford, Pa., 1944), pp. 153–78; R. L. Colie, *Light and Enlightenment* (Cambridge, 1957).

[148] *Works*, ed. A. B. Grosart (Edinburgh, 1862–63), IV, 234.

science.[149] They refer to a power dwelling in the text of the
Bible, intuitively convincing the reader and explaining to
him what he reads. "The Scriptures are the lantern and the
Spirit is the candle therein." [150] It is a light, says Thomas
Goodwin, "beyond the height of reason," and it comes when
the Bible is read to spiritualize the mind and make it "the
palate of the soul." [151] It is also a "heavenly glory" unappre-
hended by human reason.[152] More tolerant than many of his
colleagues, Richard Baxter prefers the Spirit to be assisted
by reason, memory, study, and even by books, which are
"necessary in their places"; [153] nonetheless, he "tries" the
Spirit by Scripture.[154] The reason for testing is that the Spirit
no longer gives knowledge as it once did to the Apostles; [155]
now the Word, reason, will, and Spirit must work together
for Christian ends.[156] "He moveth not a man, as a beast or
stone, to do a thing he knoweth not why, but by illumination
giveth him the soundest reason for the doing of it." [157]

In *The Arrogancy of Reason*,[158] Baxter allows reason, if it
is "sufficient," [159] to assure man that God does not lie,[160] but
limits it to this one task. On the other hand, he follows the
custom of the antiatheists in *The Reasons of the Christian
Religion*, using no testimony from Christian writings in the
first part "because I suppose the reader to be one that doth
not believe them, and my business is only to prove natural
verities by their proper evidence." [161] John Owen, though

---

[149] P. Sterry, *The Spirit's Conviction of Sin* (London, 1645), pp. 11, 16,
26, 28.
[150] Thomas Higgenson, *A Testimony to the True Jesus* (London, 1656),
pp. 14–15.
[151] Thomas Goodwin, *Works*, ed. J. C. Miller (Edinburgh, 1861), VII,
65, 143.
[152] John Owen, *Works*, ed. W. G. Goold (London, 1850–55), IV, 54–55.
[153] *The Practical Works*, ed. W. Orme (London, 1830), V, 567.
[154] V, 559; II, 198.   [155] II, 104.   [156] II, 193; IV, 226.
[157] IV, 295.   [158] XX, 405, 409, 413. 422–25.   [159] XX, 429.
[160] XX, 426.   [161] XX, 451.

ready to find God in natural light, innate ideas, and the Book of Creatures, rejects rational theology because it is what led the heathen to the opposite of truth.[162] Reason speaks the truth of revelation,[163] but "carnal reason" seldom does more than debase Gospel mysteries.[164] "Modern heathen" use it to formulate a "natural morality," which is "an obscure and partial rule of duties." [165] The world abounds in open atheism "among such as pretended unto the use and improvement of reason." [166] Reason may be employed to the confusion of atheists, but revelation is the effective weapon. Those rational theologians who reject revelation find reason totally without value.[167] John Milton, though close to the rationalists in some respects and far from the dissenters in others, almost approves this conclusion when he doubts whether a man can have "right thoughts of God" if he depends on reason and Nature "independent of the word or message of God:" [168] But the chivalrous opponents of atheism hunted the dragon with purely human arms.

III

Richard Hooker maintained that man always had an inborn idea of God, and that this innate fact was fixed by the vote of "the general and perpetual voice." [169] The idea of a spontaneous notion of God begins with the pious non-Christians, Xenophon and Cicero; [170] but it was one of the pagan ideas most helpful to Tertullian,[171] St. Augustine,[172]

---

[162] IV, 82. This is the theme of his *De Natura, Ortu, Progressu, et Studio Verae Theologiae* (Oxford, 1661).
[163] XIV, 74.   [164] II, 411; III, 371.   [165] III, 634–36.
[166] VII, 352; VIII, 612.   [167] VII, 353; IV, 12.
[168] *The Works*, ed. F. A. Patterson (New York, 1931–38), XIV, 30.
[169] I, 227.
[170] *Memorabilia*, I, 4, 4; IV, 3, 3, and *De Natura Deorum*, II, 5.
[171] PL, II, 257, 260; PL, I, 609, 612.
[172] PL, XXXIV, 21; PL, XLI, 319; PL, XXXII, 811.

and other early churchmen [173] who tried to use pagan revelations against the pagans. The Renaissance cherished the opinion as a prime ontological argument. Canephius [174] and the Jesuit Lessius [175] rely on it because, as the latter says, "all agree there is a Supreme Intelligence." Mersenne, who knew his Plato, tells how a Roman missionary, using the proper questions, evoked from the lips of a stupid savage inborn knowledge about the Christian God and the Mosaic Decalogue. [176] Amyraut, a French Protestant, thinks the innate idea of the existence of a God has "the most vogue in the world"; [177] whereas the stubborn Cromwellian, Charles Wolseley, finds it "in the blood and veins of man" and likens those who dispute this to "Torys and Moss-Troopers . . . who will come under no government." [178] Some theologians searched the classics and the moderns for further evidence [179] that the idea of God's existence was held by all men, because once one had this platform erected, the remaining towers of rational theology go up with divine magic.

The greatest of philosophical theologians expressed grave doubts about whether or not the mind is more than a *tabula rasa;* [180] and though St. Thomas is ready to call the com-

---

[173] Irenaeus, *PG*, VII, 724; Clement of Alexandria, *PG*, VIII, 326; Jerome, *PL*, XXVI, 326, 570.

[174] Pp. 7–8.   [175] P. 11.   [176] *Quaestiones*, cols. 261–62.

[177] *Traité*, pp. 74–75.   [178] Pp. 66–72.

[179] Fotherby, pp. 15–51, 164–70. Bircherod, pp. 26–28; Richard Burthogge, *Causa Dei* (London, 1675), pp. 192–218; George More, *A Demonstration of God* (London, 1597), pp. 9–26; Cousin, pp. 7–12v; Cappel, pp. 194–98; and Cudworth, II, 179–97, 305–20. There were, however, objections to common notions as expressed by Herbert of Cherbury. Johannes Musaeus complains in his *De Lumine Naturae* (Jena, 1675) that no essential doctrines of Christianity are learned in this way. In his *De Legis Mosaicae Divina Origine et Auctoritate Diatriba* (Copenhagen, 1678), pp. 12–13, Seerupius reminds his readers that Minos, Lycurgus, Numa, and Mohammed claimed a spontaneous knowledge of God, but he places Moses above them for being public in his acts and not working at night in secret caves. Abbadie (pp. 117–21) says innate ideas become more perfect as one's knowledge and experience improve.

[180] *Summa Theologica*, I, 84. 3.

prehension of God the ultimate goal of intellectual creatures,[181] he assumes this comprehension will come partly
through sense and partly through Grace. Certain intelligible
truths we can learn through the senses, but higher truths are
veiled to the intellect "unless it be perfected by a stronger
light, the light of faith and prophecy, which is called the light
of grace inasmuch as it is added to nature." [182] He agrees that
Nature informs man about God "in a general and confused
way"; but the candle of Aquinas is much smaller than the
ones lighted at Cambridge. Man's knowledge of God, he says
wisely, is "like hearing Peter coming but not knowing it is
Peter." Faith presupposes natural knowledge, and reason is
a required implement of faith, but each addresses its own
consistory. St. Thomas rejects St. Anselm's clear idea of
God, which proves God's existence, and proposes his own
famous five proofs.[183] Variously restated and extensively
adorned with rhetoric, these proofs were used by Renaissance
apologists of all creeds as weapons against atheism.

One means of convincing the atheist by reason was to
convince him of a beginning, and by beginning was meant,
of course, the one described by Moses. In the later sixteenth
century, Otho Casmannus deplores the "inane and feeble
sophistries" [184] of Plato and other ancient philosophers about
the origin of things. Other Christian cosmologists share in his
regrets.[185] The popular syncretist, Augustinus Steuchus, im-

---

[181] I, 76. 1.   [182] I, 109. 1.   [183] I, 2. 1–3.

[184] *Cosmopoeia et* ΟΥΡΑΝΟΤΡΑΦΙΑ *Christiana* (Frankfort, 1598), pp. 9–10, 38.

[185] Alfonso di Fonte, *Somma della Natural Filosofia*, trans. A. di Ulloa (Venice, 1557), pp. 17–18, 38–39; Jacobus Ambrosius, *De Rebus Creatis et Earum Creatore* (Paris, 1586), pp. 67, 81, 91–93; Joannes Gallucius, *Theatrum Mundi et Temporis* (Venice, 1588), pp. 2–3; Conradus Aslacus, *Physica et Ethica Mosaica* (Hanover, 1613), pp. 25–26; Fridericus Andraeus, *De Creatione* (Copenhagen, 1609), pp. A2–3v; Johannes Blechingus, *De Creatione* (Copenhagen, 1610), pp. A2–4; A. Libavius, *De Universitate et Rerum Conditarum Originibus* (Frankfort, 1610), pp. 4–5; Scipion de Pleix, *La Physique ou Science des Choses Naturelles* (Lyons, 1620), pp.

agined the creation of chaos, a necessary lumberyard, as God's first, formal act.[186] Less scientifically educated apologists, like Canephius [187] or George More,[188] do not bother to dispose of the arguments of the eternalists or atomists, because they *know* the "necessary, moving, rare, and worthy cause" behind all creation. Cousin is sure man is born of man, but he asks the atheist to explain "who turned his nose and pointed his lips? Not his father or his mother!" [189] The orthodox rationalists admitted they could not understand spatial and temporal infinities except in terms of an eternal God; they ask the atheist to imagine the state of a world in which all creatures had been breeding forever. The seas would be solid fish; the air dense with wings; and man would find no purchase on the earth for his feet. William Bates points out that were man eternal what he has learned but recently would always have been known.[190] Derodon refuses to accept the prevalent theory of man's spontaneous generation or the more plausible hypothesis of his evolution from mermen, who became "first amphibians and then terrestrials." He knows about a Triton brought to Holland in 1403 and about those watery peoples who hold fish picnics on the banks of a river near Cochin; but granted they exist, one still has to explain the original creation of Tritons.[191] Some atheists asked how the soul could be created and eternal and the world not? To this question one could always respond, as Richard Bentley did, that the soul is "only potentially eternal." [192] Once a beginning was prefixed to the visible world, it followed logically that there was a mover

---

12–13. A most extensive anthology of ancient Greek and Latin arguments for the world's eternity appears in Faber, pp. 238–52.

[186] *Cosmopoeia*, in *Opera Omnia* (Venice, 1591), pp. 5v–10.
[187] Pp. 34, 38–39. [188] Pp. 36–37; Goodman, p. 407. [189] Pp. 5–7v.
[190] Pp. 71–76.
[191] Derodon, pp. 5–122; Abbadie, pp. 73–92; Cappel, pp. 16–30; Good, pp. 7–16; Samuel Parker, *Disputationes*, pp. 109–17.
[192] Pp. 18–25, 30–34.

converting the potential into act,[193] a sequence of efficient causes arising to a cause,[194] a non-contingent cause in itself necessary,[195] and the existence of ultimate value established by lesser values.[196] All these proofs, adapted by St. Thomas from the nature of man or from man's world, become conventional prefaces to rational confutations of atheism, but the fifth Thomistic proof, which annotated the creatures in terms of their ends, was the proof that infatuated the seventeenth-century rational opponents of rationalism.

When a theologian like Louis of Granada, whose writings were popular with men of all credal dispositions, looked at the world, he saw it as a vast testament of order, variety, harmony, beauty, and design demonstrating a creator, the great end of all creation.[197] The full canvas of teleology, so brilliantly painted by Louis, was frequently exhibited, but some men needed only the sun working for the good of "this inferior world" [198] or the four elements "ever tending to the world's good and never failing to the world's end." [199] Bishop Fotherby is committed to his wise creator by the obvious agreement among contraries; [200] whereas Bishop Towers

[193] S. Paparella, *De Efficientia Primi Motoris*, in *Opera* (Macerata, 1582), pp. 122–30; Lessius, pp. 15–18; Towers, pp. 33–36; Parker, pp. 104–7; Cousin, pp. 2–3; Fotherby, pp. 213–17.

[194] Towers, pp. 22–23; Fotherby, pp. 212–24; Wolseley, pp. 46–60; S. Ward, pp. 12–20; Bates, pp. 62–66.

[195] De Moulin, pp. 10–12; Vincent Hattecliffe, *Aut Deus aut Nihil* (London, 1659); Cousin, p. 4; Good, pp. 5–6.

[196] R. Sault, *A Conference betwixt a Modern Atheist and His Friend* (London, 1693), pp. 4–10; Good, pp. 4–5; Bates, pp. 66–71; Goodman, pp. 408–9; Cousin, p. 4.

[197] See *De la Introduccion de Simbolo de la Fe*, translated as *God Cares for You* by E. C. McEniry (Columbus, Ohio, 1944), pp. 24–25, for a prose poem on teleology. For similar outbursts, see Yves de Paris, I, 334–35, and R. Du Pont, *La Philosophie des Esprits* (Rouen, 1628), pp. 38–40.

[198] Goodman, p. 408.   [199] G. More, p. 39.

[200] Pp. 327–45. Fotherby refers to God as a "choirmaster," the title used also by Viret, *De la Providence Divine*, pp. 335–36, and T. Raynaud, *Scalae a Visibili Creatura ad Deum* (Lyons, 1624), p. 15. See also Mersenne,

finds design inherent even in dead wood and stone, so that men can "build houses, make fires, dress meat and live." [201] Charron's Providence reduces the infinite and providential variety of creation to an "order so harmonious, a concord so firm"; [202] and Lessius, who leads his readers up the stairway of being making teleological orations on each landing, describes the moral and political confusion in a world where men, like sheep or sparrows, were physically identical.[203] Other Roman Catholics, Bellarmine and Raynaud, ascend and descend the worn rungs of the ladder of creatures; [204] but few apologists of any creed can hold a pulpit against John Edwards, a Calvinist, who assailed the "Socinian" John Locke and wrote another forty books against the various enemies of his religious convictions.

Though Edward's *A Demonstration of the Existence and Providence of God from the Contemplation of the Visible Structure of the Greater and Lesser World* (1695) is less scientific than Ray's earlier *The Wisdom of God Manifested in the Creation*, both men united to attack materialism and René Descartes, who was now revealed in his true agnostic colors. Edwards is not so sanguine as Ray about altering the minds of atheists; so he wishes only to stop the spread of "the pernicious infection." He always takes a rational stance, refusing to mention the Bible, the compendium of revelation,

---

L'Impiété, pp. 81–82; Good, pp. 19–22; Wolseley, pp. 82–90; and Derodon, pp. 136–37.

[201] P. 42.   [202] *Les Trois Vérités,* pp. 32–34.

[203] Pp. 31–109. Lessius descends and arrives finally at the "seminal principle," which is as if "a painter could impress in his pencil a permanent power to draw images." He observes that inadvertent incest, adultery, etc. would be the order of the day if all had "in the manner of sheep or sparrows" the same faces.

[204] In the *De Ascensione Mentis in Deum per Scalas Rerum Creatarum* (Cologne, 1617), Bellarmine puts man on the first stair, and God's justice at the top. In his *Scalae a Visibili Creatura,* Raynaud descends from the planets on a twelve-rung ladder. For some other texts on design, see Abbadie, pp. 23–28, 110–17; S. Nye, *A Discourse concerning Natural and Revealed Religion* (London, 1696), pp. 16–22; Parker, pp. 117–67.

because his opponents say it is no different "from the Alcoran or some Legendary Tale." [205] His argument for God is based entirely on design and he begins, like Milton's Satan, at the sun. Standing in that place, he rejects at once the Copernican hypothesis, "a modish piece of Philosophy" [206] which will shortly disappear. Descending, then, through the other creatures, Edwards sees the ultimate end of each item of creation in itself, in the ends of other creatures, and finally in God. A few parts of the world's body seem fairly useless, and Edwards uses his faithful imagination to establish their worth. Fleas, for instance, have hard, black armour to protect them in their leaping, but their value to other creatures is slight unless they "may be useful among poor people by a plentiful phlebotomy and save them the charges of a lancet and clear them of the worst of their blood gratis." [207]

This notion of creation moving in order, beauty, harmony, and economy toward final ends had been with man for centuries, and suggested a creator watching every detail of his creation, just as clearly as the notion of a creator suggested a creation with ends. Xenophon attributes the idea to Socrates,[208] although it is probably older, and Cicero's Balbus reworked the whole theory in the *De Natura Deorum.*[209] Tertullian,[210] Cyprian,[211] Lactantius,[212] St. Ambrose,[213] and St. Jerome,[214] relying on the testimony of Scriptures and of pagan philosophers, polished the non-Christian notions about the general and special Providence of God into a bright facet of Christianity. Chrysostom and Salvian wrote formal trea-

---

[205] Pp. vii–viii.   [206] Pp. 49–50.

[207] P. 237. Edwards points out, among other things, that poppy and squill, good for headaches, are "head shaped," and that kidney beans are beneficial to the kidneys (pp. 117–36). Ray directs his book against eternalists and atomists and attacks Descartes' criticism of final causes. The major part of his book is devoted to the exhibition of design; he urges men, consequently, to "converse with Nature as well as books."

[208] *Memorabilia,* IV, 1–10.   [209] II, 73–75.   [210] *PL,* II, 314–15.

[211] *PL,* IV, 576.   [212] *PL,* VII, 100–21.   [213] *PL,* XVI, 37–38.

[214] *PL,* XXV, 395, 511.

tises about it, but it was St. Augustine's practical demonstration in the *City of God* of the doctrine's missionary value which made it a sure conviction of the Church.

For St. Augustine, more than for the pagans and some Christian predecessors, God's creation and governing of his creation were separate but similar divine powers.[215] He admits the foresight of the pagans in this matter, but Christian speculation, thanks to "a better priest," was truer.[216] The force of God's government is for him so plain that it need not be proved. It controls all, from planets to insects, and establishes the harmony of the universal parts.[217] It is responsible for human time,[218] for the rise and fall of nations,[219] and for all events, ordinary or miraculous.[220] Universal in scope, it nonetheless takes care of the requirements of individuals. It minds the needs of each creature, though of some more than of others.[221] St. Thomas does little more than make shrewd distinctions among the observations of St. Augustine;[222] and in the matter of the deeds of Providence, even Calvin[223] does not dissent much from the views of the Romans. All Renaissance men who were Christians saw the hand of Providence everywhere and tried to point it out to the atheists.

Canephius, for whom the crucifixion of Christ was a convincing proof of Providence, assigns doubts on this doctrine only to atheists;[224] and De l'Épine wrote a book "not for the profane, libertines, Epicureans, and atheists" but for the "children of God" who are, nonetheless, shown the work of Providence in the quality, spaciousness, motion, and conservation of creation as well as in the special attributes of each

[215] *PL*, XLI, 600–2; XXXIV, 336–38; XXXVII, 1892–93.
[216] *PL*, XLI, 788–90.
[217] *PL*, XLI, 353–55, 472–76, 696–99; XXXII, 745; XXXI, 519.
[218] *PL*, XLI, 295.   [219] *PL*, XLI, 141–42, 153–54, 165–66, 219.
[220] *PL*, XLI, 293–95.   [221] *PL*, XLI, 435–36; XL, 19–20.
[222] *Summa Theologica*, Ia. 22, 1–4.   [223] *Inst.*, I, 16.
[224] Pp. 23–26.

creature.[225] George More knows St. Augustine and finds, consequently, a clearer reflection of God's government in the careers of great men than in those less great. It is plainly displayed not only in Adam's Fall but also in the subsequent defeats of Xerxes, Pompey, and Philip of Spain that God moves in human history and hurls down some of his finest earthly replicas. Fedele Danieli, who wrote on Providence for doubtful Italians, attributes the rise of the Valois and Lancastrians as well as the good wind "given Caesar at Brindisi" [226] to the special intervention of Providence. But the pleasant and profitable events that sixteenth-century theologians attributed to Providence were questioned with hellborn wit by the philosopher Bruno, who was yet-to-be providentially disciplined. Bruno's *Spaccio de la Bestia Triofante* begins with a conversation among Sofia, Saulino, and Mercurio on the celestial reforms being instituted by the aging Jupiter on account of the illogical complaints of Momus. Shortly, however, the reader is on earth and is learning about a set of curious pedants who insist men are pleasing to God only in terms of their religious beliefs. These pedants, Bruno implies, work for nobody, actually speak evil of work, and live on the labors of others because they are singularly engaged with "invisible things, which neither they, nor any others, ever understood." Mercury now explains to the other celestials, since the pedants cannot, the functioning of divine Providence under the Jovian scepter.

He has ordered that at noon today two melons in the plot of Franzino shall become ripe, but they are not to be gathered

[225] *Traité de la Providence de Dieu* (Rochelle, 1594); Charron, *Les Trois Vérités*, pp. 49–69; Du Pont, pp. 36–40; Boucher, pp. 534–60; W. Charleton, *The Darkness of Atheism*, pp. 95–158; Stephen Charnocke, *A Treatise of Divine Providence* (London, 1680); William Sherlock, *A Discourse concerning Divine Providence* (London, 1693); the treatises, sermons, and general observations on this matter are innumerable and rather much the same.

[226] *Trattato della Divina Providenza* (Milan, 1615), pp. 281–312.

for three days, when they will be inedible. . . . Nasta, the wife of Albenzio, will burn fifty-seven hairs on her forehead and temples by getting her curling iron too hot; whereas two hundred and fifty beetles will develop out of the dung of her bull. Of this number, thirteen will be trampled by Albenzio; twenty-six will die by being turned over; twenty-two will live in a cave; eighty will wander through the yard; forty live retired lives under the horse block; and sixteen roll their balls where they please. Antonio Savolino's bitch will conceive five puppies, of which number, two will be born dead and three alive. One of these will look like his father; one like his father and mother; and one like Polidoro's dog. At that time the cuckoo must be heard neither more nor less than twelve times, and go to the ruins of the castle, from which after seven minutes she will fly to Scaravita. . . . Twelve bedbugs will leave the boards of Constantino's bed and march to his pillow, four of them very little, seven very large, and one of them of middle size. What happens to them at candlelight we shall see.[227]

After Mercury has recounted other histories of industrious, special Providence, Sofia talks about the men loved by Jupiter and the men praised by "pedants and tellers of parables." Jupiter prefers good citizens and humanitarians, who are magnanimous, just, and merciful;[228] but the "pedants" ruin decent men who come under their instruction.[229] It is clear that Jupiter's good is really the evil of the "parable tellers." The reader now goes to Bruno's heaven and hears the Gods plan the future of constellations bankrupted by the discoveries of Copernicus. The divine synod plans to send Aquarius down to earth to convince men of the truth of such biblical stories as the Deluge.[230] Orion, on the other hand, who "can walk on the waves without sinking or wetting his feet and,

[227] *Opere,* ed. A. Wagner (Leipzig, 1830), II, 146–53.
[228] II, 164.   [229] II, 166–67.   [230] II, 235–36.

consequently, can likewise do a great many other pretty tricks," is to teach men that black is white, that reason is evil, and that Nature and her laws are foolish and contrary to divinity.[231] But at that moment a "fly buzzes in his ear," and Jupiter realizes "that Orion may give it out that Jupiter is not Jupiter but that Orion is Jupiter and that all the Gods are mere Chimeras and Whimsies."

Forty years before Bruno's caustic comment on the ways of Providence was printed, Curio had studied those "little fowlers," the spiders, to show how Providence worked through them.[232] A decade later, in 1594, Fontana glorified the demonstration of the divine government in the ant, which was seen as an allegory of human immortality, because, unique among insects, it buries its dead. Hence,[233] when Bruno's Mercury relates the divinely supervised careers of bedbugs, dung beetles, and bitches, he is writing a parody on a very orthodox method of expounding the activities of special Providence. But mockery had small effect, and, five generations later, men still found Providence exhibiting itself in the brains [234] and entrails [235] of men. Most of these works required only a few quires of paper; but George Stengel, a Jesuit, needed six hundred pages for his apology for monsters,[236] a book that shows God's benevolent justice at work

[231] II, 238–39.
[232] *Aranei Encomion in quo Aranei Erudita Natura Rhetorico Schemate Explicatur: Et in eo Loci Communes de Ente Supremo et Unico, de Divinia Providentia, de Spiritus Humani Perpetuitate, Aliisque Nonnullis Scitu Dignis* (Venice, 1540). See *Summa Theologica*, Ia, IIae, 1, 2.
[233] *Formica sive de Divina Providentia* (Bergomi, 1594) is a twenty-page hexameter poem.
[234] Wolf, *De Atheo.*
[235] Fridericus Hoffmannus, *De Atheo Convincendo ex Artificiosissima Machinae Humanae Structura Oratio* (s.l., 1705). The oration was delivered on March 27, 1692, and demonstrates Providence by the circulation of the blood and the digestive process.
[236] *De Monstris et Monstrosis, quam Mirabilis, Bonus, et Iustus in Mundo Administrando Sit Deus Monstantibus* (Ingolstadt, 1647). Stengel, a Jesuit, points out that no deformities are in vain. Protruding teeth and hairy

among the deformed, because deformity itself was a providentially miraculous defection from natural order. The same miraclous interference of Providence with natural processes [237] furnished the subject for other books and for innumerable sermons, but the so-called "problem of evil," or theodicy, was the truly soft link in the chain of Christian theology.

Men like Seneca's Lucilius sometimes asked the Stoics why evil existed in a world governed by good, and they were usually given Christian answers.[238] The Fathers, without straying too far from Job or the philosophers, made a stout brief against this irritating inquiry. Origen said evil was permitted but not ordained;[239] Tertullian [240] and Theodoret [241] thought it a necessary companion of the divine gift of free will. The Fall is, then, the source of evil,[242] but it is also "the medicine of the soul" and the minister of God's design.[243] "What can I think of," writes St. Augustine, "that is dirtier

---

chins in women are aids to chastity; deformed people are always compensated; dwarfs are often clever; the blind have finer senses of touch or hearing than the sighted. Another essay on the problem can be read in Charles Cotin, *Theoclée ou la Vrai Philosophie des Principes du Monde* (Paris, 1646), pp. 41–70.

[237] The question of miracles both in themselves and as proof of special and general Providence is the subject of a vast literature at this time. The Roman Catholic apologists are well represented by Richard Archdekin's *A Treatise of Miracles* (Louvain, 1667), by Lessius, pp. 115–27, 169–76, and Faber, pp. 55–58, 68–78, 127–29. Spinoza's critique of Providence and miracle in the *Theological-Political Treatise* produced outcries from all creeds: see Jacobus Batalerius, *Vindiciae Miraculorum* (Amsterdam, 1674) and Regnier van Mansvelt, *Adversus Anonymum Theologo-Politicum* (Amsterdam, 1674). In 1683 a London refutation of Hobbes, Burnet, and Spinoza, *Miracles: Works Above and Contrary to Nature*, was accompanied by *Miracles No Violations of the Laws of Nature*, a free rendering of Spinoza's chapters; hence, its purpose is ambiguous. Probably the best English apology is William Fleetwood's *An Essay upon Miracles* (London, 1701).

[238] *De Providentia*, I, 1–6; II, 1–4; III, 2.   [239] *PG*, XI, 1516–17.
[240] *PL*, II, 317–20; Lactantius, *PL*, VII, 115–24.
[241] *PG*, LXXXIII, 662.   [242] St. Gregory, *PL*, LXXV, 833–34.
[243] St. Augustine, *PL*, XL, 98–99; Origen, *PG*, XI, 1177–80.

than whores and pimps, but if they were removed, the lecherous would attack and ravish chaste matrons." [244] Sinners may seem to be fortunate, and God, hoping for amendment, does not immediately punish them; [245] but, as the story of Dives and Lazarus suggests, the time of reckoning will come. [246]

In his essay on Providence, Viret showed that God can slaughter infants to punish parents and that he prematurely removes the just from the world in order to prevent their moral corruption. [247] George More's God rewards according to rank and degree, and he sometimes treats a bad Priam or evil Agamemnon well so that their tragedies will be more horrible. [248] Charron's God, on the other hand, regards inner good superior to wealth, honor, health, and pleasure; [249] hence, he makes the just suffer so that they may come to know themselves, be morally tested, kept alert in virtue, and planted with the seeds of heavenly glory. [250] God made men good, says Charron, but he also made them free, and evil is the fruit of freedom; nonetheless, it is well known that man's evil makes God's good. [251] Jean Boucher expresses the widely held view that man does wrong to make God responsible for "evils of nature," such as floods, earthquakes, and volcanic eruptions, which are not evils but faults in substance. [252] All other mortal ills are merely divine opportunities for the good to win eternal prizes, which shortsighted sinners scorn. [253] As deism prospered, however, the sections on theodicy in antiatheist books grew more and more extended; and by the middle of the seventeenth century, the British, who were par-

[244] *PL*, XXXII, 977–87, 900, 999–1002.
[245] Lactantius, *PL*, VII, 137; St. Gregory, *PL*, LXXV, 627, 747.
[246] St. Ambrose, *PL*, XVI, 44–46.
[247] *De la Providence Divine*, pp. 426–32; sometimes (p. 437) the parents are too affectionate and make the children their idols.
[248] Pp. 103, 105, 122.   [249] *Les Trois Vérités*, pp. 68–71.
[250] Pp. 74–77.   [251] Pp. 86–88.   [252] Pp. 635–38.   [253] Pp. 640–49.

ticularly distressed by this spiritual ailment, were being very vigorous in their defense of special Providence.

The real brief of the atheists against Christianity, Walter Charleton contends, rests on the apparent inequality of divine justice; [254] hence, after he establishes the existence of a general Providence with all the conventional rational proofs,[255] he turns on those atheists who say with Epicurus that love and hate are incompatible with divine nature, that a just God would not maliciously set traps for man, and that a good and pitiful God could not endure the suffering of the righteous. He informs British unbelievers that God's anger is "an *ira sedata*," that the traps are sprung by man's free will, and that the evil gain only a "*bona fucata*"; whereas the good, by their suffering, exercise patience and virtue, and are eventually and piously consoled to see those "who daily bathed themselves in rivers of voluptuousness to be by Divine revenge on a sudden precipitated into the black sea of misery." [256] Samuel Herne lets the good be divinely oppressed so that they may show they "do not serve God for profit." [257] With similar good grace, he permits the wicked to go unmarked so that atheists will realize there must be post-mortem rewards and afflictions.[258] All of these apologists suggest that the rational inspection of the mysterious ways of Providence —at least in this difficult area—be avoided. Burthogge says the problem should not be judged "by the impertinence of sense"; [259] Charleton points out that "when the wit of man, wanting the ballast of piety, bears too much sail, it cannot

[254] Pp. 97–98.   [255] Pp. 101–58.
[256] Pp. 180–90. In his *Physiologia Epicuro-Gassendo Charltoniana* (London, 1654), he corrects "the poisonous" part of Epicurus (p. 126) by assigning the creation of atoms to God.
[257] *A Discourse of Divine Providence* (London, 1679), p. 23.
[258] Pp. 27–29.
[259] Richard Burthogge, Ταγαθὸν *or Divine Goodness Explicated and Vindicated from the Exceptions of the Atheist* (London, 1670), p. 54.

escape oversetting"; [260] and Nye, who permits God's thunder-bolts to strike churches where the ritual is improper,[261] urges men not to question the special acts of Providence but rather to await the "last act of the drama that opens the reason and beauty of the plot." [262] However, the disquieting facts remained that there was an Old Testament Book of Job and that the God who superintended the history of minnows and men seemed to have a hand in evil itself.

"We should not request that we be not led into temptation," wrote the Jesuit, Thomas Whitfield, "if God were not both a passive and active force in the course of evil." It would, in fact, be a reduction of the powers of Providence if God were only a "mere spectator of men in their sinful actions." [263] Nonetheless, one should not accuse God as a producer of evil because his will is good, not evil. He uses evil naturally, not morally; and, since the end of all action, both evil and indifferent, is God, it is consequently good.[264] George Gifford, an Anglican, details a series of divine means used for the promulgation of natural, but necessary, evil; [265] and Stephen Charnocke, a Puritan, writes that Providence, which watched over Jesus Christ, and cares for both good and bad angels, righteous and wicked men,[266] permits and sometimes even commands an evil action or event; [267] what it decides is an imperial edict, and no man has the right to rebel or even question its decisions. Man's duty is to admire, because the "beauty of Providence" often shines forth in the affliction

---

[260] P. 353.   [261] Pp. 29–30.   [262] P. 51.
[263] *The Extent of Divine Providence* (London, 1651), pp. 3–16. He says God allows men to follow evil, permits Satan to tempt them, withdraws his Grace, makes one sin to punish another, lets one sin, and not another, be committed, and supports the sinner in his natural motions. He not only permitted Pharaoh's heart to be hardened but hardened it!
[264] P. 27. Later (p. 29) he says God "lovingly" permitted Job to be tempted by hateful Satan.
[265] *The Great Mystery of Providence* (London, 1695), pp. 7–13.
[266] Pp. 25–32.   [267] Pp. 40–47, 66–68, 70–79.

of the just, and the wicked themselves are sometimes forged into the sword of God.[268] Milton's *Samson Agonistes*, which asserts eternal Providence in a more particularized fashion than *Paradise Lost*, is a poetical commentary on all of this. One must endure until the last act, or, as Milton puts it, the wisdom of God is "ever best found in the close." [269] When atheists question or deny this precept, sin is made moral, religion has no purpose, God is disgraced, and the natural light in man goes out. "It was," Charnocke continues, "pride, interest, self-conceit, and opinion of merit rather than any well grounded reason introduced this part of Atheism into the world." [270]

---

[268] Pp. 88–89, 106.
[269] For the treatment of this theme in *Samson* see J. D. Ebbs, "Milton's Treatment of Poetic Justice in *Samson Agonistes*," *MLQ*, XXII (1961), 377–89.
[270] P. 118.

Chapter Five

Reason and Immortality

I

FOR THE OPPONENTS of atheism, the proof of God's existence was inseparably bound with the proof of the soul's immortality. Each hypothesis supported the other and required the other's support. The concept of a life after death was, of course, a pre-Christian belief; and the earliest Christians, aided by revelation, improved, though not without intramural quarrel, the cruder speculations of pagan philosophers.[1] St. Augustine's stubborn conviction that immortality was a truth beyond question satisfied most early theologians;[2] nonetheless, they were all happy to recount the guarantees that the simple, central, spiritual substance lived consciously after the material body disintegrated. To sustain this assurance, Albertus Magnus recited proofs of the soul's existence,[3] insubstantiality,[4] immediate creation,[5] and incorruptibility;[6] and though his clever pupil, Thomas Aquinas, nowhere presents a formal demonstration, it is clear he held immortality a Christian essential. The soul is for him the first and eternal

---

[1] J. Bainvel, "Âme," *Dictionnaire de Theologie Catholique*, eds. A. Vacant, E. Mangenot, and E. Amann (Paris, 1923), I, cols. 977–1005.
[2] *De Civitate*, PL, VII, 23.
[3] *Opera Omnia*, ed. A. Borgnet (Paris, 1896), XXXV, 6–9.
[4] Pp. 14–15.   [5] Pp. 82–84.   [6] Pp. 521–30.

principle of life, the act of the body;[7] and his successors accept immortality as an essential Christian premise in the same way that the Euclidians must admit the dogma of the first theorem.

Raimond de Sebonde was one of the first, modern, rational theologians to compose a formal demonstration of immortality, because he finds it the major consolation for existence. It fences man from the animals and brings him nearer in essence to God.[8] Man is served by the sun and planets, immortal creatures, and it would be irrational were he lesser than his ministers.[9] Sebonde knows unbelievers who think the soul depends on the body and perishes with it; consequently, they scorn the rewards of eternity and find the damnation which awaits evildoers. He offers his proofs in hopes of changing doubting minds and because immortality is necessary for a reasonable morality.

God created for his everlasting honor and utility, and these divine ends require as their means the immortality of man. Sebonde discovered that repugnance and desire, volition and non-volition are the only human qualities which do not diminish with age; hence, they must be incorporeal, survive the flesh, and show the soul eternal. Immortality is established further by the reason's ability to strip quantity, quality, and place from the testimonies of the senses, so that man can understand abstract, universal form. The notion "man," for example, is understood by all men; yet it lacks sensational reality because no individual man fits the whole of the human con-

---

[7] *Summa Theologica*, I, 75, 1. V. E. Sleva, *The Separated Soul in the Philosophy of St. Thomas Aquinas* (Washington, 1940), pp. 62–63, points out the implicit proofs. For other medieval demonstrations of immortality, see those of Jean de Rochelle in B. Haureau, *Histoire de la Philosophie Scolastique* (Paris, 1880), II, 192–213, and E. Gilson, *La Philosophie au Moyen Âge* (Paris, 1947), pp. 437–40. Haureau also summarizes the *De Anima* of Guillaume d'Auvergne (II, 149–56), and Georg Bülow has edited the *De Immortalitate* of Gundissalinus in *Beiträge zur Geschichte der Philosophie des Mittelalters* (Münster, 1897), Vol. II.

[8] Pp. 121–22.   [9] Pp. 161–62.

dition. The ability to universalize is, then, a principal talent of the immortal soul. One must not, however, regard the soul as eternal in itself; it was created and only endowed with the potentiality of immortality.[10] Sebonde's rational demonstration occupies but a small portion of his larger work, but it is one of the more persuasive essays of its generation. The Middle Ages was keenly enough interested in eschatological matters, and this interest depended upon the actuality of immortality, which was accepted commonly and almost never demonstrated. The philosophical expositions of this concept really begin toward the end of the fifteenth century.

Giacomo Camforo, a Dominican, whose *De Immortalitate Animae* was printed at Cosenza in 1478, knows and rejects the psychological speculations of pagans; [11] and he agrees with Sebonde that immortality is made plain by the soul's ability to consider and resolve intellectual problems, by its intrinsic perfection and lack of extrinsic oppositions, by its innate desire for survival, and by its talent for logical abstraction.[12] His contemporary, Guillaume Houpelande, also quotes the views of Plato, Hermes, Seneca, and Cicero in his *De Immortalitate Animae* (1489); but he thinks that immortality is made certain by revelation supported by universal consent, by the extraordinary virtues of reason, by the natural yearning for life after death, and by the final rendering of divine justice.[13] But these continual discussions fade before the *Theologicae Platonicae de Immortalitate Animorum* of Ficino, friend of both Plato and Christ.

As his thesis, Ficino uses St. Matthew's opinion that the whole world has less value than the soul. Men should, he writes, look more deeply into this matter because Christ died in vain if the soul is mortal.[14] The face of the Divine is

[10] Pp. 404–13.   [11] Pp. 19v–20.   [12] Pp. 24–26.
[13] H. Busson, *Les Sources* (1957), pp. 147–48.
[14] *Opera* (Basel, 1576), I, 885.

reflected in the mirror of the soul; and when man is urged to know himself, he is at the same time urged to know God.[15] The Christian reading of the Socratic injunction enables Ficino to use the metaphors of Plotinus and the pseudo-Dionysius on the coming out of the darkness into light or the ascending from the material world to the spiritual.[16] To expound his vision of celestial progress, Ficino, mindful of the shadowy cave of Plato and the dark glass of St. Paul, erects, as his medieval predecessors had done, a spiritual ladder which enables the adept to climb over the stockade of mortality and escape to immortal blessedness. Rung by rung, the striving souls rise from quantity to quality, from form admitting change, but not division, to the immutable angelic spirits until the summit is reached, and here the eye of the soul sees the light of truth.[17]

Ficino also uses the metaphors of St. Augustine and St. Thomas to describe the immortal soul, the "copula mundi," [18] which moves itself circularly, dominates matter,[19] and is life itself.[20] The fact of immortality can be proved both *per intelligendi virtutem* [21] and *per rationalem virtutem*,[22] but no proof is clearer than the soul's own longing for goodness and truth.[23] Densely modified and cabalistically complicated by other adept Florentines,[24] this new theology competed successfully with that of the new Aristotelians. Suddenly, the proof of the soul and its eternity was of the greatest impor-

[15] I, 78.   [16] I, 763; II, 1380, 1947.   [17] I, 79.   [18] I, 135.
[19] I, 136–39, 163–72, 175, 214.   [20] I, 150–52.   [21] I, 182–202.
[22] I, 202–19.   [23] I, 307–9.
[24] G. Saitta, *Marsilio Ficino e la Filosofia dell'Umanesimo* (Bologna, 1954), pp. 131–92, and *Il Pensiero Italiano*, II, 71–156; P. O. Kristeller, *Il Pensiero Filosofico di Marsilio Ficino* (Florence, 1953), pp. 350–80; E. Garin, *Giovanni Pico della Mirandola: Vita e Dottrina* (Florence, 1938), pp. 194–208, and "Testi Minori sull'Anima nella Cultura del 400 in Toscana," *Archivio di Filosofia* (1951), No. 1, pp. 1–36. The root of Ficino's Platonic theology may possibly tap the sections on immortality in Bessarion's *Adversus Calumniatorem Platonis*, in *Opera* (Venice, 1516), pp. 6v–7.

tance; and there were disquisitions enough on the subject when the students shouted as Simone Porzio entered his classroom, "Lecture to us on the soul!" [25]

Before Porzio's *De Mente Humana* was published in Florence in 1551, the *De Anima* of Aristotle had been carefully annotated to suit the orthodox; [26] and the dangerous ruminations of Pomponazzi had been shown, to the satisfaction of many men, to be both fallacious and foolish. Nifo assaulted Pomponazzi's first five propositions in his *De Immortalitate Animae* (1518); and Contarini used "natural reason" and Aristotle, not only to overwhelm Averroes and Pomponazzi,[27] but also to answer sagaciously fifteen trenchant questions about the soul that had been proposed by Cardinal Farnese.[28]

[25] Busson, *Les Sources* (1957), p. 46.
[26] For bibliography on this limitless topic, see J. G. T. Grässe, *Bibliotheca Psychologica* (Leipzig, 1845), and pp. 29–31 of Busson's *La Pensée Religieuse Française*. Some sixteenth-century works of interest are G. F. Pico della Mirandola's *De Animae Immortalitate* (Paris, 1541), where the notions of Pythagoras, Alexander Aphrodisiensis, and Averroes are exposed and disposed of; and the lengthy sections (pp. 219–73) in Philippes de Mornay, which report all the conventional arguments and then accept or reject the views of Hermes, Phocylides, Pindar, Homer, Pythagoras, Heraclitus, Plato, Aristotle, Cicero, Ovid, Seneca, Herodotus, Epictetus, Plotinus, Alexander, Galen, Averroes, and others. Most commentaries on Aristotle take up the question, and one can consult the disquisitions in the editions of Johannes de Lutrea (1482), Spina (1519), Odoni (1557), Duodus (1575), Denisetus (1577), Schroter (1585), and Galla (1621). Petrus Martinez Toletanus begins his "Tractatus de Animorum Nostrorum Immortalitate," in his commentary on the *De Anima* (Murviedro, 1575), with a confutation of skeptics and settles the matter for believers by referring them to the affirmative pronouncements of Clement V at the Council of Vienna and Leo X at the Fifth Lateran Council.
[27] *De Immortalitate Animae adversus Petrum Pomponatium*, pp. 179–80.
[28] P. 195. Saitta has a brilliant essay, *Il Pensiero Italiano*, II, 325–449, on the philosophical reaction to Pomponazzi's *De Immortalitate Animae* and on the psychological systems of Achillini, Porzio, Zabarella, Piccolomini, and others. Bernardino Telesio, also accused of atheism, writes in his *De Rerum Natura Juxta Propria Principia* (Naples, 1586) that the soul is eternal, but the world is not (pp. 14–16); the divine soul, infused by God, instructs man in theological matters; whereas the rational soul, inherited from parents, is mortal and engages in ordinary mundane

Aristotle was clearly helpful on either side of the problem. Petrus Nicolas of Faenza, in turn, tried to shorten the intellectual mileage between Plato's Florence and Aristotle's Padua by referring to all the ancients but, especially, to the two Greeks.[29] He is, perhaps, the earliest defender of immortality to try to harmonize the doctrines of the pagan scriptures.[30] Before the mid-century, the nature of the soul and its potential durability is a major philosophical topic, and Juan Vives was one of the best examiners of the problem.

In the *De Anima*, Vives proclaims the soul as the only source of life. It is superior to the humors, although it may

---

ratiocination (pp. 178–80). Telesio protects himself by urging his readers (p. 2) to reject anything in his book not in accord with Catholic doctrine.

[29] In his *Opus de Immortalitate Animorum Secundum Platonem et Aristotelem* (Faenza, 1525), pp. IIIr–XXVIIv, he presents the notions of Thales, Anaxagoras, Homer, Hermes, Orpheus, Zoroaster, and others. The immortalist ideas of the *Phaedo, Republic,* and *Timaeus* are presented to offset the arguments of Aristotle and Themistius. The atheist arguments against immortality are based on the following assumptions: the intellect is composed of corruptible and incorruptible substances; the rational soul is an act of body and has no offices apart from body; all souls are attached to bodies; if souls are created, they are corruptible; if souls are finite in operation, they are finite. The author attacks these principal ideas and others just as bad, such as "an immortal soul would desire rather than fear death," "would reveal itself to friends after the body's death," "would not be joined to a corruptible body by a loving God," "would understand abstractions at birth," and "would more fittingly inhabit an everlasting body."

[30] Pierre Viret summarizes the theories of Galen, Plato, and others in the twenty-fourth dialogue of his *Exposition* (pp. 813–36). Like other immortalists, he has no respect for Plato's notion that souls are part of the divine substance. He thinks that early men buried both men and animals; and that when the doctrine of immortality was revealed to them, they desisted from animal burial. Nicolas Nancelius, whose *De Immortalitate Animae* (Paris, 1587) is highly conventional, sketches a history of pagan notions. Jacob Colerus, admitting that Pythagoras had sound Christian ideas, writes that the question cannot be solved without revelation. He devotes the first sixty pages of his *De Animarum Immortalitate* (Wittenberg, 1587) to restating favorable philosophical opinions. Giovanni de Fedeli's *Anima Immortale* (Venice, 1598) is a pagan-Christian history of immortality.

bring them, as Aristoxenus suggested, into harmony. The nature of the soul may not be known, but its effects are plain, and its goodness and harmony test its divinity.[31] When they discard the spiritual, materialists unwittingly reject their own wit and reason. A naked soul is, of course, never seen, and communication between material creatures and the immaterial never occurs; however, the mind's spirituality is often displayed in its comprehension of the incorporeal. In living and dying, man may be similar to plants and animals; yet he is distinguished from them by his idea of God, who created and can destroy the soul. The celestial origin of the soul is further established by other inescapable proofs. Man's desire for deathless fame is one. Another is his horror before the extinction of consciousness. Still others are his preferences for the pleasures of the intellect before those of the senses, for his reason rather than for his imagination, and for the contemplation of the spiritual and the eternal.[32] The problem of immortality was not, however, peculiar to the Roman Catholics.

Though Calvin was convinced that those who had the Bible did not need the proofs of pagan or Christian philosophers,[33] his colleague Pierre Viret unwound a long coil of logic to

[31] *De Anima et Vita* (Lyons, 1555), pp. 37–50.
[32] Pp. 128–42. This very common idea of the mind's supramaterial powers and interests is discussed in Claudius Auberius' *De Immortalitate* (Morges, 1586), pp. 9–15, 29–30.
[33] *Psychopannychia*, ed. W. Zimmerli (Leipzig, 1932), pp. 31–32. First printed in 1545, this book begins the offensive against those who taught "the sleep of the soul." The history of the context can be read in *A Short Historical View of the Controversy concerning the Immediate State and the Separate Existence of the Soul between Death and the General Resurrection Deduced from the Beginning of the Protestant Reformation* (London, 1765). See also George Williamson, "Milton and the Mortalist Heresy," in *Seventeenth Century Contexts* (Chicago, 1961), pp. 148–77. Calvin's contemporary Melanchthon says in his *De Anima*, in *Opera*, ed. C. G. Bretschneider (Halle, 1846), XIII, 172–78, that we do not have minds keen enough to talk about the matter; hence, he depends on revelation but adds to it proofs drawn from ghostly apparitions, the conscience, and the ultimate justice of God.

solve the problem of immortality. The fact that Viret accepted the traducian doctrine of Tertullian, which Calvin,
unlike Luther, rejected, may have required him to argue.[34]
For Viret the soul is not harmony nor temperament nor air
nor fire.[35] He is equally sure that the Egyptians, who con-
versed with Hebrew patriarchs, had a correct but confused
understanding of the nature of the soul.[36] His exposition is
in the form of a dialogue, and his character Nathaniel asks
how atheists, who fight against Nature and regard immortality as a fable, can be convinced of their errors? He thinks
they cling to this foolish unbelief because they fear for their
lot in a hereafter and, consequently, wish to die as animals
do. Atheists, says his friend, Philip, have only to consider the
works of man, "tant ingenieux et merveilleux," to know he
is superior to all other creatures; his top place in the hierarchy
of the created shows his possession of a soul. It is true, of
course, that separated souls are never seen; but why should
a soul, blessed in paradise, wish to return to demonstrate
immortal existence to the incredulous? [37] Viret, who knows
all of Vives' arguments, can also defend the concept of immortality by a dialectic.

Nothing can know aught greater than itself; hence, the
very notion of immortality, an incorporeal postulate, shows
the mind to be everlasting. To be sure, both animals and men
seek good and fly evil; but men, in addition to this, desire
to exist after death. For example, Epicurus, an ardent atheist,
did not believe in immortality; yet he requested an annual
celebration of his birthday. Other indications of the consciousness after death of an individual are: the terrors that
torture the dying atheist; the upright posture of men, which
enables them to look toward heaven; a common conviction
that divine justice is inevitable; and the endless search for

[34] *Exposition*, p. 813.   [35] P. 816.   [36] Pp. 834–36.
[37] Pp. 853–58.

truth, which, given infinite time, will one day be achieved.[38] Immortality is man's great hope, and Viret is astonished not only by the atheists' hardhearted rejection of the idea,[39] but also by the tender-minded rationalists' notion that the soul could be immortal through faith but mortal by nature. They simply do not realize the nature of truth: "Car vérité n'est point double, mais toujours une." [40]

A tone similar to Viret's is maintained by John Woolton, bishop of Exeter, whose *Treatise of the Immortalitie of the Soule* was printed at London in 1576. "Amongst all the works of Creation," he writes, "there is almost none more secret and hidden from carnal and fleshly reason than the substance and operation of man's soul." [41] Philosophical dissections are "witty," but they satisfy neither philosophers nor Christians; hence, Woolton summarizes the opinions of Plato, Aristotle, and Galen only to exhibit their errors. Coming to his own demonstration, he separates the reasonable soul from the understanding, which is part of it, and discovers that reason is "inorganical," functioning without the aid of matter, breeding its own knowledge, universalizing, and then judging its resultant hypotheses. The soul is clearly immaterially created by God as the principle of life, motion, and virtue. However, the rational soul is not, as Epiphanius thought, composed of divine substance, either by influence or derivation. The heretic Origen thought it a heaven-born creature descended into body, and the Manichees, following the Stoics, made souls

---

[38] Pp. 865–77.   [39] P. 890.

[40] P. 896. Coincident with Viret's exposition is the popular discussion of Pierre de la Primaudaye in his *L'Académie Française* (Paris, 1584), pp. 286–342. Other contemporary demonstrations, conventional and repetitive, are found in Cousin, pp. 28–31v; Marco Natta, *De Immortalitate*, in *Opera* (Venice, 1564), pp. 5v–6v, 17–28; and Pierre de l'Hostal, *Les Discours Philosophique* (Paris, 1579), pp. 34–54. In his *De l'Immortalité de l'Âme* (Lyons, 1596), Jean de Serres offers many proofs and "signs" of immortality, but he eventually informs atheists that they really are intruding on forbidden knowledge (pp. 421–26).

[41] Pp. 2v–3.

out of the substance of God. Tertullian believed all souls descended from that of Adam; whereas St. Jerome and St. Augustine thought them to be divinely and continually produced. Woolton agrees with Tertullian, even though he knows some men regard his traducian doctrine as atheistical. He hopes to write another book "to acquit many godly and learned men from such odious accusations." [42] His liberality toward Tertullian did not hamper his bitter criticism of those who held that the souls of the dead lie "in heavy drowsiness or deep lethargy" until the Last Day. [43]

II

Tertullian's doctrine of psychogenesis, [44] attacked by Lactantius [45] and frowned upon by St. Thomas, [46] won many adherents besides Woolton during the Renaissance. Camforo, writing at the end of the fifteenth century, deplored the idea; [47] but a century later, Rodolphus Goclenius gathered a multitude of opinion, both pro and con, in his ΨΥΧΟΛΟΓΙΑ: *Hoc est de Hominis Perfectione, Animo, et in Primis Ortu Huius Commentationes ac Disputationes* (Marburg, 1590). [48]

[42] Pp. 4v–26. [43] P. 84v. [44] *PL*, II, 693–96. [45] *PL*, VII, 70.
[46] St. Thomas objects to the emanationists because they are really material monists who oppose incorporeality, or believe in unity of intellect, or ascribe divine attributes to the human soul (*C.G.*, II, 85). He criticized traducianists (*S.T.*, I, 118, 2) for deriving intellectual principles from seminal force. On the immediate, rather than mediate, creation of souls see *C.G.*, II, 21 and *S.T.*, I, 90, 2.
[47] Pp. 4–5v.
[48] The book contains essays by Franciscus Junius, Jacobus Grynaeus, Colerus, Caspar Peucer, Egidius Hunnius, Petrus Lascovius, and Timothy Bright on both sides of the debate. The traducianists are supported, or at least not condemned, in Joannes Magirus, *Anthropologia* (Prostadt, 1603), pp. 77–80; Aslacus, pp. 332–33; B. Keckermannus, *Systema Physicae*, in *Opera* (Geneva, 1614), I, 1592. Antonio Rocco, in his *Animae Rationalis Immortalitas* (Frankfort, 1644), pp. 15–21, defends traducianism; other books with the same intent are M. Gruvius, *De Origine Animae Humanae*

A decade later, Nicholas Hill reported twenty-three theories [49] of the soul's origin in his *Philosophia Epicurea, Democritiana, Theophrastica* (Paris, 1601); but not all psycholo-
gists are so learned or tolerant as he. Simon Harward doubts
that the individual soul, some remote portion of Adam's
infused spirit, is generated in the course of copulation. If
parents, he argues, gave up parts of their souls to compose
that of their child, they would surely die.[50] Jean Boucher, on
the other hand, cannot tolerate the variant theory that souls
are created mediately by angels; God is the immediate maker
of souls, although their union with bodies depends on paren-
tal cohabitation.[51] Abra de Raconis traces the error of the
angelic creators to Seleucus and insists that the soul is made
by God at the exact moment the body needs it.[52] Jean Fevrier,
while admitting that traducianism is an attractive means of
transmitting original sin, agrees with his church's doctrine
of divine creation. He accounts for the temperamental sim-
ilarity of children to parents—a telling traducian argument—by imagining that God, "to show his infinite sweet-
ness," imprints the child's soul with the personal qualities of
its parents.[53] This contention swung back and forth, and in
1677 Henry Hills made a strong case for traducianism.

(Erfurt, 1673); Georg Lehmannus, *De Animae Immortalis Traductione*
(Leipzig, 1649); and Jacobus Thomasius, *De Origine Animae Humanae
ex Traduce* (Leipzig, 1669).

[49] Pp. 395–96 of the Geneva edition of 1619.

[50] *A Discourse concerning the Soul and Spirit of Man* (London, 1604),
pp. 33r–36R.

[51] Pp. 755–62.

[52] *Tractatus de Anima Rationali* (Paris, 1632), pp. 12–29.

[53] *Traités de Immortalité de l'Âme* (Paris, 1656), pp. 133–42. Micraelius,
imitating Bodin, presents, in his *Ethnophronius* (Stettin, 1647), theological
discussions between Theophilus, a deist, Ethnophronius, a Brahman,
Achmetius, a Mohammedan, Juda, a Jew, Romanus, a Catholic, Helvetius,
a French Protestant, and Photinus, a Polish Protestant. The first part of
Book One is about the being and immortality of the soul; Book Two is
devoted to proving God's existence from the soul's immortality. The
question of the soul's generation occupies the second dialogue (pp. 48–85),
and the speakers, Helvetius only excepted, are for traducianism.

The human soul, Hills said, is neither eternal nor created at the beginning of things and "kept in the heavens, or the stars, or in I know not what treasures of God." Some theologians believe souls are daily created "so as the parents give no natural force"; others think the soul develops in the womb or is infused by God when "the body is ripe." Zanchius, Junius, and Beza cling to the latter doctrine; but Hills takes his stand with traducianists like Keckermannus, Goclenius, Aslacus, Magirus, and Bright.[54] The antitraducianists pointed out that if angels did not procreate in heaven, it was unlikely that earthly souls would beget a child-soul. This argument, Hills contends, avoids the strict qualitative differences between created hierarchies: animals breed; men breed and reason; angels only reason. The fear, expressed by the antitraducianists, that parents will die when they provide pieces of their souls for their offspring is also totally absurd. They provide the same children with bodies without losing their own arms and legs.[55] The whole process of propagation depends on "a seed" extracted by a refining process from all parts of the body; it is no piece of a limb, no shred of an organ; and yet it contains "a virtual and potential faculty, or a symbolic character of the whole nature, and therefore (speaking of man) of the soul as well as of the body impressed in it." [56]

To his logical demonstrations, Hills appends a long exposition and reinterpretation of the biblical passages commonly quoted against traducianism. The atypical origin of Christ's soul is, for example, no argument for the creationists; moreover, God cannot continually create souls because he is no breaker of the Sabbath, of his announced sixth-day termination of creation. This divine pause was well understood by

[54] *A Short Treatise concerning the Propagation of the Soul* (London, 1667), pp. 4–7.
[55] Pp. 11–21.   [56] P. 23.

our first parents; hence, Eve is the Hebrew word for "life" and Adam properly begets the body and soul of a son "in his likeness"; both points suggest man begets souls. Moreover, nothing impure comes from the hand of God; so he would hardly place newly created but somehow or other impure and sin-tainted souls in the bodies of fresh infants.

III

The question of the soul's origin was variously answered throughout the seventeenth century; but while theologians took sides, they always presented a solid front against atheists who doubted the soul's existence and immortality. Louis Richeome, defending the cause of immortality, urged men to base their arguments on the Bible, for this truth was "as bright as the sun until the minds of men were perverted by sin." [57] An anonymous contemporary of his stood on the Christian tradition because all rational proofs of immortality are "like making glass as hard as rock." [58] Few men of any creed gave heed to these sound recommendations, and rational demonstrations went forward as before. Thanks to a fairly standard knowledge of Greek philosophy, Simon Harward recalls that the soul has been anciently defined as a thin body infused into a thick one, as fire, water, earth, as a combination of elements, as heat or complexion, as bright quality in the brain or heart, as an unattached and omnipresent point, and as an indivisible divine essence ruling all. He finds signs of immortality in the soul's ability to "pass the seas in a moment," to calculate the courses of heavenly bodies, to hesi-

[57] *Immortalité de l'Âme* (Paris, 1621), preface.

[58] *Effroyables Pactions Faites entre la Diable et les Prétendus Invisibles,* in *Varietes Historiques et Litteraires,* ed. E. Fournier (Paris, 1855–63), IX, 305.

tate and, then, to decide, and to comprehend the eternal nature of God and his angels.[59] Bishop Goodman, Harward's better-known contemporary, writes that, since miracles and oracles have ceased, the truthful and free-willed soul blessed by divine "concourse and assistance" [60] is the touchstone of Christian verity. Its prospects of eternity are also suggested by its natural desire for immortality, its shame about its bodily functions, and the character of its dreams, presages, visions, and ecstasies.[61]

The printed efforts of early seventeenth-century Christian rationalists to preserve the soul for eternity are all surpassed in weight of paper by the giant volume of Jean Silhon, a friend of Descartes, who wrote in support of "the supposedly failing validity" of the Christian religion.[62] The history of the idea of immortality is naturally well known to him; hence, he attacks all ancient philosophers in the opposition,[63] strokes the heads of those on his side,[64] and, putting aside the atheist Cremonini's injunction to search the Gospels, decides Aristotle may have found the truly reasonable way.[65] He is aware of the damage caused by the agnostic attitudes of Pomponazzi, Cardano, and Vanini, although he admits he has not been able to secure copies of the latter's books.[66] He proposes, therefore, to mend the leaking breaches in the wall of faith

[59] Pp. 42v–44v.   [60] Pp. 7–8.
[61] Goodman's arguments, all conventional, are almost verbally repeated by Amyraut, a French Protestant, in his *Traité*, pp. 74–86. Jean Boucher offers a long chain of traditional proofs (pp. 675–796), and so does Lessius (pp. 237–344). John Dove, who believes in the continual creation of souls, offers thirteen proofs of immortality based on the central idea that the soul is at its best when deprived of the body.
[62] *De l'Immortalité de l'Âme*, p. 21. The book was attacked by Antoine Sirmond in *De Immortalitate Animae Demonstratio Physica et Aristotelica adversus Pomponatium et Asseclas* because Silhon made immortality depend on God's existence, power, and will and not on "the law and condition of our nature" (pp. 1–3).
[63] P. 4.   [64] Pp. 26–34.   [65] P. 36.   [66] P. 47.

with the mortar of reason, because immortality is man's most glorious idea, and to question it darkens the world's skies [67] and ruins the foundations of society.[68]

Silhon knows his foundation stone is God's existence, so he must first destroy the Pyrrhonism which denies the innate knowledge of God, places all its faith in sensation, and derides supernatural signs and prodigies as illusory nonsense.[69] When skeptics talk of man's general ignorance, Silhon responds that man, on the contrary, knows a great deal about architecture, music, and medicine.[70] He chooses Montaigne, whose prose style influenced his, as an especial target. The essayist's doubts about the mind are repeated and dismissed, and we are once again assured of God's existence by a customary train of proofs. These proofs admit us to a series of lectures on the formation of matter, of the skies, the elements, and the two lower floors of the soul. Montaigne's estimate of animal intelligence is heavily discounted; and Silhon inspects the rational, immortal soul, which is created in time and incomplete in itself.[71] The soul, we learn, requires a body, which it leaves with reluctance because it is part of its total perfection.[72] Since creation is the evidence of God's glory and love,[73] it is necessary that he made the souls of men better than those of animals.[74] The creation of angels was, indeed, for God, glory enough; [75] therefore, man was made to bridge the chasm between spirit and matter [76] and

[67] P. 3.   [68] Pp. 5–6.   [69] Pp. 101–7.   [70] Pp. 149–75.

[71] Pp. 236–88.

[72] Pp. 493–95. He regards Platonism as a "soft" philosophy.

[73] P. 498.   [74] Pp. 754–55, 763.   [75] Pp. 788–91.

[76] Pp. 783–86. Among Silhon's contemporaries who wrote on the problem is Gassendi, who defines the soul as a "flos materiae" with a habit of symmetry in his "De Anima," *Opera* (Lyons, 1658), II, 250–52. In a synthesis of elements, he writes, new qualities appear that are not present in the components. He will not contend that sensibles can be formed from insensibles, but there are things—fire in flint—not "effectively sensible" which contain the principles of sense (pp. 344–47). In the *De l'Immortalité de l'Âme*, in *Oeuvres* (Paris, 1662), I, 492–515, La Mothe le Vayer repeats

unify the whole creation. Silhon's defence flows over the shoals of many old arguments, and, in all ways except length, his book is probably not so good as Sir Kenelm Digby's subsequent "Treatise Declaring the Nature and Operations of Man's Soul."

In his preface to this essay, Digby, who has just written about bodies as material body, proposes to examine immortality by first looking at mortality. If something has body and no parts and operations without "local translation," then we can assume it is a spiritual substance.[77] Apprehension conceives of "being" as inexpressible; what has being is "thing"; and when to this one adds a quality, color or size, one has expressed "something." All our additional knowledge is obtained by "comparisons" or "respects"; hence, we arrive at abstractions, such as "whiteness" or "heat," which are different indeed from concrete "white" or "hot." So apprehension reaches to all being, and what it cannot reach is said to be "nothing"; but even nothing can be conceptualized because man is capable of considering, unhindered by his stock of innate or acquired ideas, the impressions flowing from "things."

Given the notions in the mind and the impressions streaming into it, man can come, Digby assumes, to the active principle of a "settled judgment," or to an "opinion," which is a confession of inexact examination, or to faith, "which though it ever fail of evidence, yet sometimes is better than opinion." The evidence that results in faith "sticketh one degree on this side the thing itself," and seeing with "another's eye," we are convinced not so much by the "thing itself" as by the "goodness" of the other person. Faith, then, depends on the moral superiority of another.

---

little more than Scripture and old proofs: see also Cappel, pp. 125–76; Fevrier, pp. 70–84; and Cotin, *Traité de l'Âme*, pp. 141–48.

[77] *Two Treatises* (London, 1665), pp. 3v–4r. I shall summarize the treatise without annotation.

If the soul is both immaterial and separate, it is immortal. The fact that the soul apprehends immateriality demonstrates its own immateriality. Its process of reasoning by respect, its powers of abstraction and comprehension of universalized abstractions, says Digby most unoriginally, also prove it separate from natural bodies. The immaterial soul can balance together, as a material soul could not, contrarieties in nature such as fire and water, heavy and light. "We must allow that things are there immaterially; and, consequently, that what receiveth them is immaterial." [78] The same quality is seen in the soul's identification with "first truths," enabling her to "know that she is when she knows a thing." She also knows things without end or measure; and in her powers of motion and ordering, she is plainly of "a higher race," immaterial, void of quantity.

The soul's immateriality points, Digby supposes, to her separateness, because we notice in man both an exterior-visible and an interior-invisible motion; he is, consequently, composed "of somewhat else that is not a body." [79] This double motion also tells us we should still exist even though we lost our five senses. In addition, this separate spiritual body has no contraries to destroy it. It is more perfect than the material body, for which it supplies motion and is "the spring of life." The nature of time also enters Digby's proof. Perfection and happiness consist in "knowing all things," but completeness of knowledge is impossible in human time. The soul, which comprehends time, sets its limits, thinks of things beyond time, and "casts about for them," knows this deficiency only too well. Aware of the difference between the time of man and God, a man unconvinced of immortality has no choice but to yield to his desires and live as a beast. "The whole body of morality," says Digby, would thus be abandoned [80] if immortality were not a condition of the soul.

[78] P. 51.   [79] Pp. 79–80.   [80] P. 87.

An equally conventional, but far better-written, defence of immortality than Digby's was put together at almost the same time by John Dryden's friend, Walter Charleton. *The Immortality of the Human Soul Demonstrated by the Light of Nature* pretends to be a discussion between two Oxonians, Lucretius and Athanasius, after a dinner given by Isodicastes, a French virtuoso. Athanasius, who is the author thinly veiled, accepts the word of the Bible on immortality; but he likes to corroborate its revelation with "the concurrent testimony of my reason." [81] It is clear that the idea of immortality is the basis of religion and worship. If the soul perishes with the body, "what is the purpose of religion, of prayer, of self-denying acts, of unjust sufferings?" [82] He begins where Digby ends, and his defence of immortality is truly a defence of religion and morality.

The soul has no divisions. Those who have written treatises discussing the "animus" and the "anima," reasonable and sensitive souls, one superior, the other inferior, have completely confused the unwary. The soul is single and immortal. It could be annihilated by its creator, but this is unlikely because "what He hath once made incorporeal shall persevere to be the same to all eternity." Incorporeality is for Charleton's Lucretius, a Neo-Epicurean, incomprehensible; so Athanasius explains it by observing that men of good will

---

[81] Printed in 1657, this book bears comparison with Micraelius' *Ethnophronius* (note 53) where one learns that, although Peruvians, Mexicans, Chinese, Japanese, and Virginians believed in immortality, many famous philosophers did not (pp. 4–8). All of the conventional arguments are repeated (pp. 121–40), and there is a full parade of heretical opinions, including those of Menasseh ben Israel (pp. 77–101). Menasseh's *De Resurrectione Mortuorum* (Amsterdam, 1636) was widely read by Christians because it was the first anthology of rabbinical opinions on both sides of the question of immortality. He notices that one dreams of people who have been dead for years, but never of animals, even when they were beloved pets (p. 58). This proves, of course, that people have souls and visit with us in dreams.

[82] P. 59.

pursue the good and not the pleasant, can sort out the rational from the imaginative, construct universals, and practice psychology. This line of argument is so unoriginal that Charleton refurbishes it by adding new examples. The sufferer from jaundice, he writes, sees only a yellow world; hence, if the intellect were "wholly and entirely immersed in corporeity," it would perceive only materiality; but, on the contrary, the immaterial mind, aided by sense and imagination, informs even the body that it too is above dissolution.

After these novel views are sorted, the tired proof from common consent recurring, Athanasius admits men sometimes err en masse, but adds that common erroneous ideas quickly wither. This rule serves him in good stead when Lucretius suggests that all men desire to be young, because he can scotch this common, or perhaps innate, idea with "a vain desire!" The Oxonians finally get on the problems of theodicy; and when Lucretius complains that nice animals are battered by nasty ones, he is corrected with "animals have no claim to a concernment in justice divine." His complimentary allusion to Pomponazzi's self-rewarding justice is erased by Athanasius' "hence all virtuous persons have an eye of affection constantly leveled at somewhat beyond it." Digby's book is more scholastically logical than Charleton's; Charleton's is more literary than Digby's; neither work is as original or as tightly woven as Henry More's vast study of the soul which was printed in 1659 and provides us with a climax. Other Englishmen and numerous continentals [83] took up the chal-

---

[83] Thomas Wadsworth's Αντιψυχοθανασια: *or the Immortality of the Soul Explained and Proved by Scripture and Reason* (London, 1670) is written for "downright atheists," whose wicked lives make them abhor immortality; it relates an experiment in blood transfusion between a man and a goat (pp. 28–30). William Bates, in his *Considerations of the Existence of God and of the Immortality of the Soul*, rehearses all the usual arguments for immortality (pp. 148–207); and John Moore, bishop of Norwich, gets almost all of them into a sermon, *Of the Immortality of the Soul* (London, 1694). Richard Burthogge is more original in assuming that since only

lenge of the materialists during the last forty years of the seventeenth century, but none of them was the equal in wisdom or fear of the Platonist of Cambridge.

IV

More was not the first of the Cambridge group to ponder the soul's immortality. John Smith,[84] whose brain was nourished by the "Heavenly warmth" of his heart, cannot put by the common belief in immortality even when it was founded on "Error and Superstition"; on the other hand, he cannot accept the rationalists' definition of the soul as a material form, the definition proposed by "some hot-brained" Neo-Aristotelians. Heating his brain with heart's fire, he wonders whether the grass on which he treads could "by the help of Motion, spring up into so many Rational Souls and prove as wise as any Epicurean." But, no! The mind must actually withdraw from the material body when it would discern naked truth; moreover, the atoms of Epicurus could hardly distinguish the emergencies that exist in a train of causes which sometimes work contingently. Furthermore, if man's mind was only a compact of "fluid Atoms," he would "slide" from himself and forget what he was, because the new matter that supplied the place of the departed old atoms "would never know what the old were, nor what that should be that should succeed that." It is, of course, true that the mind does not know or control everything in the body. Pas-

God is immaterial, all other spirits must "admit of degrees of matter." *An Essay upon Reason and the Nature of Spirits* (London, 1694), pp. 162–73. Some unoriginal continental treatises are J. E. Swellingius, *Mens Immortalis Evidenter Certo contra Atheos Scepticosque Demonstrata* (Bremen, 1683); S. Ulrici, *De Animae Rationalis Immortalitate* (Wittemburg, 1696); and C. Weidling, *De Vita Aeterna ex Lumine Naturae Indemonstrabili* (Leipzig, 1685).

[84] *Select Discourses*, pp. 63–113

sions rise up, knock at its door, and disturb it in its musings; many of the bodily functions are performed without the control or perception of the mind. But the will and understanding are continually under the domination of the soul, which is, consequently, not only free from matter but knows itself immaterial.

The immateriality of the soul is established, for Smith, by its capacity for mathematical notion, its naked perception of sensation, its collation of sensations with "its own more obscure and dark ideas," its powers of discourse and reason (διανοια και λογος), and its intuition of archetypical ideas and first principles. There is also the common realization that we all know our souls better than we do our bodies. The only troublesome problem is the apparent dependency of the soul on the body, with which it seems constantly to comply "and to assume to itself the frailties and infirmities thereof, to laugh and languish as it were together with that, and so when the body is composed to rest, our soul seems to sleep together with it." Smith, who agrees with all other immortalists that religion depends on their hypotheses, reduces this central and baffling psychical inconvenience to a basic condition of humanity.[85]

Smith's charming personal essay seems somewhat philosophically naïve when one turns to Henry More's *The Immortality of the Soul, So Far as It Is Demonstrable from the Knowledge of Nature and the Light of Reason.* The question of the soul's nature engaged More for many years,[86] and his more youthful and uncomplicated speculations were revealed in 1642 with the publication of his Spenserian poem, ΨΥΧΩΔΙΑ *Platonica: or a Platonical Song of the Soul.* This poem is more than the lintel of the doorway to the later theo-

---

[85] P. 113.

[86] The first section was composed in 1640; see H. More's *Opera Omnia* (London, 1679), I, viii.

logical treatise; it must be seen as part of a poetical crusade against the dreadful third book of the *De Rerum Natura*, an armed excursion during which philosophical poets of Christendom attacked the Epicurean laureate with the metrical weapons of his own choice. Unlike other materialistic atheists who squandered their lives on prose that vanished, Lucretius lived in his poem, which, though often more philosophical than poetical, contained meadows of verse so enchanting that even Christians paused to admire them.

The classical scholars of the Renaissance who edited the *De Rerum Natura* always walked with care when they approached the morass of Book Three, in which the souls of men sank into mortality. Lambinus, one of the best sixteenth-century editors, wrote in 1563 to Charles IX that, even though Lucretius' hostility to Providence and immortality is dangerous to "our religion," the work is a great poem "ornamented, distinguished, and illuminated by the lights of genius." He thought that no Christian had been won for atheism by reading these verses, which were corrected "not only by truth but also by silence itself." Many of Lucretius' ideas, writes Lambinus, are philosophically excellent; and one should not reject a work of art because it does not coincide with Christian beliefs. To do so would require the rejection of Plato, Homer, Aristotle, and other pagan authors approved by many Fathers of the Church.[87] Subsequent editors followed the practice of Lambinus; and a century later, Tanaquil Faber sterilized his edition of the *De Rerum Natura* with an essay on Book Three cautioning the readers against the "saxa et scopuli" ahead, reminding them of their Christian heritage, and urging them to read Tertullian's *De Anima* as

---

[87] Lucretius, *De Rerum Natura*, ed. S. Havercamp (Leiden, 1725), I, C4–D4. There are several studies on the influence of Lucretius in the Renaissance: M. Lehnerdt, *Lucretius in der Renaissance* (s.l., s.d.) and E. Belowski, *Lukrez in der französischen literatur der Renaissance* (Berlin, 1934).

an antidote to the poison supplied by Lucretius.[88] But sweeter poetical remedies were by Faber's time in the pharmacy of the spirit; the earliest of these was compounded by Aonius Palearius, a victim of the Italian Reformation.

Palearius' *De Immortalitate Animorum*, three books of hexameters, was first printed in 1536, frequently reprinted (sometimes as an appendix to Lucretius), and eventually honored with a place in Alexander Pope's collection of notable Italian Latin poets. It accounts for God's existence, sings of immortality, and relates the ultimate bliss of the soul released from the body's bondage.[89] For Palearius, the soul, which is unchanged in child or old man, is different from the reason, which depends on sensation and alters with corporal alterations. Simple in essence but diffused throughout the flesh, the soul, unlike matter, has foresight and understands incorporeality. As God sees himself and is reflected in the orb of creation, the soul sees God's image in itself and rises on desire's wings to love its creator.

Its eternity, he repeats, is proved by its universalizing powers, its comprehension of contraries, infinities, and essential forms. It is shown further in its admiration of the great men of history, and in its regret that it will never know all its descendants. Because man has an innate sense of immortality, he raises monuments, diverts the courses of rivers, levels hills, and invents and cultivates the arts. For the same reason, he stands ready to die for his country or religious faith. Nature, Palearius says, has given man an instinct of immortality; this she would not have done were it untrue. While Nature has given gifts to men, she has also furnished them with evils unknown to other creatures. One of these evils is the transitoriness of all things. Change and decay, the

[88] Pp. 384–88 in the Cambridge edition of 1686.
[89] *Opera Omnia* (Lyons, 1552), pp. 51–68. In his preface (p. 12), Palearius directs his poem against atheists.

ineluctable end of the whole universe itself, were they absurd, would render man's instinct of his immortality absurd.

Although man dominates the creatures, his life, in other respects, is more miserable than that of his servants, the animals. He is born in agony, naked to the rigors of nature, strengthless, and dependent. Illnesses of body and mind assail him. To gain riches, he endures innumerable sufferings; his passions of love and hate tear him apart. None of these miseries is known to other creatures, who are contented with field fare, the water of fountains, and the shade of the wood. If man is no more than a mortal animal, life is a vicious jest. But Palearius does not permit his proofs of immortality to conclude on this tragic note. He sees in the spacious journeys of the human mind a mobility of soul suggesting immateriality. More than this, the soul, which can dart through the universe faster than any bird, can fly, thanks to its powers of prophecy, into the future. The ultimate proof of immortality is man's prophetic soul, and the poet illustrates this gift with an iambic account of David's foresight of the Messiah's coming and the fulfillment of this prediction in the life of Christ. A century later, an irate English poet tried his Pegasus on the same muddy track.

Sir John Davies' well-known *Nosce Teipsum*, a versification of popular arguments for immortality similar to those compiled by De Mornay and La Primaudaye,[90] is broader in scope but truly less poetic than the *De Immortalitate Animorum* of Palearius. A few years after its publication, the so-called atheist Theophile de Viau printed his expanded version in verse and prose of the *Phaedo* [91] as a rational rearguard action against the revelationists. Shortly afterward, Daniel Heinsius restated all the conventional immortalist

[90] *The Poems*, ed. Clare Howard (New York, 1941), pp. 113–93.
[91] *De l'Immortalité de l'Âme*, in *Oeuvres Complètes*, ed. M. Alleaume (Paris, 1855), I, 11–134.

arguments in the polished Alexandrines of Book Two of his *De Contemptu Mundi.* None of these literary efforts can compete in density of thought with More's *Psychodia Platonica*,[92] although it would be impossible for any of them to fall below him in poetic worth. Since More had thought about his subject for many years, he decided to "sing out lustily," grant his readers some "fair glimpse of Plato's hid Philosophy," and restore "deep Plotin." Plato, the Neoplatonists, and the *Theologia Platonica* of Ficino are his feathered muses, but Christian worry shapes all that he writes.

More's poem is not explicitly directed against atheism. The "putrid muse" of Lucretius is admittedly one of his competitors;[93] and the Roman son of Epicurus, Democritus, and Aristotle,[94] who regarded religion as simple silliness,[95] must be corrected by "Platonissa," nearest "allied to Christianity."[96] The ultimate beneficiary of More's rimes, as he explains in the preface of 1647, are not the sons of Apollo but the man of "melancholy temper," who needs "security" for his fading childhood beliefs. The literal story of the *Psychozoia*, the first part of the *Psychodia Platonica*, is childish enough. Psyche, daughter of Ahad, marries Aeon, and one of their children sets forth on a pilgrimage to his divine home. Those of melancholy disposition who had read the first book of the *Faerie Queene* could grasp the meaning of this story; but if the blessed soul of Spenser dictated the plot,

[92] (Cambridge, 1647), A. 1, 3–4. Although the *Psychozoia* has been learnedly edited by Geoffrey Bullough in *Philosophical Poems of Henry More* (Manchester, 1931), Grosart's 1878 edition is the only complete text. For ease of documentation, I shall record as follows: A. *Psychozoia* (three cantos); B. *Psychathanasia*, Bk. I (three cantos), Bk. II (three cantos), Bk. III (four cantos); C. *Antipsychopannychia* (three cantos); and D. *Antimonopsychia* (one canto). The *Democritus Platonissans* (infinity of worlds) is appended to B., and *The Praeexistency of the Soul* to C. There is an excellent discussion of these poems in P. R. Anderson, *Science in Defense of Liberal Religion* (New York, 1933), pp. 79–112.
[93] A. 1, 6.   [94] A. 1, 17.   [95] A. 1, 9.   [96] A. 1, 20.

stanza form, and archaic rimes, the pre-existent soul of Blake named the characters.

The *Psychozoia* describes the cosmos in which the soul lives. It is both a hierarchy of descent, the "stole of Psyche," and a series of concentric spheres, the "folds of Psyche's vest." The first cosmos has eight planes; "this number suits well with the Universe": [97] Ahad (first principle), Aeon (eternal being), Uranore (Psyche), Semele (imagination), Arachnee (sensation), Physis (*natura naturans*), Tasis (extension or *natura naturata*), and Hyle (matter, non-being). These planes have infinite extension and share in *nous*. The spheres of the second cosmos have absolute reality as their center. The outermost, visible surface is Tasis, since Hyle has no true being. The second layer is Physis, "the great womb" to which Psyche lends "a smaller fee/ Of gentle warmth." [98] When Semele and Arachnee are folded back, one finds "the inmost Center of Creation/ From whence all inward forms and life proceed." [99] Sensation and imagination removed, man can fulfill his obligation to know the true forms [100] because these superficial processes blind him to reality.

The outer layers of the concentricity are created by the inner forms. More calls these "Atom-balls" [101] or "Atom-lives" [102] and explains them as "dark little spots" or "knots" [103] pierced and warmed into life by aethereal darts. Aether for him is "the vehicle of touch, smell, sight/ Of taste, and hearing too, and of the plastic might." [104] The soul of the world possesses, as do the darts, a magnetic force by which forms are stimulated to penetrate and shape matter. Men whose attention is fixed on external forms are unaware of this hidden, eternal life-force at the center. "In Earth, in Air, in the vast flowing Plain,/ In that high Region hight Aethereal, in

[97] B. I, 3, 23.　　[98] A. 2, 13.　　[99] A. 2, 2.　　[100] A. 1, 12.
[101] A. 2, 10.　　[102] B. I, 3, 28.　　[103] A. 1, 43.　　[104] A. 1, 15.

every place these Atom-lives remain." [105] The inextinguish-
ability of these atom-lives is the basis of More's case for immortality, for the human soul is not unlike them; consequently, he does not really need to use conventional arguments to make his case.

Man's soul may share in all planes or layers of being, but
it has a greater variety of motions than do "plantal" and animal souls.[106] More finds that life begins when the "plantal"
soul awakens, but this soul lacks "animadversions" or self-
consciousness.[107] In this deficiency, it is like the world soul,
the "plastic sprite," [108] which stimulates growth but is inferior to the human soul because it "hath no perceptibility/
Of his impressions." [109] Animal souls have only "local motion," or perception and sensation,[110] which depend on the
"mundane spirit" bringing colors, figures, or "inherent light"
by a "circular diffusion" to the eyes and ears.[111] Because of
this intermediate force, man often errs, perceiving only by
"Deuteropathy." [112] The fact that reason corrects the false
perceptions of sense is for More a strong proof of immortality. To this end, he spends the third canto of Book Three
of the *Psychathanasia or The Immortality of the Soul* defending the new astronomy and demonstrating that whereas
"sense pleads for Ptolemy," reason shows Copernicus to be
right.[113]

The power of reason to grasp ideas beyond the sense is a
sign of the separateness and immortality of the soul, which
More regularly describes as a self-moving substance, "that is
the definition of souls." [114] It is the constant motion of the
soul in all its lives that assures its eternal consciousness.[115] In
the present life, the soul moves about external objects and

[105] B. I, 3, 28.   [106] B. I, 2, 12, 25–43.
[107] B. II, 1, 19; I, 2, 31; III, 1, 14–17.   [108] B. III, 3, 28.
[109] B. III, 2, 51–52.   [110] B. I, 2, 36.   [111] B. III, 1, 17–22.
[112] B. III, 1, 124.   [113] B. III, 2, 60.   [114] B. I, 2, 25.
[115] B. I, 2 and 3.

about itself; in the next life, it will be in continual movement as it extrapolates on its innate ideas.[116] For More, the soul is substance, but it is an active substance; its activity distinguishes it from passive matter.[117] This is all the argument that More really needs to establish the validity of the hypothesis of immortality; but for the sake of tradition, he recalls, in three cantos of Book Two of the *Psychathanasia*, the time-honored proofs which all men knew.

The massive poem was succeeded by the *Antidote against Atheism*, which presents the mind as an active, immaterial substance and explains how it should function in the realms of Nature and spirit. The innate ideas which make the foundation of this theory are not "a certain Number of Ideas flaring and shining to the Animadversive Faculty . . . but . . . an active sagacity in the soul or quick recollection . . . whereby some small business being hinted upon her, she runs out presently into a more clear and larger Conception." This mental power enables men to have "relative notions," such as equality and inequality, symmetry and asymmetry, as well as logical and mathematical ideas. These ideas make "no impresses" on the sense; hence, More is certain they come from within the soul. He is also convinced, as he was in the *Psychodia Platonica*, that these ideas of the soul are of a higher order; there are, for example, notions of circularity in the mind more perfect than the senses could supply.[118] This notion grows in the second book of the *Antidote*, which is consecrated to providential design. Phenomena can, if they are regular, be explained by Cartesian matter and motion, but this mechanistic theory will not manage all experience.[119] The last book, with its amazing collection of occult stories, once again demonstrates the ceaseless activity of spiritual substance and permits More to conclude

[116] C. 2, 18.   [117] B. I, 4, 9.   [118] *A Collection*, pp. 17–18.
[119] P. 38.

his case against atheism with his famous motto, "No Spirit, no God." This book concluded, he turned to his great project.

More decided to write *The Immortality of the Soul* in 1656, and in March, 1658,[120] he had four hundred quarto sheets ready, which were copied for the printer without revision.[121] The composition was rapid; the argument was hardly rethought critically; yet the whole work is more or less original; and More could honestly say it was "the genuine result of my own anxious and thoughtful Mind, no old stuff purloined or borrowed from other writers."[122] To write the book a "knowledge of Nature and the Light of Reason" joined forces, and the preface affirms the subtitle by stating that its author was "unassisted and unguided by any miraculous Revelation."[123] The force of this announcement is directed against the obstinate rationalists, whose reasoning is so unreasonable. Pomponazzi and Vanini are reproached almost at once for assuming that all things "not grossly material . . . are totally immaterial."[124] The ecstasies of Cardano are eventually mentioned as indications of the separability of the soul,[125] but his pathetically agnostic questions about man's uncertain fate are printed on the title page as one of the themes of More's inquiry.

"Perfect Scepticism" wins More's laughter or pity, but not his opposition, which would be a pointless task because skeptics refuse to acknowledge the verdict of their faculties or the clear proof afforded by reason.[126] Mechanists (whose philosophy is "but a pitiful subterfuge of fearful Souls" loath to admit a spiritual immateriality "for fear the next step must be the acknowledgment also of a God"[127]) are more malleable to the hammer of the Platonist, who was always ready to

---

[120] *The Conway Letters*, ed. M. Nicolson (New Haven, 1930), p. 146.
[121] R. Ward, *The Life of the Learned and Pious Dr. Henry More* (London, 1710), p. 153.
[122] P. Gg. 1.   [123] P. 2.   [124] P. 6.   [125] P. 128.   [126] P. 16.
[127] P. 12.

accept and philosophically employ their concepts after a careful correction. They are, consequently, never placed in the same booth of Vanity Fair with the three dubious Italians because they had helped, though inadvertently, in the creation of More's metaphysics.

The name of Hobbes appears for the first time in any of More's writings in *The Immortality of the Soul*. The *Leviathan*, which inclined so many men to include Hobbes in the sour society of non-saints, brought no protest from More, who actually respected Hobbes and with whom he had much in common. Both were Anglicans, anti-Romans, haters of religious enthusiasm, and monarchists. When More criticizes Hobbes' ideas in the first and second books of *The Immortality of the Soul*, he paused to call him "a grave philosopher" and to agree with Hobbes' self-estimate "that his peculiar eminency lies in Politics." [128] Later, Richard Ward wrote that Hobbes in his turn preferred, if his own system were untrue, "the philosophy of Mr. More of Cambridge."[129] More vigorously attacks Hobbes' theories of spirit, matter, free will, the location of the common sensorium, and second notions, describing his comments on the last concept as a "witty invention to befool his followers"; [130] but never once does he insinuate that the sage of Malmesbury is an atheist. Until this moment, More's adversaries were the Greek and Roman atomists and the religious enthusiasts of his own day; now he saw in Hobbes' materialistic philosophy a dangerous doctrine that might not be intentionally atheistic but could lead to disbelief.

The second book of *The Immortality of the Soul* concludes with stereotyped arguments based on the truth and justice of God; [131] but it is preceded by rather original, axiomatic demonstrations of the nature of spiritual substance. Since many men find the idea of spirit unintelligible, and

---

[128] P. 42.   [129] P. 80.   [130] P. 69.   [131] Pp. 139–44.

hence nonsense, More presents them with a tenable definition. *Spirit* is substance "penetrable and indiscerptible"; *body*
is substance "impenetrable and discerptible." Substance is
extension with either inherent or communicated motion.[132]
On this dogma he settles his case. The soul is, consequently,
created spiritual substance "indued with Sense and reason
and a power of organizing terrestrial Matter into humane
shape by vital union therewith." [133] But can the existence of
such a substance be rationally established? If it can, More
thinks he has just about made his case.

To clear the way, he disposes of a series of objections to
the whole idea of spirit expressed by Hobbes in the *Leviathan, Human Nature,* and the *Physics.* They are not par-
ticulary valid because they are not facts but philosophical
assumptions. Motion, visible everywhere, cannot come from
inert matter; its source must be incorporeal substance,[134] or
God, who "superadded" it when he created matter.[135] This
motion is not a mechanical "blind impetus," or the universe
would lack its "admirable wise contrivance." [136] "An Essence
absolutely perfect" and without body, the orderly phenomena of nature, and the history of apparitions [137] testify to the
reality of a spiritual substance everywhere present in this
world. More has still to show, however, that this substance
is found in man.

If Hobbes was right in his notion that the movement of
particles resulted in thought, thinking would be limited,
More writes, to particularized sense perceptions; and there
would be no possible "congeries of matter" producing "free
cogitations." If matter were endowed with sense and free
motion, it would withdraw itself "from the knocks of ham-
mers or the fury of fires." [138] A jack-in-the-box held down

[132] P. 23.   [133] Pp. 34–35.   [134] P. 44.   [135] P. 47.
[136] P. 48.   [137] Pp. 50–52.   [138] Pp. 59–60.

by its lid would be a living animal; the decaying tremor of a bell would be imagination; the stroke past, memory; "and if a stroke overtake it within the compass of this memory, what hinders but Discrimination or Judgment may follow."[139] Spiritual substance is, therefore, required for sensation, the organization of sense perceptions, memory, imagination, the apprehension of second notions,[140] and consciousness of freedom or ἀντεξούσιον.[141] The place where these activities are both co-ordinated and occur is the common sensorium, the throne of the soul. Helmont had located this center in the orifice of the stomach; Hobbes in the heart; Descartes in the conariun.[142] More rejects all these theories in turn and concludes "that the chief Seat of the Soul where she perceives all Objects, where she imagines, reasons, and invents, and from which she commands all the parts of the Body is those purer Animal Spirits in the fourth Ventricle of the Brain." [143]

The soul, "architect of the body," diffuses itself through its creation and, as the body "dilates," possesses it. Its primal faculties are plastic; but it moves upward through the levels of sense, imagination, will, and reason; hence, though the "root of the soul" is in the head, thanks to the passions, her effects are felt in the heart and stomach.[144] The power of the soul is not the same in each part of the body; and she uses instruments, the vital and animal spirits, not only to make the organs of sense pervious to the motion expressed by objects,[145] but also to convey the received motion to the common sensorium.[146] This psychology enables More to

---

[139] Pp. 65–66, 213.   [140] Pp. 82–83, 87.

[141] Pp. 69–70. He qualifies this (p. 77) by stating that men's actions are sometimes free and sometimes not, but the fact they are at any time free "is a Demonstration that there is a Faculty in us that is incompatible to mere matter."

[142] Pp. 77–88.   [143] P. 94.   [144] Pp. 102–3.   [145] P. 109.

[146] P. 106.

assume that the separate spiritual substance is connected with body and to insist that this is its necessary state while it is in the world, "thickset with matter or Body." [147]

"At one time the soul was not in union with matter." This is a pregnant statement, because More clings, in *The Immortality of the Soul*, to the concept that inspired his earlier poem on the pre-existence of souls, but he no longer accepts all his former Platonic premises. Pre-existence is, for him, the only reasonable theory because the indiscerptibility of spiritual substance makes the doctrine of traducianism illogical; and the adherents of continual creation unwittingly make God an assistant "in those abominable crimes of Whoredom, Adultery, Incest, nay Buggery itself, by supplying those foul coitions with new created Souls for the purpose." [148] All souls were made at the original moment of creation. If "it is good for men to be, they should be as soon as possible." Many nations and innumerable philosophers, Aristotle included, believed in pre-existence; but in addition to all this authority, More unhesitatingly adopts the heresy of Synesius and Origen to explain why souls become incarnate.

That their Souls did once subsist in some other state, where in several manners and degrees they forfeited the favor of their Creator. And so according to that just Nemesis that He has interwoven in the constitution of the Universe and of their own natures, they undergo several calamities and asperities of Fortune and sad drudgeries of Fate as a punishment inflicted or a disease contracted from the several Obliquities of their Apostasy. Which key is not only able to unlock that recondite mystery of some particular men's almost fatal averseness from all Religion and Virtue, their stupidity and dullness, and even invincible slowness to these things from their very childhood, and their incorrigible propension to all manner of Vice, but

[147] P. 122.   [148] P. 111.

also of that squalid forlornness and brutish Barbarity that whole Nations for many Ages have lain under, and many do still lie under at this very day.[149]

If one objects that no one recalls his antecarnal existence, More does not run to Plato for excuses but frankly agrees: there are no mnemonic objects or events in this world to start the train of celestial reminiscence!

The forfeited soul, according to More, descends to its terrestrial body by means of congruities. The soul contains three such congruities, of which the lowest is either "plastic" or "terrestrial" and is similar to the forces of growth and sense in plants and animals. This congruity is attracted by the analogous congruity in the "prepared matter either to be organized or already shaped into the perfect form of an animal." The attraction is similar to "pleasure perceived by the sense, or rather to the capacity of receiving it"; the body and soul are thus attracted or tied together "by an unresistible and unperceptible pleasure." If this explanation is beyond the homely reader, More offers an humble illustration.

Where the carcass is, there will the eagles be gathered. Not that she need use her perceptive faculty in her descent as hawks and kites, by their sight or smelling, fly directly to the lure or the prey; but she being within the atmosphere (as I may so call it) of generation, and so her Plastic powers being reached and touched by such an invisible reek (as birds of prey are that smell out their food at a distance), she may be fatally carried, all perceptions ceasing in her, to that matter that is so fit a receptacle for her to exercise her efformative power upon.[150]

[149] P. 112.
[150] Pp. 120–21. On p. 124, More turns to the materialist Vanini for the account of a drop of water changing into a frog; this is an example of

The congruities which enable the soul and the "carcass" to marry also provide the eventual bill of divorcement. The "terrestrial congruities" ceasing, their superiors, the aereal (like δαίμονς) and the aetherial (like θεοι), burgeon into act and find matter everywhere with which to unite.[151] In fact, if God "did but leave Nature to work of herself," the soul once separate from the body would not become a preliminary heavenly saint but "should act and inform the air they are in with like facility that other *Genii* do." [152] The ability of the soul to separate itself from the body is temporally illustrated for More by the trances of ecstatics or by the return to life of men who have been "perfectly dead." At true death, however, the soul collects herself together with a small residue of vital and animal spirits "that may haply serve her in the inchoation of her new vehicle." Since she could now depart, if necessary through the pores, her exit from the body terrestrial is simple; but More expects she passes from the heart into the lungs and so out through the mouth, or else she goes into the head, "out of which there are more doors open than I will stand to number." [153]

Having left her earthly body, the soul may now peruse the third book of *The Immortality of the Soul*, where her further experiences as a daemon or aereal creature are fully described. In these final pages, she will learn that further trials await her in her new state, but her dog or horse will lend her aid to survive them. Triumphant in this middle condition, the soul then assumes aetherial form and, in this shape, escapes the terrors of Doomsday. When an atheist or melan-

congruent attraction. Thanks to his pneumatology, More peoples his aereal world with creatures lesser than man. "And therefore to be short that the Souls of Brutes cease to be alive after they are separate from this Body can have no other reason than *Immorality* the Mother of *Ignorance* . . . to embolden us so confidently to adhere to so groundless a Conclusion" (p. 136).
    [151] P. 123.   [152] P. 139.   [153] P. 122.

choly Christian had digested More's mathematical analysis of the soul's nature and immortality, he undoubtedly regarded all previous rhetorical, philosophical, or biblical demonstrations as futile and hopelessly unconvincing.

Chapter Six

The Atheist Redeemed:
Blount, Oldham, Rochester

~~~~~~

I

THE CONFUTATION of atheism and the salvation of the atheist were the acknowledged purposes of all rational expositions of the existence of God and the immortality of the human soul. It is possible that some of these logical demonstrations were composed for more personal reasons; to show, for instance, the author's skill in destroying regiments of straw men, to salvage or harden his own wavering religious conviction, or to make a public statement of his piety and orthodoxy. There is little reason, however, to doubt the sincerity of most of these books. Christians had been told so much about the prevalence of atheism that they rushed to aid heaven in subduing it. Some authors say they have friendly atheists in mind and describe the sad state of the unbelievers who are made miserable by spiritual doubts, which the writers then proceed to correct. Others, gifted with dramatic powers, write dialogues in the manner of morality plays between Firmianus and Scepticus. These argumentative comedies all have happy endings; the spiritually weak questioner is reclaimed for Christian truth by the right reason of his faithful comrade. The supporter of orthodox belief takes a firm grip on the scruff of Agnosticus' intelligence and, after dragging him through the morass of natural theology, gets him finally on the dry, sunny bank of revelation. Unknown in Italy, and not too common in France, the natural approval of reason was in the England of Falkland, Chillingworth, and the Cambridge Platonists a requirement of substantial conversion. Not all Englishmen trusted in the convincing powers of natural theology. For Thomas Manningham, for instance, any improvement in philosophic argument was attended by an enfeeblement of divinity.

> They are our too eager disquisitions after the *Internal* Varieties of things that have led the Witty World into so large a Field of *Scepticism*. Men must be pressing and breaking into the *Recesses* of Nature, as that Conqueror heretofore into the *Sanctum Sanctorum*, then mistake the thing, return dissatisfied, cry all is *Pageantry*, and that we worship Clouds. I had rather consider the *Rainbow* as the *Reflection* of God's Mercy, than the Sun's Light; and when I call to mind, that *Thunder* throughout the Scriptures is styled his *Mighty* Voice, I'm satisfied at what I *Tremble*, and though this may debase my Philosophy, yet it heightens my *Divinity*.[1]

One of the better dramas of rational conversion, *A Conference betwixt a Modern Atheist and His Friend*, was published by J. Sault just as the seventeenth century ended. In it an atheist, Eugenes, agrees, as all atheists did, to discuss religion provided all proofs are made as evident as those of mathematics. Erastus, his orthodox friend, proposes that their basic theorem be, "I am a thinking being." From this not very original leaping block, they jump to the proof by perfection of God's existence, because it is evident "that which communicated to me what I am and what I have, cannot be inferior to me." To this tired idea the atheist objects: wise

[1] Pp. 97–98.

men sometimes beget sons who are foolish. Erastus cannot deny this fact, but reminds Eugenes that men always beget in their kind. The wise man, he observes, never begets an angel anymore than the horse sires an elephant. Neglecting to point out that foolish parents sometimes have wise children, the atheist inquires whether our first ancestors might not have been produced by spontaneous fermentation. "In your Chymical Experiments," he says, "many things of different nature will at length produce a Phaenomenon very different from the first Ingredients." Pious Erastus brands this as "equivocal generation," because all things produce their kind, and there is no "Mechanick Formation of a man according to the Gravation and settled Laws of the Motion of Matter."

Eugenes, the atheist, illogically suggests that in the jiggling of atoms "there might have been just such a lucky hit as the Formation of a Man." Against this frayed atomic doctrine, Erastus marshals his shock troops: the delicate nature of the body's internal organs, the basic laws of mathematical probability, and the Newtonian hypotheses. It then turns out that atheism can hold its ground only against Sir Isaac's assault. Is it not true, Eugenes asks, that heavy things sometimes get above lighter? Then he points to the bark and boughs of a tree as examples. Erastus admits this point: "Naturally, the tree is made by God." The overwhelmed atheist admits that few of his doubting breed really deny God's existence, "for the wise Constructure of the World, the Wonderful Contrivance of Humane Bodies, nay, even the most contemptible Insects, if examined by a Microscope, do exhibit to us the most legible Characters of a Deity." [2] The only obstacles to his conversion are his doubts about the soul's immortality.

In the last three dialogues, the nature of the human soul is examined. Once again it is proved not to be "thought,"

[2] Pp. 1–31.

but "the thinker," not a passive "modification of matter," but "continually thinking, or in other terms, existing." The soul, Erastus notices, is constantly "Compounding, Dividing, Concluding, Rejecting, Choosing, Doubting"; hence, they both agree that it must be "an immaterial thinking substance." As such a substance, it exists without matter by definition, and so it must not be compared to a wheel in a clock but rather to an artisan, "who leaving one Mechanic Employ can Busy himself in another." Eugenes, the infidel, is not so easily put down. Throughout the piece, he has felt a connection between his body and soul. When his soul was buoyant, he was in good health; when he was ill, his soul was melancholy. Erastus states that he has reversed matters. It is the soul that establishes the state of the body. He must learn to regard his soul as a highly talented musician forced to play on a very inferior instrument. Since the soul has been proved master of the flesh and a separate substance, Erastus can now lead his friend to comfort with a logical account of the misery or happiness of the soul in its final separation from the flesh.[3] The anonymous atheist was imaginatively converted in this manner, but accounts of actual conversions are not easy to find. Most of the foes of atheism held that no man ever died an atheist and, then, emphasized this observation with lists of men dead in atheism and accounts of the violent conclusions of atheist lives. Mauduit, for example,

[3] Pp. 34–53. A similar debate, *A Dispute betwixt an Atheist and a Christian: The Atheist Being a Flemming, the Christian an Englishman* was published anonymously at London in 1646. The atheist believes in general Providence and Immortality, but not in the Christian religion; he also states that the more southeasterly one goes, the more intelligent people become; hence, the religion of China is the best (pp. 6–8). He inquires why Abraham never mentioned Adam and whether or not Jews prior to Jacob are saved? (p. 12). The atheist mentions a list of fake messiahs and Josephus' silence about Christ (p. 40). The Christian, who identifies his opponent as one of the new-style atheists "who believe in God but not in Christ," answers his arguments and, finally, subdues him with a variant of Pascal's wager: if the possibility of hell is only one out of a million, it would be better to believe than be damned for one's opinion (pp. 50–51).

compares the deaths of an atheist and a Christian centenarian. The atheist leaves pleasure to begin pain; the Christian dies happily because he is through with pain.[4] The misery of the atheist's death is described by Jean Cousin: "Having lived as an animal, he dies as an animal." [5] The death throes of these men are approved by Martin Fotherby, who describes the dreadful atheist deaths of Pharaoh, Socrates, Epicurus, and Bion. All of them, with the exception of the tyrant of Syracuse, Dionysius, died horribly, and, as for "this last; *whose damnation* yet slept not; being, though respited, yet not removed." [6] The same sad story is told by Bonhome of some seventeenth-century atheists known to him but never introduced by name to us. One wrote a dialogue against religion, but soon "grew Frantick" and died insane. Two others argued with Bonhome about the existence of God; the first "fought a duel and died upon the place"; whereas the second "in as short time he died (fearfully mad) with the Plague." He knows many other atheists besides these, but they all either "died very strangely" or "suffered violent Deaths." [7] Snatched away in sin, none of these faceless atheists is given, as Eugenes is, a chance at Christian rehabilitation.

The foes of atheism seem to have had no better results with named atheists. Of course, these godless men often died violently on the block, at the stake, or with a rope round the neck. This final misery might be providential planning, but it is difficult at this distance to say. Vanini went out to a violent death saying, "Come let us die like a philosopher." But this was not to be the case. "He died," said one reporter, who may have read Cousin, "like an animal, bellowing like an ox when his tongue was cut out." Other atheists, less sensational than Vanini, died, contrary to Mauduit's belief,

[4] M. Mauduit, *Traité de Religion contre les Athées, les Déistes, et les Nouveaux Pyrrhoniens* (Paris, 1677), pp. 22–29.
[5] P. 14.   [6] P. 153.   [7] Derodon, pp. A7–A7v.

"safely in their nests." On his deathbed, Prince Maurice of Orange rejected the comforts of a religion in which he saw nothing of "mathematical certainty." [8] The *Mercure Français* relates the final blasphemies of the well-known atheist Ruggieri,[9] but there is no hint of misery or violence. Estienne, a man of orthodox beliefs, sets down the agnostic remarks of Marechal Strozzi, who died well enough.

> He often admitted that he would like to believe in God, as others did, but could not, and in spite of this desire, it was his delight to utter such blasphemies against God that those of Julian the Apostate seem in comparison to be nothing. . . . He was not ashamed to say that God was unjust when he condemned mankind for a piece of apple and that he had learned nothing in the New Testament except that Joseph, being so old, and she, being so young, was a fool not to be jealous of his wife.[10]

The English casebooks reporting God's judgments against sinners can be compared with anthologies of pious deaths like the *Abel Redivivus*, but, even then, the facts are embarrassing. True enough, atheist Marlowe died with a knife in the eye, and atheist Raleigh with an ax in the neck, but St. Thomas More died no better. The records of conversion are so sadly limited in number that the atheist hunters found in the happy-miserable end of John Wilmot, Earl of Rochester, the perfect example they wanted.

[8] G. Tallement des Réaux, *Les Historiettes,* ed. G. Mongrédien (Paris, 1932), I, 312.

[9] *Mercure Français* (1615), p. 45. He is reported to have summoned a priest only to say: "Fool that you are, get out! The only devils are our enemies, who torment us in this life, and there are no gods except the kings and princes who reward us."

[10] I, 179–206.

II

In December, 1678, Charles Blount,[11] a disciple of Lord
Herbert of Cherbury and Thomas Hobbes, wrote to "the
Right Honourable and most ingenious Strephon." His letter,
inspired by an earlier London conversation on political and
religious revolutions, was really an essay on the rise of Christianity which intended to show that the "general pretence of
Piety and Religion, was but like Grace before a Meal" and
that all human actions were based on "a Temporal Interest."
The Earl of Rochester, the recipient of this letter, is ad-
dressed under the pastoral name he used in poetical conversations with Alexis, Daphne, and Sylvia.[12] He is informed
by Blount that the whole Jewish messianic theory results
from the attempts of "anathematized" sects to justify tenets
they took over from Greek philosophy; hence, Jacob's prediction about the advent of a Redeemer was "insinuated
thereby."

Enumerating the various messianic impostors and their
ultimate political purposes, Blount, while maintaining a Christian detachment, attempts to destroy all his century believed
about the Old Testament prophecies of Christ's mission. At
the time of Christ's birth, he says, there "arose an universal
expectation of a Messiah to come, excepting among the
Herodians, who thought Herod the Messiah." Though he
was pressed to do so, Christ never claimed this title except
in his conversation with the woman of Samaria. At the time

[11] For Blount's place in English Deism, see G. V. Lechler, *Geschichte des
Englischen Deismus* (Stuttgart and Tübingen, 1841), pp. 114–27, which
draws to some degree on John Leland, *A View of the Principal Deistical
Writers That Have Appeared in England in the Last and Present Century* (London, 1757), I, 37–43.

[12] *Collected Works*, ed. John Hayward (London, 1926), pp. 3–7, 67,
140–41.

of "his Cavalcade upon an *Asinego*," he was urged to do so, but his immediate apprehension and death caused all of his frightened and disappointed followers to fly. "But after that he was risen again, and they assured thereof, they reassume their hopes of a temporal Messiah, and the last Interrogatory they propose unto him, is, *Lord wilt thou at this time restore the Kingdom to Israel?*" It is obvious to Blount that all early Christians were "millenaries" who invented the Second Coming of Christ as a "pretense . . . that stopped the Mouths of the unbelieving Jews, who before, upon his Death and suffering like other Men, began to doubt very much of the Power of his Messiaship . . . wherefore this *Millenary* Invention of his coming again to reign in Glory salved all." [13]

During the winter of the next year, Rochester discussed the basic tenets of religion with Gilbert Burnet; [14] and the poetic fruit of this discussion appears to be his "After Death Nothing," a translation of a chorus from Seneca's *Troades*, [15] which he sent to Blount on February 6, 1679/80. Blount praised the verses as a refutation of their content, "since what less than a divine and immortal Mind could have produced what you have written." The arrival of the poem, which stated that "Devouring Time swallows us whole,/ Impartial Death confounds Body and Soul," impelled Blount to furnish Rochester with a compilation of his own and others' ideas about the prospects of human immortality. The Bible is filled, he states, with conflicting statements on the idea; and, outside Christian doctrine, one has only a choice between the Arab notions of Averroes and Avicenna on human im-

[13] All of the letters to Rochester are contained in the final section of Charles Gildon's edition of the *Miscellaneous Works* (London, 1695); this one appears on pp. 158–68.

[14] *Some Account of the Life and Death of John Wilmot, Earl of Rochester* (Boston, 1812), pp. 21–22.

[15] *Works*, pp. 48–49. According to Patin (II, 478–79) these lines were frequently in the mouth of Naudé's atheist professor, Claude Belurget, at the College of Navarre.

mortality. He quotes Pomponazzi's paradox of the three religions and approves the Paduan's theory that immortality was invented by lawgivers to win men to virtue. As a former student at Padua, Rochester may have known all of this, but Blount also expresses his very sensible belief that one cannot believe in immortality unless one accepts literally the concepts of hell and heaven.[16] This rather pointed assertion may refer to an earlier conversation because Rochester later told Burnet that, though he accepted immortality, he could not subscribe to the doctrine of post-mortem rewards and punishments: "the one . . . too high for us to attain by our slight services, and the other . . . too extreme to be inflicted for sin." [17] This is one of the topics of the Senecan chorus that found English voice when Rochester describes hell and its keepers as the creatures of "senseless Stories, idle Tales, Dreams, Whimsies," which were "Devised by Rogues, dreaded by Fools."

The day after he sent his thanks to Rochester for the translation of Seneca, Blount sent him a series of axioms on the soul that had been written in Latin by his father, Sir Henry Blount. These ruminations are correctly described by Charles Blount as "an undigested heap of my Father's Thoughts concerning the Soul's acting, as it were in a state of matrimony with the Body." The marriage metaphor is not improperly used, because Sir Henry imagined the soul and body as in a tight, interdependent, and perpetual union. The soul is a fire, kindled and fed, but altered each moment, by spiritual aliments from the body's concoction; it is really refined substance, subject to all the vicissitudes of the body's cruder

[16] Pp. 117–27.

[17] Burnet, *Some Account*, p. 60. Rochester's belief in the immortality of the soul arose, as he told Burnet (pp. 35–38), from his experience in 1665 when Montague's premonition of death came true; and it was enforced when his mother-in-law's chaplain's dream of dying plus the unlucky coincidence of thirteen at the table ended with the death of the chaplain.

matter. Man makes a brief appearance as an effigy in God's hall, says the older Blount; "he is a momentary apparition in God's eternity." In his second letter to Rochester, Blount had advised him to read Pomponazzi and Cardano's *Theonoston;* now he writes a postscript to his father's thoughts in which he agrees that, at best, man can have only "twilight Conjectures" about the soul, the "Divinum Aliquid" of the ancient philosophers.[18] Further letters between the two young men are unknown; hence, we do not know whether or not the discussions continued into the spring of 1680 when Rochester was wrestling with his angel, Burnet. That industrious theologian says nothing (perhaps he was unaware) about his his competitor for Rochester's soul; and he, of course, being an experienced historian, always sees to it that he has the last word. But if the author of the *History of the Reformation* was qualified to tug in a heavenward direction, Blount, at this moment, had strength enough to pull to the contrary.

Blount began his public confession of doubt in 1678/79 with the *Anima Mundi: or an Historical Narration of the Opinions of the Ancients concerning Man's Soul after This Life: according to Unenlightened Nature.* Clandestinely printed in London (there were three editions in a year), the book's title page claimed origination at Amsterdam in the "anno mundi 00000." In the same year, Blount was responsible for a broadside, *The Last Sayings, or Dying Legacy of Mr. Thomas Hobbs,* a collection of antireligious remarks lifted from the context of the philosopher's writings. From this sheet, the average Londoner picked up the information that "God is almighty matter" or that "The best prophet is the best guesser." Shortly after this, in 1680, appeared Blount's *Great is Diana of the Ephesians: Or The Original of Idolatry.* It was followed by his best-known work, *The Two First*

[18] Pp. 154–56.

Books of Philostratus concerning the Life of Apollonius of Tyaenus, Written Originally in Greek, with Philological Notes on Each Chapter. This last work presented the public with a full-length portrait of the rival Christ, whose career and deeds of wonder enabled the annotator to make cynical footnote comments.[19] It is clear, then, that in the last year of Rochester's life, Blount was at his deistic busiest.

The *Anima Mundi* opens by advising the reader that this is not "an Atheistical, Heretical Pamphlet" because in it neither the existence of God nor his Providence is denied. Real atheists are the "ignorant Vulgar people" who liken themselves to God and "think that everyone they Hate, are God Almighty's Enemies." [20] The purpose of this book, Blount states, is to banish the superstitions invented by the self-interest of religious innovators who always claim divine revelation. Hippocrates pretended that medicine had been revealed to him; Numa, Zamolxis, Pythagoras all pretended that during sleep or death they had revelations. Mohammed retired to a cave in Arabia, where with the assistance of

[19] The anthology from Hobbes is reprinted in *Somers Tracts,* ed. W. Scott (London, 1812), VII, 368–70. The translation and commentary on Philostratus, published at London in 1680, is a fascinating compendium of learning, some of it ravished without acknowledgment from Herbert and others, some of it carefully attributed, and the remainder the result of Blount's own researches. Although it was known from Eusebius that Hierocles (confused in the seventeenth century with the commentator on Pythagoras and the author of the *De Providentia*) had compared Christ and Apollonius (a task attempted in the reverse by More in his *Grand Mystery of Godliness,* in *Theological Works* [London, 1708], pp. 71, 74–75, 83–89, 94), Blount points out in his preface that this was not the purpose of Philostratus, who nowhere mentions the name of Christ. His own project, as translator and commentator, is to provide descriptions of "remote countries," "ancient customs," and "Philosophical discourses of Morality." He knows word has been spread about this "dangerous book" and that common folk may be made to think him an atheist, but he has decided to let "the two Millstones of Knavery and Folly grind on to the end of the World." A sampling of his *obiter dicta* will suggest what the incipient dangers were: see, for example, pp. 4–6, 13, 18–21, 27–28, 34–39, 42, 69, 81, 95–96, and 243.

[20] P. A4. I use the so-called Amsterdam edition of 00000.

Sergius and two Jews, he wrote "that fabulous Law which he after divulged unto the World, as coming from the Angel *Gabriel*, with whom he pretended himself very familiar." [21]

Primitive heathens, Blount thinks, assume the soul is as mortal as the body, but some of the ancient philosophers thought up a hereafter filled with the immortal souls of the voluptuous and the ambitious. "In which way they adapted eternal terrours to evil doers, and everlasting glory to the virtuous. This they not improbably hoped would make their Sect to be admitted and cherished by Princes, as commodious to Government." So any notion of immortality was wrested "far from mere illuminate Nature" and changed into a kind of dream. Subsequent generations, "like Carriers-Horses in a track," followed without question the beliefs of their ancestors, which they improved "with such dotages of their own, as surpassed all Poetic Fictions."

Blount proposes, taking full advantage of patristic helpers, that man's soul is begotten as his body is. He bases his espousal of the *ex traduce* theory on its reasonableness. It is the only way to explain the transmission of the original taint of sin; it is supported by Genesis 46:26 and Exodus 1:5; it makes man better than an animal; it supports both the theory that like produces like and God's command to increase. If God creates each soul, theological difficulties follow, because God not only creates a soul to be punished for another's sin but also concurs in acts of fornication and adultery. Suppose a man copulates with an animal and begets a monster, Blount asks: would God furnish a soul? would the monster be immortal? Questions of this nature lead Blount to Montaigne's *Apologie*, and he quotes the French Pyrrhonist on the wisdom of animals (especially on his cat) [22] and on the benighted human belief in witches.[23] He looks for many pages at the doctrines of the World Soul and of metempsychosis and

[21] Pp. 2–6.   [22] Pp. 26–39.   [23] P. 44.

puts them aside.[24] Erasmus, he states, said that immortality was a matter of faith, not reason; but he, himself, is ready to admit that "there may be much more said for the Immortality of the Soul, than can be urged against it." But, it must be added, not too much.[25]

Most of the arguments for immortality stem, Blount assumes, from the belief in future rewards and punishments. He has not, however, noticed that this idea has had much effect on human conduct. Men leave vice only when they die; if they are virtuous, they often appear to lead miserable lives. Is there really such a thing as virtue? The Stoics held "that Poverty, Contempt, a Dungeon, Nakedness, Ulcers, and rotting in the Streets, are not really evils, especially to a noble mind that can defy Fortune." So much for the Stoics, Blount says, but are not remarks of this sort the reason why the French "call a learned Ass *Un Philosophe?*" Are not virtues in many cases also a matter of self-interest? Chastity gets high praise, but it may spring from lack of opportunity, physical inability, or the fear of pregnancy and scandal. He remembers, too, that in "our late Civil Wars" and in the risings of the German Anabaptists, what was called "the Work of the Lord" was what the sectarians, themselves, wanted. They all "turn the other cheek" when they are minority groups; but when they grow strong, they begin to use "another of Christ's sayings, Blessed are the meek (meaning themselves)," and fall "to doing the work of the Lord diligently." It is manifest, says Blount, that when the virtuous lose out, it is a result either of inferior wisdom or of lack of effort.[26]

From Vanini, Blount borrowed the anti-Christian method of making pious sport of pagan myths and religious notions, especially those paralleled by Bible story. He uses this solemn practice to some degree in the *Anima Mundi* and more com-

[24] Pp. 51–75.   [25] P. 76.   [26] Pp. 103–7.

pletely in *Great is Diana*. In the second book, an examination
of "soft-hearted" superstitions, Blount reminds the reader
that all religions, "excepting ours," are tainted "with the
Interest of the Clergy" and should, consequently, be examined with care.[27] He also repeats the Machiavellian theory
of the princely invention of religious creeds, "afterwards
Educated by Ecclesiastics." [28] To animate this stale hypothesis, he relates the silly myths told by the pagan priesthood
to keep the superstitious in awe. Some of them are slightly
modern. Jupiter, he recalls, had no other way "to reduce the
Trojans to himself, but was forced to suffer his own Son
Sarpedon to be knocked on the Head by them." Common
sense, he thinks, should have informed pagans, as it does us,
that the claim of the mother of Remus and Romulus to have
lain with Mars "was only a sham upon the credulous multitude" by which she hoped "to save both her Credit and her
Life." The children of ancient superstition accepted false
miracles, believed that Apollonius raised "a Maid from the
Dead," that the sun was darkened at Caesar's death, and that
Vespasian healed the lame and blind.[29] Blount would write
later on miracles as natural events and compose a *Religio
Laici*, copied from Herbert of Cherbury and directed at
Dryden; [30] but he had written, or was writing, the *Anima*

[27] Pp. F3–4.   [28] P. 7.   [29] Pp. 24–26.

[30] In 1693, the year of his death, there appeared a series of Blount's essays
and letters under the title, *The Oracles of Reason. In Several Letters to
Mr. Hobbs and Other Persons of Eminent Quality and Learning*. This
volume shook more hornets' nests than any of Blount's previous publications. In 1696 came William Nicholls' *A Conference with a Theist*; it was
followed by Josiah King, *Mr. Blount's Oracles of Reason Examined and
Answered* (London, 1698) and James Lowde, *Moral Essays. Together
with an Answer to Some Chapters in the Oracles of Reason concerning
Deism* (London, 1699). Nicholls, a pupil of Thomas Gale and a great
opponent of Socinianism, expanded his book to two volumes in the edition of 1723. Actually, the first complaint against Blount appeared in
1695 at Edinburgh in an appendix to *The Charge of Socinianism against
Dr. Tillotson Considered*.

Mundi and *Great is Diana* when he was contending with
Burnet for the soul of Rochester.[31] Though he may have won
a few games, the deist lost the set. Later, he would have
momentary luck with the lapsed Roman, Charles Gildon; [32]
but, even then, he could not keep this poor hack in his
church; and Leslie, the hammerer of deism, finally gained possession of the scribbler's soul.

These were the ideas advanced by Rochester's dark angel,
Charles Blount, in an attempt to convert his lordship to a
philosopher's religion which "borrowed the best of all others." The orthodox saw in Rochester the perfect example
of the practical atheist, Satan's talented altar boy, but Blount
knew better. There was Rochester the London roisterer,
and there was the Rochester who retired to the country and
turned over books in search of a satisfying religious philosophy. The Earl of Mulgrave informs us that Charles II was a
deist because it was too much trouble to seek out the best
religion; "for his quickness of apprehension at first view
could discern through the several cheats of pious pretenses,
and his natural laziness confirmed him in an equal mistrust
of them all." [33] This is not the case with Rochester. No man
ever tried harder to believe something.

III

Rochester's religious speculations begin, perhaps, with his
amused contempt for man and all the fictions man had in-

---

[31] For biographical fact, I have constantly consulted J. Prinz, *John Wilmot, Earl of Rochester, His Life and Writings* (Leipzig, 1927); V. de
Sola Pinto, *Rochester, Portrait of a Restoration Rake* (London, 1935);
K. B. Murdock, *The Sun at Noon* (New York, 1939); and Charles Williams, *Rochester* (London, 1935).

[32] *Miscellaneous Works* was edited by Gildon, who wrote the prefatory
biography of Blount.

[33] *The Works* (London, 1740), II, 55.

vented to keep himself safe and warm in his world. "A Satyr against Mankind," Rochester's sour hymn to self-important man, written in 1675/76 and printed in 1679, was preceded (if one may play games with a canon that cannot be untangled) by symptoms of poetical amusement with man's religious innovations. In Lucretius, Rochester found some lines, as he did in Seneca, that suited his personal convictions and were, consequently, worth translation.

> The *Gods* by right of Nature, must possess
> An everlasting Age of perfect Peace:
> Far off removed from us and our Affairs;
> Neither approached by *Dangers*, or by *Cares;*
> Rich in themselves, to whom we cannot add:
> Not pleased by *Good* Deeds; nor provoked by *Bad.*[34]

Led by this text, Rochester sometimes writes innocently-cynically about a Providence "that never made a thing in vain,/ But does each Insect, to some end ordain." [35] At other times, when he is lecturing on the paucity of wit in England, he leaves no doubt about his intent.

> The *World* appears like a great Family,
> Whose *Lord* oppressed with *Pride* and *Poverty*,
> (That to a few great Bounty he may show)
> Is fain to starve the numerous Train below.
> Just so seems *Providence*, as poor, and vain,
> Keeping more Creatures than it can maintain:
> Here 'tis profuse, and there it meanly saves,
> And for One *Prince*, it makes Ten thousand *Slaves.*[36]

Attitudes of this nature undoubtedly forced the village yokel, whom the Earl describes as tortured by London girls, to rail in another poem at the town's "Wits and Atheists"; [37] they are reflected again in his account of the dubious circum-

---

[34] "Satyr," p. 45.   [35] P. 32.   [36] P. 34.   [37] P. 32.

stance under which "*Physicians*, shall believe in *Jesus*." [38] So
if Providence did not provide Rochester with the hymns
of orthodox praise that it gave some of his contemporaries,
the loss of rimes did not trouble his conscience. In fact, one
of the few good things he may have said about his monarch is
that Charles gave "liberty to Conscience tender," because
he was himself a lukewarm "Faith's Defender," who could
tolerate all sects and "please us,/ With *Moses, Mahomet,* or
Jesus." [39]

In many of his poems Rochester's true creed is always before us.[40] We should follow the doctrine of pleasure until,
physically disqualified for proper erotic worship, we can let
virtue come.[41] Love is the best religion, and as one convert,
Artemisa, writes another, Cloe, it is:

> That Cordial drop, Heaven in our Cup has thrown,
> To make the nauseous Draught of Life go down:
> On which one only Blessing God might raise,
> In Lands of Atheists, Subsidies of Praise;
> For none did e're so dull, and stupid prove,
> But felt a God, and blest his Power in Love.[42]

This medal of pleasure, with its embossed animal faces, could
be turned in the hand not to see, as one might expect, the
skull crowned with libidinous ivy but the intellectual face of
the thinking man.

[38] *Poems on Several Occasions,* ed. James Thorpe (Princeton, 1960),
p. 18.
[39] *Collected Works,* p. 87. This poem is probably not by Rochester; it
does not appear in the 1680 edition, and David Vieth does not accept it
in his *Attributions in Restoration Poetry* (New Haven, 1963).
[40] Pp. 41–42.
[41] Rochester, of course, was quite capable of blasphemous inventions and
puns, a practice common enough in Donne and Dryden. In "The Fall"
(pp. 17), he compares impotence, a disease of postlapsarian times, with the
Marvellian age: "How blest was the Created *State*/ Of Man and Woman,
e're they fell,/ Compar'd to our unhappy Fate;/ We need not fear another
Hell."
[42] Pp. 27–28.

During the spring of 1675/76, a poem of more than three hundred lines, "Faith and Reason," was handed about London in manuscript and thought to be Rochester's. Actually, it was copied from Davenant's *Works* (1673), where it is found among his "Occasional Poems." Its attribution to Rochester is difficult to understand. It presents the position of an honest doubter, who wants the gift of faith, is unsure of knowledge, despairing of reason, yet would live according to Heaven's will.[43] John Verney, son of Rochester's former guardian, Sir Ralph, thought it similar to "A Satyr against Mankind." This is not really the case. There are stanzas in the poem with which Rochester might agree, but he could not have written the whole poem. The voice and the hands are those of Davenant. Pinto thinks that the "Satyr" was written about this time,[44] and connects the monkey mentioned in its fifth line with the pet crowned by Rochester with laurel in the Huysman portrait. Actually, this monkey has a larger role in "A Letter from Artemisa," and reappears in a letter of June, 1678, in which the Earl, contemplating the nonsense of human affairs, writes to Savile that "it is a Fault to laugh at the monkey we have here, when I compare his Condition with Mankind."[45]

The "Satyr" begins with the poet's hope that granted his choice at next incarnation, he will be "a Dog, a Monkey or a Bear," any animal except "rational" man, who prefers Reason "before certain Instinct."

> Reason, an Ignis fatuus of the Mind,
> Which leaves the Light of Nature, Sense behind.
> Pathless and dangerous wandering ways, it takes,

[43] The poem appeared in Davenant's *Works* (London, 1673), I, 326–33. Pinto sees it as an English counterpart of the famous *Quatrains du Déiste*, which was answered at too great length by Mersenne.
[44] P. 174.
[45] *The Rochester-Savile Letters, 1671–1680*, ed. J. H. Wilson (Columbus, Ohio, 1941), p. 60.

Through Errour's fenny Bogs, and thorny Brakes:
Whilst the misguided Follower climbs with pain,
Mountains of Whimsies, heaped in his own Brain,
Stumbling from thought to thought, falls headlong down
Into Doubt's boundless Sea, where like to drown,
Books bear him up a while, and make him try
To swim with Bladders of Philosophy,
In hopes still to o'ertake the skipping Light:
The Vapour dances, in his dazzled sight,
Till spent, it leaves him to eternal night.
Then old Age, and Experience, hand in hand,
Lead him to Death, and make him understand,
After a search so painful, and so long,
That all his Life he has been in the wrong.
Huddled in Dirt, (the) reasoning Engine lies,
Who was so proud, so witty, and so wise:
Pride drew him in, as Cheats their Bubbles catch,
And made him venture to be made a wretch:
His Wisdom did his Happiness destroy,
Aiming to know the World he should enjoy.

The Earl's philosophy of life is epitomized in this score of lines. Man is given life to enjoy, and he wastes it and comes to naught trying to find what it is. But at this moment "formal Band and Beard," the British version of Boileau's Claude Morel, "Docteur de Sorbonne," enters to take the "Wit" to task.

The "mighty Man," who provides Rochester with his second poetic wind, will have neither man nor reason mocked. Man has been given "an everlasting Soul" and the powers of reason "to dignify his Nature above Beast." Reason, says this graduate of what Rochester calls "a reverend Bedlam," enables man to transcend his senses, "dive into Mysteries," and search heaven and hell to give "the World true grounds of hope and fear." But the poet, who has read dull divines like Simon Patrick and Richard Sibbes, knows this already; in fact, one cause of his scorn for reason is that it permits these little men to think they are reflections of God's image and to compare their short, restless lives "to the eternal and the ever Blest." Reason excogitates theologies, and then discovers them; but it is also the father and mother of doubt. Through its ministrations, men fail in life by mistaking the purpose of living. *Sense* is the word with which to conjure; "by Sense" man learns to curb his desires so that they are always vigorous and never satiated. This is what Rochester, contrary to all theology, calls "right Reason." The other kind of reason, recommended by the "mighty Man," suppresses and destroys all desire.

> My Reason is my Friend, yours is a Cheat:
> Hunger calls out, my Reason bids me eat;
> Perversely yours, your Appetite does mock;
> This asks for food, that answers what's o'Clock? [46]

Boileau, whose eighth satire inspired but had little more to do with Rochester's poem, confronts men with animals and finds a comparison favors the beasts. His ultimate thrust at "ce roi des animaux" is to let his donkey visit Paris and watch the children of reason pursue their daily round. The ass, says Boileau, then spoke from a good heart, without envy, munching a thistle, and shaking its head: "My word, man is no more than we; he, too, is an animal." [47] Rochester is not so good humored. He observes that animals, wiser than men, attain their ends more certainly. Unlike men, too, they kill only for love or hunger; whereas, man, beset by fear,

[46] Pp. 35–39.
[47] *Oeuvres Complètes*, ed. A. C. Gidel (Paris, 1872), II, 9–32. In "The Originality of Rochester's *Satyr against Mankind*," *PMLA*, LVIII (1943), 393–401, J. F. Moore demonstrates that Rochester owed his inspiration, rather than his words, to Boileau.

will betray a friend out of sheer wantonness. Fear, says the Earl, is the mainspring of all man does, the source of his virtues. From it come honor, fame, the quest for power—all means of obtaining security. Cowardice has made cowards of us all, but it has also made us men. Such were the thoughts on man expressed in 1679 by the bitter young nobleman.

Some weeks after this broadside struck the city, it was answered in rime by either the Reverend Mr. Griffith or by Dr. P——ck (Pococke). The reply to "Earl Bear" defends reason and miserable man against appetite and sensation and the pleasures of happy animals. "An Answer to the Earl of Rochester's Satyr against Man" has a certain pulpit humor, for its author points out that a rational man can be more adroit and various in sinning than a mere man of sensations. He, however, would rather be a "reasoning *Engineer*" and "post Gazettes of Divine Intelligence" than be the dull pupil of "Spirit *alias* Appetite." Animals, he admits, go more efficiently to their goals than men; but the animal's road is shorter, and his goal is not hard to reach. There is no question that man has become corrupted, but corruption came from irrational actions. Provided that man does not "barter Reason with a Beast,/ But purge the Guilt with which he is oppressed," he may overcome the penalties of Adam's Fall.[48]

It is not impossible that Rochester answered this "Answer" in his curious "Epilogue to the Satire on Man," which does not appear in the 1679 folio leaflet but in the edition of 1680 and most subsequent texts. In this poem he describes a pride-puffed parson, who reproves sin from his pulpit, and yet all the while vents lies, "railings, scandals, calumnies." Clergymen of this type hunt preferments (a favorite Rochester complaint) as avidly as they seek the chastity of

[48] *Poems on Affairs of State* (London, 1703), II, 432–37; Vieth has an excellent section on these responses (pp. 178–80).

the parish wives; thus, at the end of twenty years of spiritual service, they can see "Half a large parish their own progeny." If anyone can find a preacher who is meek, modest, pious, the poet will recant his paradox; but "if such there are, yet grant me this at least,/ Man differs more from man, than man from beast." [49]

IV

When Rochester had been dead six years, his memory was once again made poetically green by the appearance in print of a translation from the Greek, "Bion, a Pastoral in Imitation of the Greek of Moschus, Bewailing the Death of the Earl of Rochester." The well-known classical lament is not only translated into English but transported to Britain, where it is watered with English rivers and planted with English flowers. Bion is granted a succession of English ancestors, too: Chaucer, "who first taught the use of verse"; Spenser, "the Muses' glory"; Milton, "Blest Cowley," "soft Orinda"; and Waller, "sweetest of living Bards." The translation (a prose preface speculates on whether it was begun by Rochester or not) [50] then concludes with the customary testimony of the celebrating poet.

> And I, the meanest of the British Swains,
> Amongst the rest offer these humble strains:
> If I am reckoned not unblest in Song,
> 'Tis what I owe to thy all-teaching tongue:

[49] Pp. 40–41.
[50] Oldham's *Poems and Translations* (London, 1683), p. A, states that the first fifteen lines were said to be by Rochester; "but I could not well believe it, both because he seldom meddled with such Subjects, and more especially by reason of an uncorrect line or two to be found amongst them, at their first coming to my hands, which never used to flow from his excellent Pen."

> Some of thy Art, some of thy tuneful breath
> Thou didst by will to worthless me bequeath
> Other thy Flocks, thy Lands, thy Riches have
> To me thou didst thy Pipe and Skill vouchsafe.[51]

The literary heir of the dead Strephon was known in the poetic pastures as Menalcas, Adonis, and Astrophel;[52] but John Oldham is more properly remembered as Dryden's "Marcellus of Our Tongue," the promising young satirist whose life was briefer than that of Rochester.

This translation is Oldham's acknowledgment of his debt to the Earl, a debt probably tacitly admitted in October, 1682, when he changed, perhaps influenced by Rochester's example, the French *ecus* of Boileau's "Satire against Mankind" into English shillings and pence.[53] The friendship of the two poets began in the late sixteen-seventies. Oldham was at Oxford until 1674, and his undergraduate reputation for irreverent wit is perhaps suggested in Thomas Wood's poem on his death;[54] but in 1675 he went as an usher to Whitgift's school at Croydon, where he "beat Greek and Latin" and wrote poetry that passed in manuscripts from hand to hand. Some of these poems came to Rochester's attention and caused him to visit Oldham at his school.[55] One cannot know exactly which of Oldham's poems pleased the Earl. Those to Cosmelia, particularly the lascivious "The Dream," would, in spite of their obligations to Donne and Cowley, have interested him. He would also have found the so-called "Ode against Virtue" ("Now Curses on you all!

[51] Pp. 73–87.

[52] He is called by these names in the prefatory poems to Oldham's *The Remains* (London, 1684), pp. A3–B5.

[53] Oldham's translation, "The Eighth Satyr of Monsieur Boileau imitated," is dated October, 1682. He usually renders the original as closely as rime permits, but he often makes a scene or allusion more familiar.

[54] Oldham, *The Remains*, pp. B1v–B2v.

[55] Edward Thompson, *The Compositions in Prose and Verse . . .* , ed. E. Thompson (London, 1770), I, ii–iii.

ye virtuous Fools!") consonant with his own doctrine of sensation.

The "Ode," omitted from all editions of Oldham since those of the eighteenth century, is not worthy of the importance that its suppression implies. It opens with an imprecation against moral Aristotle and all founders of law and religion, who have deprived man of his "primitive liberty" and made him in pleasure inferior to the "more happy Brutes." Virtue is commanded to join Astrea in "Airy Mansions," where she may "converse with Saints and holy Folks," "Christian fools," who bled "to be thought Saints, and dye a Calendar with red." The poet plans to adore virtue when he is in his dotage; but until then, he proposes to exile conscience, the "Great Wheadle" used by "gowned Impostors" to frighten the rabble. The vicious are praised, beginning with Jove, who turned heaven into a Seraglio crowded with bastards, and founded the order of Satanic Grandees, the Royal Society of Vice, in which Oldham, a new Columbus, must "new Worlds in Vice descry/ And fix the pillars of unpassable iniquity." Father Adam is proclaimed unimaginative, unworthy to sire "noble Cain" and "me/ And all the braver part of his Posterity." Adam's crime is that he was a niggardly sinner; the poet in his place would have "acted somewhat, which might merit more than Hell." [56]

When he wrote this poem, which was widely transcribed by connoisseurs and pirated by printers, the parson's son reckoned without the tenderness of his own conscience. Eventually, he printed the "Ode" with a verse "Apology," and later there were further amends in the form of "A Counterpart to the Satyr against Virtue." Oldham's change of heart is obvious in his adapted translation of Juvenal's thirteenth satire, where there is a sarcastic reference to "great

[56] *Satyrs upon the Jesuits* (London, 1685), pp. 93–115. This reference includes the "Apology."

Hobbes," [57] who had undeceived the world about God and
hell. In addition, the notions of both deists and lax Christians
are held up to poetic scorn. When the cheated friend, whose
misfortune is the occasion of the poem, complains that
priests are liars if he does not get prompt heaven-sent justice and protests that if his experience is a sample of providential care, "Bless'd Saint Vaninus I shall follow thee,"
Oldham reminds him that God is not mocked and promises
that his deceiver will either be transported or "hung up
like Boroski for a Gibbet-Sign." The converted and spiritually changed Oldham, who translated an Ambrosian hymn,
paraphrased Psalm 137, and wrote pious verse for Madam
L. E. and Mrs. Kingscourt, comes frighteningly to the fore
in "A Sunday-Thought in Sickness," a prose meditation followed by a poetic laud.

Job and Faust stand together in the horror of a seventeenth-
century British sickbed in this strange work. Smitten with
the terrors of death, which arise, he knows, from his inward
conviction of a life after death with rewards and penalties,
the poet regards his short life with shuddering dismay. Devils
stand by to tear him to shreds, and he can only hope that
God will reduce him to naught. He regrets he was not
created a plant or animal, that he did not die in the womb
or as he stepped from it. The various recollections of a wasted
and debauched life, during which God was forgotten, appear to his fearful eyes. Then, as in other dramas of salvation, just as he reaches despair, he remembers God's mercy.
An angel descends, bearing the book of his account with

---

[57] Oldham, *Poems and Translations*, pp. 29–39. For this end of the century, Hobbes and Spinoza are the great devils, taking the pews occupied
earlier by Pomponazzi, Vanini, Charron, and Bodin. Most young English
wits were assumed to be damned in Hobbes; in fact, Seward reports
Rochester saying during his last illness, "Mr. Hobbes and the philosophers
have been my ruin." He then put his hand on a Bible and, "with great
rapture," said, "This, this is the true philosophy." *Biographiana* (London,
1799), II, 509.

his sins blotted; a voice whispers his pardon. The prose ends, and the wit writes humorless poetry.

> Hail sacred envoy of the Eternal King!
> Welcome as the blessed tidings thou dost bring
> Welcome as heaven from whence thou cam'st but now;
> Thus low to thy great God and mine I bow,
> And might I here, O might I ever grow,
> Fixed and unmoved, an endless monument
> Of gratitude to my Creator sent.[58]

We know nothing about Oldham's last year except that it was spent at Holmes-Pierpont in Nottinghamshire, where the poet lived by the kindness of the Earl of Kingston and where he died of smallpox on December 9, 1683. Thompson blames Rochester for Oldham's fall from Grace;[59] but Anthony Wood states more reasonably that the Earl sought Oldham out because of his delight in "the mad, ranting, and debauched specimens of poetry of this author." [60] There is no evidence, but it is not unlikely that Oldham read Burnet's account of the last ten months of Rochester's life.

V

The Earl of Rochester, richly apparelled for heaven, died on July 6, 1680. Before the year had ended, Gilbert Burnet had given to the press and seen printed *Some Passages of the Life and Death of the Right Honourable John, Earl of Rochester*. This book passed through many printings, and sometimes it was even given a sensational title.[61] It was translated

---

[58] Oldham, *The Remains*, pp. 59–68.
[59] Thompson, *The Compositions*, I, xiii.
[60] *Athenae Oxonienses*, ed. P. Bliss (London, 1813–20), IV, 120.
[61] In the same year, it appeared as *A Mirror for Atheists* and in 1690 as *The Libertine Overthrown*.

into German at Halle and into Latin at Utrecht. In 1715 there was a French version; and a year later, the whole tale was recapitulated when Philipps concluded his exhaustive history of atheism with an account of the last days of the Earl.[62] Until this moment, the last minute conversions of atheists had mainly been anonymous fictions; now the believing world had a case which made all printed dialogues between Christians and atheists seem the pallid inventions they were.

Gilbert Burnet, the author of Rochester's conversion, was born in Edinburgh in 1643 and educated at Aberdeen. A visit to England in 1663 enabled him to meet and admire Cudworth, Pearson, Thomas Burnet, Henry More, Fell, Pococke, Wallis, Boyle, Tillotson, Stillingfleet, Patrick, Whichcote, Wilkins, and Robert Murray. In the year following, he was perfecting his Hebrew at Amsterdam with the help of a learned rabbi and associating in that tolerant city with Arminians, Lutherans, Unitarians, Brownists, Anabaptists, and Roman Catholics. "Among each of whom he used frequently to declare he had met with men of such real piety and virtue, that there he became fixed in that strong Principle of universal charity, and of thinking well of those that differed from him." In this broad view, he was encouraged, of course, by the tenets of the liberal Christianity he had learned

---

[62] See T. E. S. Clarke and H. C. Foxcroft, *A Life of Gilbert Burnet* (Cambridge, 1907) for a bibliography (pp. 526–27), but they missed *Rostae Comitis in Extremis* Μετανοια *seu Poenitentia Salutaris*, trans. G. Gaesbecius (Utrecht, 1698). Thereafter, Rochester's conversion is described in the larger histories of atheism, and he joins the calendar of Protestant saints; he receives in 1722 the accolade of Pierre de Laroque, a compiler of two earlier anthologies of pious deathbeds, who placed the mortuary couch of the Earl in his *La Science de Bien Mourir* between that of Madame du Plessis Mornay and Mademoiselle de Ciré. In spite of this beatification, his unregenerate days were often remembered. Richard Burridge wrote the unbelievably pompous and vulgar *Religio Libertini: or the Faith of a Converted Atheist* (London, 1712), in which he relates his seduction by Lucretius and Lucian, his eventual salvation, and proudly recalls that he was known as "young Rochester."

from the Cambridge Platonists, especially from Smith's *Discourses*, which he had read in Scotland, and by his association in London with the new men of latitude, Patrick and Tillotson.

Returning to Edinburgh, Burnet was appointed minister of Saltoun, then professor of divinity at Glasgow, where he set a course of theological study for his students "that seemed to require the labour of four or five, instead of one man." A partisan of the Duke of Hamilton, who was his patron and for whom he wrote his *Memoirs of the Dukes of Hamilton*, he quarreled with the Duke of Lauderdale, resigned his professorship, and went to London in 1675 as chaplain to the Rolls and lecturer at St. Clement.[63]

Thanks to "the abundance of his fancy" and his "good-nature," he made many important London friends. Among them was George Savile, Marquis of Halifax, whose "Character" of Burnet is quoted at the end of Thomas Burnet's biography.[64] The Marquis was, of course, the elder brother of Rochester's playful, fat friend, Henry, but Burnet saw him as a proper candidate for salvation. He was a witty man, Burnet writes in *The History of His Own Time*, and one who "passed for a bold and determined Atheist." This title he disowned, and Burnet calls him "a Christian in submission" unable to swallow all the divines "imposed on the world." He trusted God would forgive him "if he could not digest iron, as an ostrich did, nor take into his belief things that might burst him." The Marquis never read an "atheistical book"; and on at least one occasion, Burnet thought he had Christianized him. "In a fit of sickness, I knew him very much touched with a sense of religion. I was then often with him. He seemed full of good purposes. But they

[63] Thomas Burnet, "The Life of the Author," *History of His Own Time* (London, 1724), II, 67–85.
[64] II, 725–26.

went off with his sickness. He was always talking of morality and friendship." [65] But it was not Burnet's friendship with Halifax that brought him together with Rochester.

In *The History of His Own Time*, Burnet, looking backward, first describes Rochester as corrupted by court life and then recounts some of the Earl's amusing and scandalous escapades. He also ran the same spiritual course as Halifax. Debauchery led to illness; illness brought remorse; recovery cured repentance. But Burnet is generous to his convert's memory. "In the last year of his life I was much with him, and have writ a book of what passed between him and me. I do verily believe, he was then so entirely changed, that if he had recovered, he would have made good all his resolutions." [66]

In his preface to *Some Passages*, Burnet states that he had met the Earl several times before the wonderful "last year" but attributes their religious conversations to two factors: the Earl's reading of his *History of the Reformation* during his convalescence of October, 1679; and Burnet's spiritual ministrations to a girl, "one well known to him, that died the summer before." [67] His son, Thomas Burnet, adds that the "well-known" one had been engaged in "a criminal Amour with Wilmot, Earl of Rochester." [68] The essential facts are reported in Burnet's autobiography. Here, he says, he was called on to assist "many who lay a dying particularly one with whom . . . Rochester had an ill concern." [69] The Earl, knowing that his former mistress had been treated neither "with a slack indulgence nor an affrighting severity" sent for Burnet, who during a half year of conversation "saw

[65] I, 267–68.   [66] I, 264–65.   [67] *Some Account*, pp. 21–22.
[68] *History*, II, 685.
[69] H. C. Foxcroft, *A Supplement to Burnet's History of My Own Time* (Oxford, 1902), pp. 486–87. It is possible that *The Conversion and Persecution of Eve Cohan . . . Who Was Baptized the 10th of October, 1680* (London, 1680), which is attributed to Burnet, is another sample of the good Scot's skill.

into the depths of Satan" and subdued Rochester's wayward understanding. The Earl trusted the Scottish divine because, unlike other clergymen about the court of Charles, there was "nothing in him aspiring to preferment." With this commendation banked to his account, Burnet paid off by writing "with utmost sincerity and truth."

Not all men believed his account. Alexander Cunningham, a contemporary historian, accused him of violating the confidences of the confessional and of voicing Spinozian impieties through the dead mouth of Rochester.[70] Burnet anticipated both charges. In his preface, he says libertines will naturally dislike the book; others will object that the clergy are always composing "such discourses for carrying on what they are pleased to call *Our Trade*"; and still others will say he had made public a private confession. Rochester, Burnet writes, "gave me in charge not to spare him in anything which I thought might be of use to the living; . . . he was not unwilling to take shame of himself, by suffering his faults to be exposed for the benefit of others." [71] At the book's end, he insists he wrote with caution and tenderness but was strict in truth. He would not "lie for God." He admits that he had no notes on the winter's conferences and his narration may be more systematic than the conversations were. "I do not pretend to have given the formal words that he said, though I have done that, where I could remember them." Looking ahead to Cunningham's accusation of atheist-by-association, Burnet trusts that no reader "will drink up only the poison that may be in it" or wrest parts to an evil intention. Burnet hopes also to have written what he did "in the best manner I could." [72]

Burnet's discussions with Rochester began in October, 1679, and were broken off in April of the following year.

[70] Clarke and Foxcroft, *A Life*, p. 167.　　[71] *Some Account*, pp. 19–20.
[72] Pp. 131–33.

At precisely this time, Rochester was in correspondence with Blount and was reading his anti-Christian essays, but he was never, in the modern sense, an atheist. When his former tutor, Francis Giffard, chided him for his debauchery and atheism, he replied to the old gentleman, of whom he "had always a good opinion," that he was guilty "of extravagances, but I will assure you I am no Atheist." [73] The same fact comes out in his discussions with Burnet, who writes: "As to the Supreme Being, he had always some impression of one; and professed often to me, that he had never known an entire atheist, who fully believed there was no God." [74]

Since he believed in a Supreme Being, Rochester also believed in creation, and perceived in "the regular course of Nature . . . the eternal power of its Author." These admissions both pleased and confused Burnet because he discovered the Earl thought the Deity no more than a "vast power that wrought everything by the necessity of its nature." As a consequence of its nature, this force had no love or hate, and offered no rewards or punishments; moreover, to love God, said Rochester, is presumptuous and "the heat of fanciful men." [75] Actually, the young poet was probably more of a penetrating religious thinker than Burnet; he sought a faith, however, that would not sicken his reason. Believers, he admits, must be happy, but not all men can believe.[76] Believing is a form of opinionism which all men cannot master.[77] Why is a man damned for not believing the irrational? [78] Burnet, learned, decent, honest man that he was, never understood a man who struggled to find God; hence, the established Anglican and the atheistic seeker talked together at variance about topics in natural and revealed reli-

---

[73] Thomas Hearne, *Remarks and Collections*, ed. C. Doble (Oxford, 1885), III, 263.
[74] P. 39.   [75] Pp. 59–60.   [76] P. 72.   [77] Pp. 76, 92.
[78] P. 93.

gion. Sometimes others were present, says Burnet mysteriously, although he never names them.[79]

Rochester admitted to believing in a Supreme Being who created but did not care for his creatures; he also believed in a soul, separated at death from the body, but enduring then no punishment, receiving then no bliss. "The soul began anew, and . . . her sense of what she had done in this body, lying in the figures that are made in the brain, as soon she dislodged, all these perished, and that the soul went into some other state to begin a new course." [80] Though scorning professional moralists, Rochester had moral beliefs, and thought an ethical philosophy might be invented which could redeem mankind. His own golden rule, he confessed, was to do no hurt either to himself or others. He clung to his religion of sensations and bodily pleasure, "the gratifications of our natural appetites." [81] Not believing in a special Providence, he considered prayer and priest to be superfluous and proposed to celebrate his Supreme Being with a "short hymn." [82]

For Burnet, ethical philosophy—mere speculation, without common consent, shaped by men's fancies and the customs of nations—"lacked the authority to suppress the evil inclinations of nature and appetite." [83] Such a philosophy would not even save its philosopher "till he applied himself to God for inward assistance." [84] Suggesting that the order Rochester saw in the world created by his Supreme Being was evidence of wisdom and goodness, Burnet concluded that such a creator must love the wise and good and help them in this world or the next.[85] Employing the amazing opening gambit afforded him by the Earl's belief in a separate soul, Burnet argued that man, who has other ideas besides those lodged by "material figure," will, when his soul

[79] Pp. 45–46.   [80] Pp. 38, 53–54, 60.   [81] P. 50.   [82] Pp. 59–60.
[83] Pp. 48–49, 83.   [84] P. 55.   [85] Pp. 61–63.

is separated from its brain and organs of sensation, have thoughts and memories from the soul's inherent strength or "by means of some more subtile organs." [86] Having thus confuted Rochester's primitive notions of God, Providence, and the human soul, Burnet had next to face his opponent's views on revelation. It was, of course, one thing to offer natural proofs of the supernatural, another to defend Christianity point by point.

Rochester had always described miracle, even when the miracles were wrought by Christ, as "the showing of tricks." [87] He had other irreverent things to say about the Bible and Christian history. The theory of inspiration gave him mental indigestion; the authors of the Bible, the holy sages, wrote "in heats" as poets did. He also objected strenuously to the idea that God was partial in his respect for his creatures; he could not believe that a wise God would communicate his commands to one man, like Moses, and place him in the position, if he was so inclined, to cheat everyone. He had trouble with the unreasonable doctrine of original sin and with various other items of Christian belief.

For prophecies and miracles, the world had always been full of strange stories; for the boldness and cunning of the contrivers meeting with the simplicity and credulity of the people, things were easily received; and being once received, passed down without contradiction. The incoherencies of style in the Scriptures, the odd transitions, the seeming contradictions, chiefly about the order of time, the cruelties enjoined on the Israelites in destroying the Canaanites, circumcision, and many other rites of the Jewish worship, seemed to him unsuitable to the divine nature; and the first three chapters of Genesis, he thought, could not be true, unless they were parables.[88]

[86] Pp. 69–70.   [87] P. 82.   [88] Pp. 73–74.

For Rochester's rational questions, Burnet had all the orthodox responses. No one would have objected, he said, if God destroyed the Canaanites with plague, but he chose to give them the merciful death of the sword instead of destroying them with a painful epidemic. Innocent children were killed, of course, but God would rectify this injustice to them in heaven. As for the creation story in Genesis—it might be parabolic, but "there is nothing in it that may not be historically true." [89] It is also possible that the literal account of the Fall is hard to believe, but, says Burnet, we mortals, who can never fathom God's secrets, should not reject the divine writings and holy system of doctrine "because we cannot satisfy ourselves about some difficulties in them." [90]

In matters of revelation, Burnet informed Rochester, it is the simple question of the nature of evidence. The courts of law depend on evidence; and testimony in Scripture, as in the legal chambers, is validated by the number, innocence, disinterestedness, and confirmation of witnesses. "It is a vain thing to say it is possible for so many men to lie." [91] It is evidence of this nature which establishes Christ's miracles and resurrection and all revelation itself. There may be apparent difficulties in the Old Testament, Burnet allows, but this fact does not astonish him; these faults will be cleared when scholars know more about the language, history, and customs of Old Testament times. The importance of the Old Testament, however, does not reside in its historical accuracy but in its adventual prophecy.[92] Its critics, who proclaim it so faulty, are themselves at fault to reject the whole corpus because of some doubtful or confused readings.[93] The mysteries of Christianity are known only through revelation, and Rochester, Burnet assured him, should not

[89] Pp. 85–87.   [90] Pp. 81–82.   [91] Pp. 74–75.   [92] P. 84.
[93] P. 91–98.

be dismayed by his inability to comprehend them. They both have the same trouble, and so do all men, with far more simple natural mysteries, such as the generation of children or the growth of plants from seed.

But Burnet, honest Scot, is not one to deny that the Christian mysteries have been "darkened" by "too many niceties" and "illustrated by theological similes not always so very apt and pertinent." Because he takes this same attitude towards his colleagues, he is equally tolerant of Rochester's observations on the materialism and professional hypocrisy of the practiced clergy. A great deal of irreligion and atheism, he thought, could be credited to his ambitious associates, whose actions led men to think "not only are they hypocrites," but "religion itself is a cheat." These talks did not convince Rochester of Christian truth; but he promised Burnet, when they parted in the spring, that "he would never employ his wit any more to run it [religion] down or to corrupt others." Burnet recommended clean living to him to clear his mind and enable him to see "through all those flights of wit that do feed atheism and irreligion." [94]

Properly edified but still in doubt, Rochester left London to go to his estate, was taken ill on the way, and conveyed to the lodge in Woodstock Park where he would end his days. Burnet wrote him a letter, but Rochester, though attended by his mother's chaplain, Robert Parsons, by Dr. Fell, bishop of Oxford, and by Dr. Marshall, rector of Lincoln College, yearned for his spiritual comforter. On June 25 he wrote Burnet about his repentance and change of heart. He described the decay of his body and spirits, his hopes that he would be spared to practice contrition, and his doubts about the divine acceptance of deathbed conversion. He asks Burnet to pray. Burnet thought, he admits, that it would be evangelical vanity to hurry to Rochester and, "not hearing

[94] Pp. 105–10.

that there was any danger of a sudden change," put off his visit until July 20, six days before Rochester's death. When he arrived, Rochester was humble, repentant, and hopeful of heaven. They talked, when the Earl was able, for four days. On one occasion the "old man" in Rochester reappeared when he damned a servant for his slowness. In all other respects, the days between Monday and Saturday were of a holiness of conversation equaled only by the deathbed scenes of Anglican saints.

Burnet wrote all of this down. It furnished a long *exemplum* to the short sermon to the libertines that followed it; but before it was in print, there was, it is clear, laughter under the hill. Some libertines must have said that the story was a pious fiction, that Rochester died an unconverted rationalist. There is evidence against this, and the rumor is clearly not so. There is Rochester's letter to Burnet; [95] there is his similar letter to Dr. Thomas Pierce, of Magdalen College, asking for his prayers. "Take Heaven by force," writes the Earl, "and let me enter with you, as it were in disguise!" [96] They are not forgeries. There is Parson's printed funeral sermon, which corroborates Burnet's account of Rochester's latter days and appends, as pious evidence, an almost legal statement of conversion signed by the Earl and witnessed.[97] With this official instrument in hand, Rochester knocked at heaven's door. Could it have been forged? There are also five letters, with supporting detail, written by Ann, countess dowager, to her sister.[98] They describe her son's conversion

[95] Burnet reprints the letter (*Some Account*, pp. 114–15), modestly disavowing the compliment in it, and admitting that it was in reply to one of his. The letter "was printed since his death, from a copy, which one of his [Rochester's] servants conveyed to the press," writes Thomas Burnet (p. 22).

[96] *Collected Works*, pp. 298–99.

[97] *A Sermon Preached at the Funeral of the Rt. Honorable John, Earl of Rochester* (Oxford, 1680).

[98] *Collected Works*, pp. 321–26.

and his response to poor, unbelieving Fanshaw, who hoped "he would recover and leave those principles he now professed." If these are forgeries, few secular connivances have ever equaled them. There are here, as Burnet said in his proof of Christ's resurrection, "too many witnesses."

There is no doubt that atheist Rochester, like atheist Oldham, reached Christian conviction. Burnet knew the story would be doubted, and he is painfully careful to close all entrances to doubt. One door he could not shut. Fanshaw walked through it when he ascribed the Earl's novel piety to sickness and hoped he would recover his health and repossess his senses. The unregenerate who did not question the conversion attributed Rochester's change of heart to delirium. Burnet knew this; there were those who said it was "a part of his disease." Some men disrespectful of Providence thought "he died mad." [99] Blount, who frequently quotes Rochester's "Satyr" in his notes to his translation of Philostratus, probably refers to the rumor in his commentary on Apollonius' remarks to the sick King of Babylon.

> Now some are so base spirited to judge of men according to their Deaths if they be of a Persuasion different to their own; when if the Heretic (as they call him) repent on his Deathbed, then they boast of such repentance as a victory over his former Opinions, although perhaps it was occasioned only by the decay of his understanding with sickness. Also if he keeps firm and resolute to his old Principles then they cry his heart is hardened; so that in effect it is no more than, "Cross I win, Pile you lose." [100]

Nonetheless, Burnet attests to his own belief in the sincerity of the conversion by reporting the doubts of others. He remembered how Lord Halifax had dashed his hopes for

[99] Pp. 123–24.   [100] P. 160.

conversion by recovering, and he, as a Protestant, had undoubtedly heard of Roman pious fraud.

The only vocal witnesses to Oldham's spiritual change are his contrite verses and his Sunday vision. Verses similar to his were eventually circulated as Rochester's deathbed compositions.[101] Blount, the dark angel, survived both poets to die as all atheists must. Widowed, he sought to marry his wife's sister, but the laws of Church and State forbade him. He did research and wrote a paper, "To Justify the Marrying of Two Sisters One after Another"; however his comments on Leviticus did not convince Canterbury, and his discussion of the case of Henry VIII did not persuade the Crown. Acting, as Charles Gildon wrote, "according to the precepts of nature and reason," [102] he took his own life. Burnet, on the other hand, survived two wives and supplied the loss of the second, as Thomas Burnet says, by marriage to a "Mrs. Berkely," a lady of substantial fortune. The bright angel, though eldest of all, survived his dark opponent by almost twenty-five years and died quietly and prosperously in the palace of the Bishop of Salisbury. God, as he had explained to Rochester, loved virtuous men and helped them in this world and in the next.

[101] Pinto thinks the poem "Consideratus Considerandus" (*Collected Works*, p. 59) was written in the spring of 1680 as a result of the conversations with Burnet. It was probably not written by Rochester at all; but if it was, it is from the pen of the poet who wrote the "Satyr." It may recommend virtue without defining it, but it also regards man's situation as genuinely hopeless. Pinto (p. 242) also thinks that Rochester wrote a rough copy of "Rochester's Farewell" on his deathbed; if he did, someone else wrote the lines alluding to affairs after Rochester's death. Prinz, who prints (pp. 136-39) Woodforde's "Ode," which complains of the rhymes fathered on the dead Earl, rejects this poem, and Vieth does not accept it.

[102] Pp. A6-A7v. One should notice that Blount, recommending Donne's *Biathanatos* as the best apology for suicide, writes in his *Philostratus* (pp. 154-55): "Moreover I do believe that he who hangs himself in a Garret (as the late Parson of Newgate did) feels less pain, horror, and trouble than such as die of Fevers in their Beds with Friends and Relations weeping about them."

Appendix

De Tribus Impostoribus

~~~~~~

FEW IMAGINARY books, even those in the collection of Jean Nepomucene Pichauld, comte de Fortsas, have been sought with such diligence or discussed with such pious fascination as the *De Tribus Impostoribus*. This famous, but invisible, polemic against the three major religions of Europe was assumed by men of the Renaissance and the early eighteenth century to be the charter of the atheists' confederation, a truly horrid protocol awaiting the signatures of the godless of all nations. It was a book to be talked about whenever two or three nervous citizens of the Christian community were gathered together, and witnesses could be found of "an agreeable veracity" who had seen the book in some obscure library or in the possession of someone of dubious orthodoxy. In spite of this visual testimony to the book's existence, it was a long time before a responsible person admitted any knowledge of its contents. After more than a century of pious clamor, the book, which by then had been attributed to many pens, finally got written in several forms. Thus, unlike other mortal things, it put off immortality to put on corruption and became more confusing in its incarnation than it had been in its essence. Its genesis began in the thirteenth century.

Pope Gregory IX, who had excommunicated his obdurate temporal opponent, Frederick II, in 1229, only to be immediately humiliated by the Emperor's divinely sent victory over the

Turks and miraculous recovery of the Holy Lands, decided in 1239 once again to cut his mighty opposite's spiritual throat. This time he denied him the sacraments on the ground that he had incited the rebellious Romans to rebellion. The Papal pretext was so thin that it was generally regarded as the sort of pious hoax only an Italian could invent; hence, Frederick, speaking with the angelic tongue of his chancellor, Pier della Vigna, had no trouble clearing himself before the Parliament of Padua. The rhetorical coup was so brilliant that Gregory lost all restraint and issued an encyclic: "A beast rose from the sea filled with the names of blasphemy, furnished with the claws of a bear, the jaws of a lion, and a body resembling a panther." The letter maintained the tone of its *incipit,* going on from its apocalyptic preamble to accuse the Emperor of blasphemous utterance. He had described the world, it stated, as deceived by three worthless fellows (*baratatores*), Jesus Christ, Moses, and Mohammed. To this foul observation, the Pope continued, the Emperor had added a fouler biological suggestion that virgin birth was incredible because no woman had ever conceived a child without first enduring the shattering experience of sexual congress. To offset the bad publicity of this letter, Frederick replied, in full imperial innocence, that it was downright malicious to say he had called the founders of the religions "three seducers" when everyone knew he openly and regularly confessed there was only one Son of God.[1]

It is not improbable that Frederick, who was one of those men who find the orthodoxies of their age outmoded and irrational,

---

[1] Mario Esposito, "Una Manifestazione d'Incredulita Religiosa nel Medioeva," *Archivio Storico Italiano,* XVI (1931), 1–48. Louis Massignon traced the remark to a tenth-century Arabic text in "La Legend 'De Tribus Impostoribus' et Ses Origines Islamique," *Revue de l'Histoire des Religions,* LXXXII (1920), 74–78. The major study is Jacob Presser, *Das Buch "De Tribus Impostoribus"* (Amsterdam, 1926). W. Kraemer maintains, in "Ein seltener Druck des Traktats 'De Tribus Impostoribus, 1598,' " *Zeitschrift für Bücherfreunde,* N.F., XIV (1922), 101–11, that the book was written in the sixteenth century.

said in private exactly what the Pope reported. But even if he did, there is no evidence he ever wrote an unorthodox book; on the other hand, it is obvious that when the notion of a *De Tribus Impostoribus* was invented, he was an excellent candidate for authorship.[2] The Papal charge against Frederick was such a fine example of political mud-slinging that it was not only recorded by ecclesiastical chroniclers but applied in turn to other possible victims, such as Averroes, Simon de Tournai, Thomas Scotus, Zanino da Solcia, and Diego Gomez, who were, then, held up for the abhorrence of religious men. Most of these tarnished names were also to be credited in due course with the writing of the wicked manifesto of the atheists. Considering the eventual title of the book, it is surprising that none of these villains were alleged in the initial indictments to have used the term *impostors*. With great care, they all seem to have avoided the word and described Christ, Moses, and Mohammed as "worthless fellows" (*baratatores*), "mountebanks" (*truffatores*), or "seducers" (*seductores*). Once, however, news of the book's existence was noised about, almost anyone—and Pomponazzi is a good example —who mentioned the three religious leaders in one breath was accused of calling all of them *impostores*.

The teasing question, which can only be satisfied by whispered conjecture, is who started the rumor that a book about the Three Impostors existed. This question is, however, no more

---

[2] Esposito reprints the repetitions of these charges until 1500. The same accusations occur later when Justus Lipsius, a most careful scholar, pointed again at Frederick II, in his *Monita et Exempla Politica*, in *Opera Omnia* (Antwerp, 1637), IV, 185. Lipsius, it must be observed, does not speak of a book, and how this famous statement first got attached to Frederick, I do not know. Seventy years later, Grotius confuses Frederick of Sicily with Frederick Barbarossa, but he also denies the book exists. *Appendix ad Commentationem de Antichristo*, in *Opera Theologica* (London, 1679), IV, 502. Voltaire puts the case succinctly: "Des que l'empereur Frédéric II a des querelles avec les papes, on l'accuse d'être athée, et d'être l'auteur du livre des Trois Imposteurs, conjointment avec son chancelier de Vineis." *Dictionnaire Philosophique*, in *Oeuvres Complètes* (Paris, 1878), XVIII, 469.

troublesome than those about the authorship of the texts that now exist. Brunet, who edited the Latin *De Tribus Impostoribus* in the middle of the last century, thought that the existence of the book was first mentioned in 1611 by Geronimo de la Madre.[3] This is a strange statement because it is clear from his essay that Brunet had heard of the "ridiculous Florimond de Raemond," who claimed in a treatise against heresy, published in 1623, to have seen a copy of the horrible book, when he was a student at the Collège de Presle, "entre les mains de Ramus." He states that he would not have mentioned the matter at all if Genebrard and Osius had not earlier testified to its existence.[4]

If we follow De Raemond's lead, we can come to a preface written in 1581 by Gilbert Genebrard for François Jordan's critical commentary on Lambertus Danaeus' theories about the Trinity. In this preface, Genebrard defends Guillaume Postel, who had been charged with heresy, and observes that his doctrinal errors, unlike those of Calvin, did not convert some men to Islam and others to atheism. It is Calvin, he thinks, who is responsible for the fact that some "unknown author" wrote a "little book, the *De Tribus Impostoribus*, about the Lord Jesus, Moses, and Mohammed." [5] This preface is dated 1581; and La Monnoye, who wrote the earliest bibliographical essay on the *De Tribus Impostoribus*,[6] thinks he has found a mention of the

[3] *De Tribus Impostoribus*, ed. Philomneste Junior (Paris, 1861), p. 7.
[4] *L'Histoire de la Naissance, Progrès, et Décadence de l'Hérésie de Ce Siècle* (Paris, 1623), p. 236. Mersenne, whom Voltaire describes as "minime et tres-minime," makes several references to this book in his *Quaestiones* (cols. 15–16, 533, 1829–30) and catalogues it with the books of Pomponazzi, Cardano, Vanini, and Des Periers; he had hoped to read the book before he refuted it; but he had to make do with the narration of a friend, who had seen the book, memorized large sections of it, and recited them to him.
[5] *Ad Lambertum Danaeum Bellianismo Doctrinam ad Sancta Trinitate . . . Responsio* (Paris, 1581), p. 39. I have not been able to see all the works of Hieronymus Osius; but if any of his writings contains a certain allusion to the *De Tribus Impostoribus*, and if he actually saw the book, the date is no earlier than 1556, no later than 1569.
[6] In his "Lettre à Monsieur Bouhier," in *Ménagiana* (Paris, 1715), IV,

book in 1543. I am inclined to be a little more cautious and to date the first sound reference to this book in the second half of the sixteenth century. It is quite possible a rumor about the existence of such a book might run about for several decades before it got fixed in print; but, even then, I cannot assume a book existed unless I have the ocular testimony of a reliable authority.

After the first quarter of the seventeenth century, men talked about the author of the *De Tribus Impostoribus* and not about the book. The register of possible composers was large, and Presser has devoted his main effort to listing them by nationalities and writing their guilty biographies. The two Fredericks —the "stupor mundi" and the "Redbeard"—were natural candidates. Pier della Vigna was a popular nomination as a reliable "ghost-writer." Pomponazzi was honored for his unchristian remarks in the *De Immortalitate Animae.* Postel, who said burned Servetus was the author, was blamed in retaliation by Mezeray.[7] Mezeray refers the reader to Henri Estienne, who reported that, among other blasphemous utterances, Postel said that to get a reasonable religion one had to make a mélange of Judaism, Mohammedanism, and Christianity.[8] Boccaccio and Pietro Aretino [9]

291–92, Bernard de la Monnoye states that Guillaume Postel, who was also reputed to be the author of the book, referred to it when he wrote in his *Alcorani . . . et Evangelistarum Concordiae Liber* (Paris, 1543), p. 72: "Id arguit nefarius tractatus Villanovani de tribus Prophetis, Cymbalum mundi, Pantagruellus, & Novae insulae, quorum auctores olim erant Cenevangelistarum antesignani." Naudé as Monnoye points out, thought that this Villanovanus was Arnaud de Villenauve; whereas it is clearly Postel's intent to name Michael Servetus, who was born at Villa Nueva in Aragon. I see no firm reason to read *De Tribus Prophetis* as *De Tribus Impostoribus,* but given the hot intellectual climate of the period, I can see the temptation to do so was enticing.

[7] *Mémoires Historiques et Critiques* (Amsterdam, 1732), II, 143.

[8] *Apologie pour Hérodote,* I, 192; II, 187. Postel came under the suspicion of subsequent generations not only on account of his unique erudition but also because of his unguarded statements (Presser, pp. 69–70). In his *Des Histoires Orientales et Principalement des Turcs* (Paris, 1575), p. 43, he writes, for instance, that God, having given men laws through Moses, laws which they did not obey, sent Christ with softer requirements. When men gave these new precepts no observance, God sent Mohammed with a sword.

[9] *Naudaeana et Patiniana* (Paris, 1701), p. 83. Naudé's own views against

were also listed as authors of this invisible book. According to Prosper Marchand, who wrote in 1758, Alfonsus X, Poggio, Ryswick, Machiavelli, Erasmus, Leonardo Aretino, Dolet, Francesco Pucci, Nicolas Barnaud, Muretus, Bruno, Campanella, Bodin, Vanini, and Milton could be added to the Stygian list.[10] The crowd of unwilling authors put together by Marchand has been augmented by others uncovered since his time, but it is scarcely impolite to mention them. As a matter of fact, it may have been considered an insult to one's intelligence and powers of liberal thought after 1700 not to be included on this enormous panel. But while many pious huntsmen were searching through the thickets and trapping possible authors of the *De Tribus Impostoribus,* men of more exquisite rational powers were exploring the question which should first have been asked: "Has the book ever been written?"

Dr. Thomas Browne, a skeptic in all matters except religion, writes as if he had read the notorious book and discovered a speck of piety in its anonymous author. "That Villain and Secretary of Hell, that composed that miscreant piece Of the Three Impostors though divided from all Religions, and was neither Jew, Turk, nor Christian, was not a positive Atheist." [11] Shortly after Browne signed this bill of spiritual health, Grotius, removing the onus of authorship from Frederick Barbarossa, stated that no one had ever seen the book, which, in his judgment, did not exist.[12] On the other hand, Jean Chapelain wrote on Feb-

---

the existence of the book are: "Je ne crois pas qu'il ait jamais existé in *rerum natura*" (pp. 119–20). How early this honor was bestowed on Aretino is hard to know; but in his *La Vie de Pierre Aretin* (Hague, 1750), Benigne Dujardin lays the blame at the door of Pier della Vigna and refutes Mersenne's accusation by stating that Aretino knew no Latin and, hence, could not have written it (p. 155). His opinion is seconded by Giovanni Maria Mazzuchelli, *Gli Scrittori d'Italia* (Brescia, 1753), p. 1019.

[10] *Dictionnaire Historique* (Hague, 1758), I, 312–30. In 1699 Johannes Micraelius described the book in his *Historia Ecclesiastica* (p. 878) as the skeptics' bible and ascribes its authorship to Aretino, Ochino, or Poggio.

[11] *Religio Medici,* in *The Works,* ed. G. Keynes (London, 1928), I, 28.

[12] *Lettres Choisies* (Amsterdam, 1730), I, 166, 212.

ruary 4, 1662, to Pierre Huet that once he had thought the book did not exist, but now he had changed his mind thanks to Claude Hardi (a friend of Descartes and an editor of Gassendi), who knew a man who had seen the book. It was printed, he continued, in a small town in Silesia or Moravia in the same type used for printing the writings of Socinus; but the text is obviously the product of an Italian mind, and he is inclined to think its author was Ochino rather than Dr. Thomas Browne. Chapelain hopes Huet can find a copy; he would like to see whether or not it conforms to the one seen and read by Hardi. He advises Huet that they must be circumspect because not everyone would use the book for the innocent purpose they intend. After the work is in their possession, they could refute it "pour désarmer l'impiété et désabuser les faibles." [13] Rational Mr. Bayle also wrote in his essay on Aretino that after examining the matter carefully, he was of the opinion no text of the *De Tribus Impostoribus* had ever existed. Thus the votes went in all directions; but shortly after Bayle made his public confession of doubt, he received a manuscript from La Monnoye which weighed all the evidence and concluded that the book had never been written. [14]

It is a question how similar the manuscript acknowledged by Bayle in 1704 was to La Monnoye's "Lettre à Monsieur Brouhier," which was supposedly written in 1712 and published as an appendix to *Ménagiana* in 1715. La Monnoye describes in this paper the 1706 and the 1710 versions of Burchard Struve's *Dissertatio de Doctis Impostoribus:* in the first version, the German Jesuit had doubted the existence of the *De Tribus Impostoribus;* in the second version, he reversed his position. [15] It was, I expect, Struve's

[13] *Lettres*, ed. P. Tamizey de Larroque (Paris, 1883), II, 199–200. Jean Fischer, who supplied Buddeus' *Traité de l'Athéisme* (pp. 53–54) with annotations, claims to have read a French manuscript and says it is clearly by a recent author.

[14] *Lettres de Mr. Bayle*, ed. P. des Maizeau (Amsterdam, 1739), pp. 1005–6.

[15] Struve had been told by Tentzel, says La Monnoye, that a friend had seen the manuscript and that the text was divided into eight chapters:

change of heart that impelled La Monnoye to revise and publish
the manuscript he had, perhaps, sent Bayle. In the published text,
he dismisses, with fine reasonableness, the charges against Frederick II, Pier della Vigna, Simon de Tournai, Gruet, Aretino,
Bruno, Beauregard, Postel, and a dozen other hellish scribes. Because he was not convinced the book existed, he took great pains
to cast sensible doubt on all witnesses who claimed to have seen
it.[16] The type of his book had hardly been distributed before
the curious evidence of the German polyhistor Ernst Tentzel,
who had described the book to Struve and brought the turn
about in the opinion of the Jesuit, was supported by J. L. R. L.,
who printed in 1716 a *Réponse a la Dissertation de Monsieur de
la Monnoie sur le Traité de Tribus Impostoribus.*

The author of the *Réponse* did not have to write a lengthy
disquisition because, as he loudly stated, he had a copy of the

---

the nature of human belief; why men believe in an imaginary god; religion
the invention of princes; several chapters on the frauds of the founders;
and the nature of the supernatural. The reason Struve changed his mind
in the second version was his reading of Campanella's *Atheismus Triumphatus;* there Campanella, to exculpate himself from the charge of
writing the *De Tribus Impostoribus,* said the book was extant in 1538.
In his preface, he puts the blame on Boccaccio, or that failing, on Muret;
see also *Ménagiana,* IV, 290–91, 309–10.

[16] Dreyer's attempt to prove that Ochino wrote the book is an example
of the sort of method that La Monnoye opposed: see V. Placcius, *Theatrum
Anonymorum et Pseudonymorum* (Hamburg, 1708), I, 184–97. By this
time, the title had been imitated by a number of authors. J. B. Morin's
*Vincentius Panurgi Epistola ad Cl. Virum Joannem Baptistum Morinum
. . . de Tribus Impostoribus* (Paris, 1654) is an attack on Gassendi, Bernier,
and Neure. The last impostor had previously attacked Morin's *De Atomis
et Vacuo; De Tribus Nebulonibus* (1655), a polemic against Mazarin,
Cromwell, and Masaniello. John Evelyn's *The History of the Three Late
Famous Impostors* (London, 1669) on the pretenders, Padre Ottomanno,
Mahomet Bey, and Sabbati Levi, was more or less translated by J. B. de
Rocoles as *Les Imposteurs Insignes* (Amsterdam, 1683) and also rendered
into German as *De Tribus Impostoribus.* In 1680 Christian Kortholt published a *De Tribus Impostoribus Magnis* at Kilon, an attack on Descartes,
Herbert of Cherbury, Hobbes, and Spinoza. In the same category is
F. E. Kettner's *De Duobus Impostoribus* (Leipzig, 1694), an indictment
against Balthasar Bekker and Spinoza. The custom of imitating this title
continued well into the eighteenth century.

De Tribus Impostoribus in his library, and he had acquired it in a romantic yet orthodox manner. In 1706, according to his narrative, he was in Frankfurt am Main with his friend, a student of theology named Frecht. Sitting in their inn and looking learned, they were naturally approached by a German army officer, who asked them about a parcel of books and manuscripts he was about to sell to a local bookseller. The first of these, they noticed, was a rare early imprint of Bruno's *Spaccio*, the second was "Un Système d'Athéisme Démontre," and the third was a manuscript of the *De Tribus Impostoribus*. The two scholars were so pleased to come at last on this rare manuscript that they got the German, a Captain Trawsendorff, drunk and obtained his permission to take the manuscript to their chambers by promising not to copy it. Reading the work with great excitement, they decided that *translating* it from Latin into French was not a breach of promise since it was not *copying*. So they turned it into French, returned the original manuscript to Trawsendorff, who sold it to the bookdealer, who had been commissioned to buy it by a prince of the Saxon house. Why did the prince commission its purchase? J. L. R. L. tells us.

> Because he knew that this manuscript had been stolen from the Library at Munich when that town, after the French and Bavarians were defeated at Kochstadt, was occupied by the Germans. Trawsendorff, wandering from room to room in the Electoral Palace, saw a parchment manuscript tied with a yellow silk cord and, assuming that it was a curious work of some sort, could not resist putting it in his pocket.[17]

The anonymous author of this bibliographical *conte*, who is my nominee for the authorship of the *De Trois Imposteurs*

[17] P. 12. The authorship has been regularly assigned to P. F. Arpe, the apologist for Vanini, but there is no evidence to prove this. Presser (pp. 95–96) puts his finger on Jean Rousset de Missy, but I see no certainty in his case. The letter is dated January 1 and the *Réponse* was regularly reprinted as an appendix to the *Traité*.

because he here supplies himself with a literary alibi, goes on to state that the manuscript began with a letter from F. I. d. s. (initials that he expands to "Fredericus Imperator salutem dicit") to "Othoni Illustrissimo amico meo charissimo" (clearly the then Duke of Bavaria), whom he informs that the document was copied by his man of learning (Pier della Vigna beyond doubt) from the original Otho had seen in the imperial library. With this piece of foolery, the blame of authorship is shifted from the shoulders of score of recent and contemporary suspects and safely loaded on the back of a man who had been dead for almost five hundred years. The author of the *Réponse* spends the remaining pages of his thin pamphlet summarizing his French translation of the manuscript *sigla Trawsendorff*, which varies from the one described earlier by Tentzel in that it had six instead of eight chapters.

This story of the manuscript's provenience is so fictional one can assume it was invented to cover up its teller's composition of an atheist manuscript of his own; however, the manuscript described in the *Réponse* is very real, although by no means original. It is derived, as Marchand long ago discovered, from the second half of the *Vie et l'Esprit de Spinoza*, first printed in 1719/20 and reprinted in 1735, 1768, 1775, and 1777.[18] Actually, the *Traité de Trois Imposteurs*, printed in 1721, 1768, 1776, and 1793, is a compression into six chapters of the eight chapters (Tentzel's book?) of *L'Esprit de Spinoza*, a slanderous misrepresentation of the philosopher's *Korte Verhandeling*. Throughout most of the eighteenth century, the two books, the profane rewriting of Spinoza's short tract and the *Traité de Trois Imposteurs*, supposedly translated from the Trawsendorff Latin manuscript, circulated side by side among the wicked.

The *Traité* begins by stating that the idea of God was invented

[18] Marchand claims to have seen three manuscripts: one from the library of Prince Eugene or Baron von Hohendorff, one in the library of Hulst at the Hague, and one in the possession of a Walloon preacher in Amsterdam (I, 322–23). See also Paul Verniere, *Spinoza* (Paris, 1954), pp. 362–65.

to prejudice the lazy and ignorant against the teachings of the philosophers; but only a little good sense is needed to see "that God is neither passionate nor jealous, that justice and mercy are falsely attributed to him, and that nothing said of him by Prophets or Apostles constitutes his nature or his essence." This God, it was said, made himself known to men through ignorant prophets, who communicated with him in dream or vision. But the ancients had no respect for these men. "When they were tired of their babble, which often resulted in turning the people from the duty they owed their rulers, they restrained them by punishments; for this reason Jesus, who did not like Moses have an army back of him, failed to escape his merited punishment." Actually these Prophets and Apostles—and the author of the *Traité* furnishes examples—consistently contradict each other.

Man's ignorance and fear cause him to people the universe with "phantoms of his imagination," which he invokes in adversity, praises in prosperity, and, finally, makes into gods. Encouraged by individuals to whom it was important that man should possess such fancies, priests create gods like men and agree that "God has made nothing except for man, and, in turn, man is made only for God." This conclusion accepted, men use it to make false ideas of good and evil, merit and demerit, praise and blame, order and confusion, beauty and deformity. Also, supposing everything was made for him by a God susceptible of human passions, each man adores a God according to his own humor, in order to attract His blessing and to encourage Him "to make all Nature subject to his desires." But since this Nature causes them inconvenience, man assumes he has incurred the wrath of God because he is unaware that blessings and evil are common to both pious and impious. On this experience of man, God's attribute of incomprehensibility depends.

Actually, God has no end, and to state he has implies divine imperfection. "If God tries for a result, either for Himself or another, He desires what He lacks and we are forced, then, to

admit that at times God is without power. He has merely de-
sired, and is, hence, impotent." A rational man would avoid all
of these pitfalls and define God as a being whose attributes are
extended substance, constancy, infinity, indivisibility, and eternity; but the God men prefer is like a human king in his actions
and passions. "In a word, the God of the people of today is
subject to more shapes than pagan Jupiter." To learn about this
God "one consults the Bible as if God and Nature were specially
expounded therein. However, this book is only a tissue of fragments gathered in various ages, heaped up by many people, and
published only after the rabbis' fancy had approved some parts
and rejected others, because they conformed to or opposed the
law of Moses."

Before religion was introduced into the world, the author
states, man lived according to natural laws and his common
sense; but fear refused the aid of reason and nature, and men
"subjected themselves by vain ceremonies and superstitious worship to frivolous phantoms of the imagination, whence arose
this word *Religion*, which makes so much noise in the world."
The founders of religion, basing their doctrines on the hopes
and fears, the ignorance of the people, took great care to maintain their impostures through the adoration of images, which
they pretended were inhabited by the gods. This resulted in a
rain of gold and benefices, called "holy things," pouring down
on the priests. To deceive the people more, the priests made
prophecies and divinations, pretending to an ability (thanks to
their commerce with the gods) to penetrate into the future.
"There is nothing so natural as to wish to know destiny." Some
set up business at Delos; others at Delphos. The Romans consulted the Sybilline books. The future was read in bird flights,
the guts of animals, and, as a result, fools paraded as inspired
men. "Les fous passaient pour des inspirés." The *Traité* now
turns to Moses, earliest of known impostors.

Pagans had no system of religion; each state or city had its own rites and worshiped a divinity according to its fancy. The primitive heathen leaders were succeeded by deceptive legislators who employed means more studied and sure in the establishment of cults and ceremonies suited to the nourishment of the fanaticism they wished to maintain. Asia produced them all. Moses is the most ancient. Jesus attempted to preserve his own doctrine by abolishing all others. Mohammed, a more recent charlatan, derives from the others, and, hence, is generally declared "the enemy of the gods." Moses was really a magician's son, who fled from Egypt because of his numerous homicides and retired to Arabia Petra, where he wedded an idolatress and did not even "think of having his sons circumcised." This ritualistic omission clearly indicates that he had no knowledge "of the redoubtable God whom he invented later" in order to avenge himself on the King of Egypt, who had justly exiled him. At any rate, he succeeded in convincing the Israelites, an ignorant and credulous shepherd folk, by various miraculous tricks, of the existence of Jehovah. Once his authority as a legislator was confirmed by them, in order to perpetuate it and establish the worship of the supreme God, whose lieutenant he claimed to be, "he made his brother and his children chiefs of the Royal Palace, that is to say, of the place where oracles were uttered out of the sight and presence of the people." Fortunately, he had the army back of him, for "deceit without force has rarely succeeded." He also encouraged jealousies among the tribes, took care that members of his faction held powerful office, and eliminated the "esprits forts" who censured his government.

"With such precautions and by calling his punishments 'divine vengeance,'" he reigned an absolute despot. To end in the way he began, that is to say by deceit and imposture, he went to an abyss he had dug in a place of solitude, whither he had retired from time to time, under the pretext of going to confer secretly with God, in order to gain by this trick the respect and submission of his subjects. Finally, he threw himself in this abyss, prepared long before, so his body being undiscovered, "it would be believed God had taken him to make him like Him."

Since Moses, the *Traité* continues, there has never been a highly successful governor who has not claimed blood connections with divine beings or, failing that, a grave mission personally entrusted to him by God. Numa, Alexander, and even the philosopher Plato adopted this handsome trick. "Jesus Christ, who was not ignorant of either the maxims or magic of the Egyptians, availed himself of this deception, which he considered fitting for his designs." A bastard child, he returned to Jerusalem from Egypt, whither his mother had fled, at the exact moment when the Hebrews were wishing they had a visible god like the ones worshiped by neighboring peoples. He lacked Moses' supreme cleverness and political foresight; hence, he failed where his sharper predecessor succeeded, because "no matter how many sick he healed, nor how many dead he raised, having no money and no army, he could not fail to perish."

Although Jesus was less adept than Moses in some respects, he was more skillful in others. He never, for example, was caught in an incriminating statement. When he was asked about the tribute owed Caesar, or the woman taken in adultery, or "by what authority he set himself to instruct and preach to the people," he saw the traps in each question and slipped out by an evasive answer. He improved on the method of Moses, who "only promised earthly benefits as the reward for keeping his law," by offering "the hope of the advantages of another life, a hope that was never realized." As a consequence of this promise and others like it, Christ was careful not to choose scholars or philosophers for apostles, but the "poor in spirit," the simple and crazy. "Les pauvres d'esprits, les simples et les imbéciles." Rational men, says the author, should console themselves with having nothing in common with these harebrains.

The author of the *Traité* now points out that Christian legends and ethics are borrowed from, but not so good as, those of the pagans. The account of creation in the *Timaeus* is better than the one in Genesis, and Plato's Androgynus is better conceived than Moses' "extraction of Eve from the side of Adam." The fall of Lucifer is copied from Jupiter's casting down of the giants or the fall of Vulcan. Samson follows the story of Hercules; Elijah that of Phaeton; Joseph is a secondhand Hippolytus; Nebuchadnezzar, a Lycaon; and original sin, another version of the myth of Pandora. In short, "it is unquestionable that the authors of the Scriptures have transcribed word for word the works of Hesiod and Homer." The morals of Christ are no more original than the Bible stories; they are not a patch on those of Epicurus (to name a man of better life than Jesus) and Epictetus.

Why the Jews quit the laws of Moses to follow those of Jesus is, indeed, a mystery; nevertheless, the same type of ignorant Jew who ran after Moses followed Jesus.

> After his death, his disciples, in despair at seeing their hopes frustrated, made a virtue of necessity; for, banished from all places and pursued by the Jews who wished to deal with them as they had with the Master, they spread into neighboring lands, where by the report of some women they retailed the story of his resurrection and divine connections and the other fables that fill the Gospels. Their ill success among the Jews made them resolve to seek their fortunes among the Gentiles; but, as it was necessary for them to be more learned than they were (the Gentiles being philosophers and, consequently, too great friends of reason to fall for these bagatelles), the sectarians of Jesus won over a young man of an eager and active mind, somewhat better educated than illiterate fishermen, or at least more able to get his babbling listened to. . . . By the pretended fears of a Hell borrowed from the fables of ancient poets, and by the hopes of a Paradise (not so attractive as the one invented by Mohammed), where he had the au-

dacity to say he had been raised, this fellow won over weak minds.

Thanks to all this, the *Traité* continues, they procured for their master the honor of passing for a God, an honor that Jesus could never obtain while alive.

After devoting a few pages to Mohammed, an impostor more lucky than Jesus, the author dismisses as absurd the common ideas of God, of heaven, and of hell. He admits that the question of the nature of the soul is more delicate, but he subscribes, as does Cardano, to a subtility of heat, drawn from the sun, as the central principle of life, which "disperses at the death of man in the same manner as in other animals." From this discussion (which was not written in the Middle Ages because it reviews the notions of Descartes), the author passes to a final chapter on spirits and demons. The fiction of a Satan, a powerful opposite of an all-powerful God, strikes him as almost comical.

> Now how is it possible to conceive of a God who would conserve a creature who not only mortally hates him and curses him without ceasing, but who also tries to debauch his friends in order to embarrass him. How can it be possible that God would maintain this Devil, who constantly mortifies Him, who would dethrone Him if possible, and who turns from His service His elected friends? What is there in it for God? What can we say in speaking of Satan and Hell? If God does all and naught can be done without Him, how does it happen the devil hates Him, curses Him, and carries off His friends. God either agrees to this or not. If He is agreeable, the Devil in cursing Him does what he should, since he can only do what God wishes. Consequently, it is not the Devil but God who curses Himself. This is about as absurd as one can get.

With this observation, the *Traité*, a composition by one of those "sincere minds" which throughout the ages have written against "the injustice of the doctors in tiaras, mitres, and gowns," concludes.[19]

It is clear this book has nothing to do with the *De Tribus Impostoribus*, from which, according to its legend, it was translated. The Latin work, invisible for so long, finally made an appearance in print, and can now be found in libraries.[20] It has been reprinted by Edward Weller and Hermann Raster (H. R. Aster) at Leipzig in 1846 and by Brunet (Philomneste Junior) at Paris in 1861 and 1867. The so-called original *De Tribus Impostoribus*, M. D. IIC, is a small book of forty-six pages. Brunet thinks that it was printed in 1698 and that it had circulated in manuscript before this date.[21] Louis Chaudon states that it was printed in Vienna by Straubius, but he fails to tell how he knows this fact.[22] If the book was really printed in 1598, the statements about its existence made by Postel and Campanella would be acceptable; but anyone (and it is hard to understand how Brunet missed) even slightly familiar with the physical aspects of typography knows at once the book was published east of the Rhine during the eighteenth century. It was only then and there that one could obtain works printed "on grey paper with blunt

[19] I summarize, without giving page references, the *Traité des Trois Imposteurs* (En Suisse, 1793); the edition also contains the usual appendices: a short version of De la Monnoye's article and the *Réponse*. The text is similar to that printed by Heinrich Dubi in *Das Buch von den Drei Betrügern und das Berner Manuskript* (Bern, 1936). There are, however, differences between it and the Amsterdam edition of 1776, which concludes (pp. 72–92) by arguing that no religion is worth anything. Natural religion is vague and uncertain; paganism is infamous because it adores dumb things and permits human sacrifice; Judaism is cruel and odious; Christianity is blasphemous and uncertain; Mohammedanism is merciless and carnal. A rational man refuses all dogma because he can believe in a God who is the source of being, but no more than this. All religions, in fact, that offer aught beyond this are invented by politicians, who are aided by priests, so they can adorn their personal crimes with the name of God as copartner.

[20] M. Barbier, *Dictionnaire des Ouvrages Anonymes et Pseudonymes* (Paris, 1824), III, 355; Brunet, pp. xxxv–xxxvii; Presser, pp. 121–22.

[21] Pp. xxi–xxv.

[22] *Nouveau Dictionnaire Historique* (Lyons, 1804), XII, 367.

type"; the rest of Browning's famous lines fit equally well.

Unlike the *Traité des Trois Imposteurs,* the *De Tribus Im-postoribus* [23] is not divided into chapters and sections, but rambles through a maze of foul Latin and badly placed emphases. It is scarcely the work of a cogent thinker or a philosophic mind, resembling in a large degree the cogitations of a Hyde Park atheist who, like Cardano, had intimations of the Latin tongue, divinely given. The treatise begins by stating that those who agree on God's existence define him in terms of their personal ignorance. Since they do not understand his origin, they say he has none. If pressed, they say he sprang out of nothing or created himself. There have been a diversity of gods, and from them have arisen a diversity of religions. Christians object to the murders and concubinage of the pagan gods; but Moses and Joshua slaughtered many tribes at Jehovah's request, and both Christians and Mohammedans talk about the universal killing of their enemies and the subjugation of all to their religions. In addition, both Moses and Mohammed have permitted polygamy; and Jehovah, according to the New Testament, was rather partial to the daughters of men. "Did not God, the Holy Spirit, beget the son of God by a peculiar union with a betrothed virgin?"

One thing which characterizes most religions, the *De Tribus Impostoribus* states, is that they are seldom clear or harmonious in their principles. Some of them call the *Ens,* in which the intellect concludes its extent, "God"; others call it "Nature." A third religious group, holding the world is eternal, defines God as "the nexus of things"; whereas a fourth party says God is an *Ens separatum,* invisible and incomprehensible. They are all similarly divided on the meaning of religion. Some say it is "the fear of an unseen power"; others state it is love. According to one sect, love of God is man's gratitude for God's benevolence. This, writes our author, is a touching idea, for who could have endowed man with this odd emotion? Did it come from

---

[23] I summarize Brunet's text.

a benevolent God who, knowing the weakness of his creatures, put a tree in Eden in order to trap not only Adam and Eve but all their descendants as well? We should worship this God because we fear his power and hope for his rewards? We should worship this God, as they say, because he is? Is there any reason better than this for adoring the Grand Mogul! Or one's parents? But, naturally, visible powers are less esteemed than invisible ones. Other religious thinkers say God should be worshiped because he created us. "To what end? That we should fall! Because certainly he foreknew they were going to fall and, consequently, set before them the means, the forbidden fruit, without which they could not fall." But all religious people agree that God delights in worship and should be honored. "The desire for honor is a sign of imperfection and impotence."

It is really no secret, the book states, that religion and its attendant moral codes were invented by the ruling rich to "calm the passions of the people." Without question, those men in command of public affairs, deriving profit from the credulity of the people, told fear-inspiring stories of the power of the invisible gods and lied about their own occasional meetings and associations with them. They demanded, in proportion to their own luxury, divine beings suitable for them or even surpassing them. These notions were promulgated by their priests, whose living depended on the acceptance of these fictions.

The *De Tribus Impostoribus* admits that all the visible universe might go back to a Supreme Being, a Prime Mover; but there is no reason to think he visits all the elements and parts of the universe as a physician does a sick man. The idea of conscience is, likewise, no proof of a provident God. Evil-doing is really an interruption in the exchange of services on which society depends; hence, conscience is really the fear that we will incur the hatred of others, or that, in return, others will refuse to satisfy our needs. Considering what religion is and how it has been used, men would obtain more tranquillity if they simply followed the guidance of their own natures, imperfect as they are.

No one has knowledge of God; no one has seen him. He dwells in unapproachable light or in allegory. How clear allegory is everyone knows. "At, quanta aenigmatis claritas sit, cuique notum credo." Some religious leaders say they speak from "special revelation," but what a mess of revelations there are. Others rely on priestly testimony, but one priest contradicts the other. Christians study the writings of Moses, the Prophets, and the Apostles; but Mohammed, who has emended the Christians with the sword, says the Bible is corrupt. The conflicting claims of all religions are known to all men. Christianity claims to be the oldest, and hence the finest religion; but the writings of the Brahmins, the Vedas, to say nothing about the writings of the Chinese, are 1300 years older than Christianity. "You, who are disputing in some angle of Europe, neglect and condemn these writings, you should also realize that with the same ease they can reject all of yours!"

Religion, says the author of this book, is a human, not a divine, institution, and is culturally evolved in one of two ways. Moses learned the magic arts of the Egyptians; then, like his successor, Mohammed, subdued Palestine by force of arms; finally, he and his brother set themselves up as king and priest, "dux magnus et sacerdos maximus." This is the first method. A second method, employed by milder messiahs, is to establish the holiness of one's sect through pious fraud, through miracles that dazzle and control the irreligious and rough peasants. This feat will bring it about that princes uncertain of their subjects will quickly accept and strongly support the new doctrine. Rules are now offered to enable one to tell a "teacher of true religion from an impostor"; and it is impartially pointed out that all that Christians condemn in Mohammed can be found, perhaps in a different guise, in Moses, whose pious impostures occupy the concluding sections of the *De Tribus Impostoribus.*

Bibliography

PRIMARY SOURCES

Editions of Greek and classical Latin authors
are registered only when references have been
made to prefaces or annotations of editors.

ANONYMOUS. *The Charge of Socinianism against Dr. Tillotson . . .
Considered . . . to Which Is Likewise Annexed a Supplement
. . . Wherein Likewise Charles Blount's Great Diana Is Con-
sidered.* Edinburgh, 1695.
———. *A Dispute betwixt an Atheist and a Christian: The Atheist
Being a Flemming, the Christian an Englishman.* London, 1646.
———. *Ménagiana.* Paris, 1715. 2 vols.
———. *Miracles No Violations of the Laws of Nature.* London,
1683.
———. *Miracles: Works Above and Contrary to Nature.* London,
1683.
———. *Poems on the Affairs of State.* London, 1703. 3 vols.
———. *Traité des Trois Imposteurs.* En Suisse, 1793.
———. *The Voice of the Nation.* London, 1675.
ABBADIE, J. *Traité de la Vérité de la Religion Chrétienne.* Rotter-
dam, 1684.
ALBERTUS MAGNUS. *Opera Omnia,* ed. A. BORGNET. Paris, 1890–99.
38 vols.
AMBROSIUS, J. *De Rebus Creatis et Earum Creatore.* Paris, 1586.
AMYRAUT, M. *De l'Élévation de la Foi et de l'Abaissement de la
Raison.* Paris, 1644.

————. *Traité des Religions contre Ceux Estiment Toutes Indifférentes.* Samur, 1631.

ANDRAEUS, F. *De Creatione.* Copenhagen, 1609.

ANDREWES, L. *Minor Works.* Oxford, 1846.

AQUINAS, ST. THOMAS. *Summa contra Gentiles.* Paris, 1925.

————. *Summa Theologica.* Paris, 1856. 8 vols.

ARCHDEKIN, R. *A Treatise of Miracles.* Louvain, 1667.

ARPE, F. P. *Apologia pro J. C. Vanino Neapolitano.* Amsterdam (?), 1712.

ASCHAM, R. *English Works,* ed. W. A. WRIGHT. Cambridge, 1904.

ASLACUS, C. *Physica et Ethica Mosaica.* Hanover, 1613.

ASSONLEVILLE, G. *Atheomastix.* Antwerp, 1598.

AUBERIUS, C. *De Immortalitate.* Morges, 1586.

BACON, F. *The Works.* London, 1778. 5 vols.

BALZAC, G. DE. *Oeuvres.* Paris, 1665. 2 vols.

BARCLAY, A. *Argenis.* Rouen, 1643.

BARROW, I. *The Works,* ed. J. HAMILTON. London, 1861. 3 vols.

BATALERIUS, J. *Vindiciae Miraculorum.* Amsterdam, 1674.

BATES, W. *Considerations of the Existence of God and of the Immortality of the Soul.* London, 1676.

BAXTER, R. *The Practical Works,* ed. W. ORME. London, 1830. 23 vols.

BAYLE, P. *Lettres de Mr. Bayle,* ed. P. DES MAIZEAU. Amsterdam, 1739.

BEAUREGARD, C. *Circulus Pisanus.* Padua, 1661.

BELLARMINE, R. *De Ascensione Mentis in Deum per Scalas Rerum Creatarum.* Cologne, 1617.

BESSARION, J. *Opera.* Venice, 1516.

BIRCHEROD, J. J. *Exercitationes contra Atheos de Aeterna Divinae Existentiae et Providentiae Veritate.* Copenhagen, 1660.

BLECHINGUS, J. *De Creatione.* Copenhagen, 1610.

BLOUNT, C. *The First Two Books of Philostratus, concerning the Life of Apollonius Tyaenus.* London, 1680.

————. *Miscellaneous Works,* ed. C. GILDON. London, 1695.

BOCLO, R. W. *De Gentilium Atheismi Falso Suspectis.* Brema, 1716.

BODIN, J. *Colloque . . . des Secrets,* ed. R. CHAUVIRE. Paris, 1914.

————. *Colloquium Heptaplomeres de Rerum Sublimium Arcanis Abditis,* ed. L. NOACK. Giessen, 1857.

————. *Les Six Livres de la République.* Paris, 1579.

————. *Universae Naturae Theatrum . . . V Libris.* Lyons, 1596.

BOILEAU, N. *Oeuvres Complètes*, ed. A. C. GIDEL. Paris, 1872. 4 vols.

BOSSUET, J. B. *Sermons*. Paris, 1929. 4 vols.

BOUCHER, J. *Les Triomphes de la Religion Chrétienne*. Paris, 1628.

BOUELLES, C. DE. *Opera*. Basel, 1576.

BOURGUEVILLE, C. DE. *L'Athéomachie*. Paris, 1564.

BREDEHOLL, G. H. *De Existentia Dei ex Lumine Naturae Cognoscenda*. Helmstadt, 1681.

BROWNE, T. *The Works*, ed. G. KEYNES. London, 1928–31. 6 vols.

BRUNO, G. *Opere*, ed. A. WAGNER. Leipzig, 1830. 2 vols.

BUDDEUS, J. *Traité de l'Athéisme et de la Superstition*. Trans. L. PHILON. Amsterdam, 1740.

BURNET, G. *History of His Own Time*. London, 1724. 2 vols.

————. *Some Account of the Life and Death of John Wilmot, Earl of Rochester*. Boston, 1812.

BURRIDGE, R. *Religio Libertini: or the Faith of a Converted Atheist*. London, 1712.

BURTHOGGE, R. *Causa Dei*. London, 1675.

————. *An Essay upon Reason and the Nature of Spirits*. London, 1694.

————. Τἀγαθὸν *or Divine Goodness Explicated and Vindicated*. London, 1670.

CALVIN, J. *Opera*, eds. W. BAUM, E. CUNITZ, and E. REUSS. Berlin, 1863–1900. 59 vols.

————. *Psychopannychia*, ed. W. ZIMMERLI. Leipzig, 1932.

CAMFORO, G. *De Immortalitate Animae*. Cosenza, 1478.

CAMPANELLA, T. *Atheismus Triumphatus seu Reductio ad Religionem per Scientiarum Veritates*. Rome, 1631.

CANEPHIUS, B. *Athéomachie ou Réfutation des Erreurs . . . des Athéistes, Libertins, et Autres Esprits Profanes*. Geneva, 1582.

CANUS, M. *Opera*. Cologne, 1678.

CAPPEL, L. *Le Pivot de la Foi ou Preuve de la Divinité contre les Athées et Profanes*. Samur, 1643.

CARDANO, G. *Opera Omnia*, ed. J. SPON. Lyons, 1663. 10 vols.

CASE, J. *Ancilla Philosophiae*. Oxford, 1599.

CASMANNUS, OTHO. *Cosmopoeia et* Οὐρανοτραφια *Christiana*. Frankfort, 1598.

CAUSSIN, N. *La Cour Sainte*. Paris, 1624.

CHAPELAIN, J. *Lettres*, ed. P. T. DE LARROQUE. Paris, 1883.

CHARLETON, W. *The Darkness of Atheism Dispelled by the Light of Nature*. London, 1652.

————. *The Immortality of the Human Soul Demonstrated by the Light of Nature.* London, 1657.

————. *Physiologia Epicuro-Gassendo Charltoniana.* London, 1654.

CHARNOCKE, S. *A Treatise of Divine Providence.* London, 1680.

CHARRON, P. *Traité de la Sagesse.* Paris, 1783.

————. *Les Trois Vérités contre Tous Athées, Idolâtres, Juives, Mohammedans, Hérétiques, et Schismatiques.* Bordeaux, 1593.

CHEFFONTAINES, C. P. DE. *Novae Illustrationis Christianae Fidei adversus Impios, Libertinos, Atheos.* Paris, 1586.

CHILLINGWORTH, W. *The Works.* London, 1704.

CLAUSSEN, M. *Atheus Convictus.* Kilon, 1672.

COEFFETEAU, N. *Premier Essai des Questions Théologiques.* Paris, 1607.

COLBERG, D. *Unicum, Proprium, Adaequatum Remedium Therapeuticum Atheologiae.* Rostock, 1680.

COLERUS, J. *De Animarum Immortalitate.* Wittenburg, 1587.

CONTARINI, G. *Opera.* Paris, 1571.

COTIN, C. *Theoclée ou la Vari Philosophie des Principes du Monde.* Paris, 1646.

————. *Traité de l'Âme Immortelle.* Paris, 1655.

COUSIN, J. *Fundamenta Religionis.* Douai, 1598.

CRADDOCK, W. *Gospel Liberty.* London, 1648.

CRESPET, P. *Instruction de la Foi Chrétienne.* Paris, 1589.

CUDWORTH, R. *The True Intellectual System of the Universe,* ed. J. HARRISON. London, 1845. 3 vols.

CUPERUS, F. *Arcana Atheismi Revelata Philosophice et Paradoxe Refutata.* Rotterdam, 1676.

CURIO, C. S. *Aranei Encomion.* . . . Venice, 1540.

DANDINI, G. *De Corpore Animato.* Paris, 1611.

DANIELI, F. *Trattato della Divina Providenza.* Milan, 1615.

DAVENANT, W. *Works.* London, 1673.

DAVIES, J. *The Poems,* ed. C. HOWARD. New York, 1941.

DEL RIO, M. *Disquisitionum Magicarum Libri Sex.* Mainz, 1624.

DERODON, D. *L'Athéisme Convaincu.* Orange, 1659. (Trans. by J. BONHOME as *The Arraignment and Conviction of Atheism.* London, 1679.)

DESCARTES, R. *The Works.* Trans. E. S. HALDANE. Cambridge, 1931. 2 vols.

DIECMANN, J. *De Naturalismo cum Aliorum Tum Maxime Jo. Bodini.* Kilon, 1683.

DIGBY, K. *Two Treatises*. London, 1665.

DONNE, J. *LXXX Sermons*. London, 1640.

———. *Fifty Sermons*. London, 1649.

———. *Six and Twenty Sermons*. London, 1660.

DOVE, J. *A Confutation of Atheism*. London, 1605.

DU HAMEL, J. B. *De Mente Humana*. Paris, 1677.

DU PONT, R. *La Philosophie des Esprits*. Rouen, 1628.

DURAND, D. *La Vie et les Sentiments de Lucilio Vanini*. Amsterdam, 1712.

EDWARDS, J. *A Demonstration of the Existence and Providence of God*. . . . London, 1695.

———. *Some Thoughts concerning the Several Causes and Occasions of Atheism*. London, 1695.

ELLIS, C. *The Folly of Atheism Demonstrated to the Capacity of the Most Unlearned Reader*. London, 1692.

ESTIENNE, H. *Apologie pour Hérodote*, ed. P. RISTELHUBER. Paris, 1879. 2 vols.

EVELYN, J. *The History of the Three Late Famous Impostors*. London, 1669.

FABER, P. *Adversus Impios Atheos*. Venice, 1627.

FABRICIUS, J. L. *Opuscula Varia*. Heidelberg, 1688.

FEDELI, G. DE. *Anima Immortale*. Venice, 1598.

FERGUSON, R. *The Interest of Reason in Religion*. London, 1675.

FEVRIER, J. *Traités de l'Immortalité de l'Âme*. Paris, 1656.

FICINO, M. *Opera*. Basel, 1576. 2 vols.

FLEETWOOD, W. *An Essay upon Miracles*. London, 1701.

FONTANA, M. P. *Formica sive de Divina Providentia*. Bergamo, 1594.

FONTE, A. DI. *Somma della Natural Filosofia*. Trans. A. DI ULLOA. Venice, 1557.

FOTHERBY, M. *Atheomastix*. London, 1622.

GALLUCIUS, J. *Theatrum Mundi et Temporis*. Venice, 1588.

GARASSE, F. *La Doctrine Curieuse des Beaux Esprits de Ce Temps*. Paris, 1624.

GASSENDI, P. *Opera*. Lyons, 1658. 6 vols.

GENEBRARD, G. *Ad Lambertum Danaeum Bellianismo Doctrinam ad Sancta Trinitate . . . Responsio*. Paris, 1581.

GIFFORD, G. *The Great Mystery of Providence*. London, 1695.

GIOVIO, P. *Elogia Doctorum Virorum*. Antwerp, 1557.

GOCLENIUS, R. Ψυχολογια: *Hoc est de Hominis Perfectione, Animo, et in Primis Ortu Huius Commentationes ac Disputationes.* Marburg, 1590.

GOOD, T. *Firmianus and Dubitantius.* Oxford, 1674.

GOODMAN, G. *The Fall of Man.* London, 1616.

GOODWIN, T. *Works,* ed. J. C. MILLER. Edinburgh, 1861.

GRAMMONT, G. B. DE. *Historiarum Galliae ab Excessu Henrici IV Libri XVIII.* Toulouse, 1643.

GRAVELLE, F. DE. *Abregé de Philosophie.* Paris, 1601.

GROSSE, J. G. *An Atheismus Necessario Ducat ad Corruptionem Morum.* Rostock, 1696.

GROTIUS, H. *Lettres Choisies.* Amsterdam, 1730. 2 vols.

———. *Opera Theologica.* London, 1679. 4 vols.

GRUVIUS, M. *De Origine Animae Humanae.* Erfurt, 1673.

GUNDISSALINUS, D. *De Immortalitate,* ed. G. BÜLOW (in *Beitrage zur Geschichte der Philosophie des Mittelalters*). Münster, 1897.

HALES, J. *Golden Remains.* London, 1673.

Harleian Miscellany. London, 1810. 12 vols.

HARTNACK, D. *Sanchez Aliquid Sciens.* Stettin, 1665.

HARWARD, S. *A Discourse concerning the Soul and Spirit of Man.* London, 1604.

HATTECLIFFE, V. *Aut Deus aut Nihil.* London, 1659.

HEARNE, T. *Remarks and Collections,* ed. C. DOBLE. Oxford, 1895. 11 vols.

HERNE, S. *A Discourse of Divine Providence.* London, 1679.

HIGGENSON, T. *A Testimony to the True Jesus.* London, 1656.

HILL, N. *Philosophia Epicurea, Democritiana, Theophrastica.* Paris, 1601.

HILLS, H. *A Short Treatise concerning the Propagation of the Soul.* London, 1667.

HOBBES, T. *English Works,* ed. W. MOLESWORTH. London, 1839–45. 11 vols.

HOFFMANNUS, F. *De Atheo Convincendo ex Artificiosissima Machinae Humanae Structura Oratio.* S.l. 1705.

HOOKER, R. *Laws of Ecclesiastical Polity,* ed. J. KEBLE. Oxford, 1888. 3 vols.

HUET, P. *Alnetaneae Quaestiones.* Paris, 1690.

ISRAEL, MENASSEH BEN. *De Resurrectione Mortuorum.* Amsterdam, 1636.

JAEGER, J. W. *Cuperus Mala Fide aut ad Minimum Frigide Atheismum Spinoza Oppugnans.* Jena, 1710.

KECKERMANNUS, B. *Opera*. Geneva, 1614. 2 vols.

KETTNER, F. E. *De Duobus Impostoribus*. Leipzig, 1694.

KING, J. *Mr. Blount's Oracles of Reason Examined and Answered*. London, 1698.

KORTHOLT, C. *De Tribus Impostoribus Magnis*. Kilon, 1680.

L. J. L. R. *Réponse à la Dissertation de Monsieur de la Monnoye sur le Traité de Tribus Impostoribus*. Amsterdam, 1716.

L'HOSTAL, P. DE. *Les Discours Philosophiques*. Paris, 1579.

LA MOTHE LE VAYER, P. DE. *Oeuvres*. Paris, 1662. 2 vols.

LA PRIMAUDAYE, P. DE. *L'Académie Française*. Paris, 1584.

LA RIVIERE, P. DE. *Angélique*. Lyons, 1626.

LAROQUE, P. DE. *La Science de Bien Mourir*. Amsterdam, 1722.

LATIMER, H. *Works*, ed. G. E. CORRIE. Cambridge, 1844. 2 vols.

LAUNOY, J. DE. *De Varia Aristotelis in Academia Parisiensis Fortuna*. Paris, 1653.

LEHMANNUS, G. *De Animae Immortalis Traductione*. Leipzig, 1649.

LELAND, J. *A View of the Principal Deistical Writers That Have Appeared in England in the Last and Present Century*. London, 1757. 3 vols.

LESSIUS, L. *De Providentia Numinis et Animi Immortalitate Libro Duo adversus Atheos et Politicis*. Antwerp, 1613.

LIBAVIUS, A. *De Universitate et Rerum Conditarum Originibus*. Frankfort, 1610.

LIPSIUS, J. *Opera Omnia*. Antwerp, 1637. 4 vols.

LOUIS OF GRANADA. *God Cares for You*. Trans. E. C. McENIRY. Columbus, Ohio, 1944.

LOWDE, J. *Moral Essays. Together with an Answer to Some Chapters in the Oracles of Reason concerning Deism*. London, 1699.

LUCRETIUS. *De Rerum Natura*, ed. T. FABER. Cambridge, 1686.

———. *De Rerum Natura*, ed. S. HAVERCAMP. Leyden, 1725. 2 vols.

MAGIRUS, J. *Anthropologia*. Prostadt, 1603.

MALDONATUS, J. *Commentarii in Quattuor Evangelistas*. Paris, 1596.

MALEBRANCHE, N. *Conversations Chrétiennes*, ed. L. BRIDET. Paris, 1929.

———. *De la Recherche de la Vérité*, ed. G. LYON. Paris, 1925.

MANNINGHAM, T. *Two Discourses*. London, 1681.

MANSVELT, R. VAN. *Adversus Anonymum Theologo-Politicum*. Amsterdam, 1674.

MARCHAND, P. *Dictionnaire Historique*. Hague, 1758. 2 vols.

MARTINEZ, P. "Tractatus de Animorum Nostrorum Immortalitate," in ARISTOTLE. *De Anima*. Murviedro, 1575.

MAUDUIT, M. *Traité de Religion contre les Athées, les Déistes, et les Nouveaux Pyrrhoniens*. Paris, 1677.

MAZZUCHELLI, G. M. *Gli Scrittori d'Italia*. Brescia, 1753.

MELANCHTHON, P. *Opera*, ed. C. G. BRETSCHNEIDER. Halle, 1834–46. 28 vols.

MENCKEN, G. H. *Dissertatio Moralis de Juramento Athei*. Leipzig, 1713.

MERSENNE, M. *Correspondance*, eds. C. DE WAARD and R. PINTARD. Paris, 1932–45. 7 vols.

——. *L'Impiété des Déistes, et des Plus Subtils Libertins Découverte, et Réfutée par Raisons de Théologie et de Philosophie*. Paris, 1624.

——. *Quaestiones in Genesim*. Paris, 1623.

MEZERAY, F. DE. *Mémoires Historiques et Critiques*. Amsterdam, 1732.

MICRAELIUS, J. *Ethnophronius*. Steetin, 1647.

——. *Historia Ecclesiastica*. Magdeburg, 1699.

MIGNE, J. B. (ed.). *Patrologia . . . Series Graeca*. Paris, 1886–1912. 162 vols.

——. *Patrologia . . . Series Latina*. Paris, 1844–90. 217 vols.

MILTON, J. *The Works*, ed. F. A. PATTERSON. New York, 1931–38. 18 vols.

MONTAIGNE, M. DE. *Les Essais*, eds. H. MOTHEAU and D. JOUAUST. Paris, 1886–89. 7 vols.

MOORE, J. *Of the Immortality of the Soul*. London, 1694.

MORE, G. *A Demonstration of God*. London, 1597.

MORE, H. *A Collection of Several Philosophical Writings*. London, 1662.

——. *The Grand Mystery of Godliness*. London, 1660.

——. *Opera Omnia*. London, 1675–79. 3 vols.

——. *Philosophical Poems of Henry More*, ed. G. BULLOUGH. Manchester, 1931.

——. *The Poems*. Cambridge, 1647.

——. *Theological Works*. London, 1708.

MORIN, J. B. *Vincentius Panurgi Epistola ad Cl. Virum Joannem Baptistum Morinum . . . de Tribus Impostoribus*. Paris, 1654.

——. *De Vera Cognitione Dei ex Solo Naturae Lumine*. Paris,

1655. (Trans. by H. CARE as *The Darkness of Atheism Dispelled by the Light of Nature*. London, 1683.)

MORNAY, P. DE. *De la Vérité de le Religion Chrétienne*. Paris, 1585.

MOULIN, P. DE. *A Treatise of the Knowledge of God*. Trans. R. CODINGTON. London, 1634.

MUSAEUS, J. *De Lumine Naturae*. Jena, 1675.

NANCELIUS, N. *De Immortalitate Animae*. Paris, 1587.

NATTA, M. *Opera*. Venice, 1564.

NAUDÉ, G., and PATIN, G. *Naudaeana et Patiniana*. Paris, 1701.

NEUFVILLE, J. DE. *De Pulchritudine Animi*. Paris, 1556.

NICHOLLS, W. *A Conference with a Theist*. London, 1696.

NICOLAS, P. *Opus de Immortalitate Animorum Secundum Platonem et Aristotelem*. Faenza, 1525.

NICOLSON, M. (ed.). *The Conway Letters*. New Haven, Conn., 1930.

NIFO, A. *De Immortalitate Humane Animae adversus Petrum Pomponacium*. Venice, 1518.

NYE, S. *A Discourse concerning Natural and Revealed Religion*. London, 1696.

OLDHAM, J. *The Compositions in Prose and Verse . . .*, ed. E. THOMPSON. London, 1770.

———. *Poems and Translations*. London, 1683.

———. *The Remains*. London, 1684.

———. *Satyrs upon the Jesuits*. London, 1685.

OLEARIUS, J. G. *Dissertatio Prior: De Vita et Fatis J. C. Vanini; Dissertatio Posterior: De Vanini Scriptis et Opinionibus*. Jena, 1709.

OWEN, J. *Works*, ed. W. G. GOOLD. London, 1850–55. 24 vols.

PALEARIUS, A. *Opera Omnia*. Lyons, 1552.

PARIS, Y. DE. *La Théologie Naturelle*. Paris, 1640.

PARKER, S. *Disputationes de Deo et Providentia Divina*. London, 1678.

PARPARELLA, S. *Opera*. Macerta, 1582.

PARSONS, R. *A Sermon Preached at the Funeral of the Rt. Honorable John, Earl of Rochester*. Oxford, 1680.

PASCAL, B. *Entretien avec de Saci sur Epictète et Montaigne*, ed. M. GUYAU. Paris, 1875.

———. *Pensées*, ed. L. BRUNSCHVIG. Paris, 1904. 3 vols.

PATIN, G. *Lettres*, ed. J. H. REVEILLE-PARISE. Paris, 1846. 3 vols.

PEREIRA, B. *De Rerum Natura*. Paris, 1579.

PETRUS, H. *De Atheismi Eversione*. Helmstadt, 1689.

PHILIPPS, J. T. *Dissertatio Historico-Philosophico de Atheismo sive Historia Atheismi.* London, 1716.

PICO DELLA MIRANDOLA, G. F. *De Animae Immortalitate.* Paris, 1541.

———. *Examen Vanitatis Doctrinae Gentium.* Mirandola, 1520.

PLACCIUS, V. *Theatrum Anonymorum et Pseudonymorum.* Hamburg, 1708. 2 vols.

PLEIX, S. DE. *La Physique ou Science des Choses Naturelles.* Lyons, 1620.

POIRET, P. *Cogitationes Rationales de Deo, Anima, et Malo.* Amsterdam, 1685.

POLLOT, L. *Dialogues contre la Pluralité des Religions et l'Athéisme.* Rochelle, 1595.

POMPONAZZI, P. *De Fato, de Libero Arbitrio et de Praedestione,* ed. R. LEMAY. Verona, 1957.

———. *De Immortalitate Animae.* Leyden, 1534.

———. *De Naturalium Effectuum Causis sive de Incantationibus.* Basel, 1567.

PORZIO, S. *De Mente Humana.* Florence, 1551.

POSSEVINUS, A. *Judicium de Nuae . . . Scriptis.* Lyons, 1593.

POSTEL, G. *Alcorani . . . et Evangelistarum Concordiae Liber.* Paris, 1543.

———. *Des Histoires Orientales et Principalement des Turcs.* Paris, 1575.

POULLET, C. *Réponse aux Athéistes de Tours.* S.1., 1590.

RACONIS, A. DE. *Metaphysica.* Paris, 1624.

———. *Tractatus de Anima Rationali.* Paris, 1632.

RAEMOND, F. DE. *L'Histoire de la Naissance, Progrès, et Décadence de l'Hérésie de Ce Siècle.* Paris, 1623.

RAY, J. *The Wisdom of God Manifested in the Creation.* London, 1691.

RAYNAUD, T. *Scalae a Visibili Creatura ad Deum.* Lyons, 1624.

REIMANN, J. F. *Historia Universalis Atheismi et Atheorum Falso et Merito Suspectorum apud Judaeos, Ethnicos, Muhamedanos.* Hildesheim, 1725.

REISER, A. *De Origine, Progressu, et Incremento Atheismi ad Spitzelium.* Augsburg, 1669.

RICHEOME, L. *Immortalité de l'Âme.* Paris, 1621.

ROCCO, A. *Animae Rationalis Immortalitas.* Frankfort, 1644.

ROCOLES, J. B. DE. *Les Imposteurs Insignes.* Amsterdam, 1683.

RUST, G. *A Discourse of Reason.* London, 1683.

SAINTE HONORINE, C. DE. *Le Discernement et l'Usage que le Prince Doit Faire des Livres Suspects.* Paris, 1672.

SANCHEZ, F. *Opera Philosophica,* ed. J. DE CARVALHO. Coimbra, 1955.

SAULT, R. *A Conference betwixt a Modern Atheist and His Friend.* London, 1693.

SCALIGER, J. C. *Exotericarum Exercitationum Liber XV de Subtilitate.* Frankfort, 1612.

SCHELLING, C. H. *Oeconomiam Systematis Moralis Atheorum.* Helmstadt, 1718.

SCHRAMM, J. *De Vita et Scriptis Famosi Athei Julii Caesaris Vanini.* Küstrin, 1709.

SEBONDE, R. DE. *Theologia Naturalis.* Frankfort, 1635.

SEERUPIUS, G. N. *De Legis Mosaicae Divina Origine et Auctoritate Diatriba.* Copenhagen, 1678.

SERRES, J. DE. *De l'Immortalité de l'Âme.* Lyons, 1596.

SEWARD, W. *Biographiana.* London, 1799. 2 vols.

SEXTUS EMPIRICUS. *Opera,* ed. J. A. FABRICIUS. Leipzig, 1718.

SHEFFIELD, J., EARL OF MULGRAVE. *The Works.* London, 1740. 2 vols.

SHERLOCKE, W. *A Discourse concerning Divine Providence.* London, 1693.

SIBBES, R. *Works,* ed. A. B. GROSART. Edinburgh, 1862–63. 6 vols.

SILHON, J. DE. *De la Certitude des Connaissances Humaines.* Paris, 1661.

———. *Les Deux Vérités.* Paris, 1626.

———. *De l'Immortalité de l'Âme.* Paris, 1634.

SIRMOND, A. *De Immortalitate Animae Demonstratio Physica et Aristotelica adverus Pomponatium et Asseclas.* Paris, 1635.

SMITH, J. *God's Arrow against Atheists.* London, 1622.

SMITH, J. *Select Discourses.* London, 1660.

SPITZEL, G. *De Atheismi Radice.* Augsburg, 1661.

———. *De Atheismo Eradicando.* Utrecht, 1669.

———. *Scrutinium Atheismi Historico-Aetiologicum.* Augsburg, 1663.

STAEDELEN, J. C. *De Atheismi Origine.* Jena, 1720.

STENGEL, G. *De Monstris et Monstrosis, quam Mirabilis, Bonus, et Iustus in Mundo Administrando Sit Deus Monstantibus.* Ingolstadt, 1647.

STERRY, P. *The Spirit's Conviction of Sin.* London, 1645.

STEUCHUS, A. *Opera Omnia.* Venice, 1591.

SWELLINGIUS, J. E. *Mens Immortalis Evidenter Certo contra Atheos Scepticosque Demonstrata.* Bremen, 1683.

TALLEMENT DES RÉAUX, G. *Les Historiettes,* ed. G. MONGRÉDIEN. Paris, 1932. 8 vols.

TAYLOR, J. *The Works,* eds. A. TAYLOR, R. HEBER, and C. P. EDEN. London, 1883. 10 vols.

TELESIO, B. *De Rerum Natura juxta Propria Principia.* Naples, 1586.

THOMASIUS, J. *De Origine Animae Humanae ex Traduce.* Leipzig, 1669.

THORNDIKE, H. *Works.* Oxford, 1845–56. 6 vols.

THOU, J. A. DE. *Historia Sui Temporis.* Orleans, 1626. 4 vols.

TIETZMANN, H. *Atheismi Inculpati Monstrum.* Wittenberg, 1696.

TILLOTSON, J. *The Works,* ed. T. BIRCH. London, 1820. 10 vols.

TOWERS, W. *Atheismus Vapulans, or a Treatise against Atheism.* London, 1654.

TURRETINUS, F. *Theologiae Elencticae Institutio.* Geneva, 1688.

ULRICI, S. *De Animae Rationalis Immortalitate.* Wittenberg, 1696.

VALLA, L. *Opera.* Basel, 1543.

VANINI, J. C. *Ampitheatrum Aeternae.* Lyons, 1615.

——. *De Admirandis Naturae Reginae Deaeque Mortalium Arcanis.* Paris, 1616.

——. *Oeuvres Philosophiques de Vanini.* Trans. M. X. ROUSSELOT. Paris, 1842.

——. *Le Opere,* ed. L. CORVAGLIA. Milan and Rome, 1933–34. 2 vols.

VIAU, T. DE. *Oeuvres Complètes,* ed. M. ALLEAUME. Paris, 1855. 2 vols.

VILLEMANDY, P. DE. *Scepticismus Debellatus.* Leyden, 1697.

VIRET, P. *De la Providence Divine.* Lyons, 1565.

——. *Exposition de la Doctrine de la Foi Chrétienne.* Geneva, 1564.

VIVES, J. L. *De Anima et Vita.* Lyons, 1555.

——. *Opera.* Basel, 1550. 2 vols.

VOETIUS, G. *Selectae Disputationes.* Utrecht, 1648–60. 4 vols.

VOIGT, F. Συν θεω *De Atheismo.* Leipzig, 1695.

VOLTAIRE, F. M. A. DE. *Oeuvres Complètes.* Paris, 1877–85. 52 vols.

WADSWORTH, T. Αντιψυχοθανασια: *or the Immortality of the Soul Explained and Proved by Scripture and Reason.* London, 1670.

WAGNER, T. *Examen Elenchticum Atheismi Speculativi.* Tübingen, 1677.

WARD, R. *The Life of the Learned and Pious Dr. Henry More.* London, 1710.

WARD, S. *A Philosophical Essay towards the Eviction of the Being and Attributes of God.* Oxford, 1677.

WEDDERKOPFF, G. *Dissertationes Duae, Quarum Prior De Scepticismo Profano et Sacro . . . Posterior de Atheismo Praeprimis Socinianorum.* Strasbourg, 1665.

WEEMSE, J. *The Works.* London, 1636. 4 vols.

WEIDLING, C. *De Vita Aeterna ex Lumine Naturae Indemonstrabili.* Leipzig, 1685.

WHICHCOTE, B. *Moral and Religious Aphorisms,* ed. W. R. INGE. London, 1630.

———. *The Works.* Aberdeen, 1751. 4 vols.

WHITFIELD, T. *The Extent of Divine Providence.* London, 1651.

WILD, V. *Quod Aliquid Scitur.* Leipzig, 1664.

WILMOT, J., EARL of Rochester. *Collected Works,* ed. J. HAYWARD. London, 1926.

———. *Poems on Several Occasions,* ed. J. THORPE. Princeton, 1960.

———. *The Rochester-Savile Letters, 1671–1680,* ed. J. H. WILSON. Columbus, Ohio, 1941.

WOLF, J. C. *De Atheo ex Structura* του Σγκεραλου *Convincendo.* Ratisbon, 1708.

WOLSELEY, C. *The Unreasonableness of Atheism Made Manifest.* London, 1669.

WOOD, A. *Athenae Oxoniensis,* ed. P. BLISS. London, 1813–20. 4 vols.

SECONDARY SOURCES

ANDERSON, P. R. *Science in Defense of Liberal Religion.* New York, 1933.

ANDREA, M. DE. "Fede e Ragione nel Pensiero del Pomponazzi," *Rivista di Filosofia Neoscolastica,* XXXVIII (1949), 278–97.

BAKER, H. *The Wars of Truth.* Cambridge, Mass., 1952.

BARBIER, A. A. *Dictionnaire des Ouvrages Anonymes et Pseudonymes.* Paris, 1822–27. 4 vols.

BAUDOUIN, A. "Histoire Critique de Jules César Vanini," *Revue Philosophique,* VIII (1879), 48–71, 157–78, 259–90, 387–410.

BAUDRILLART, H. *J. Bodin et Son Temps.* Paris, 1853.

BELLINI, A. *Gerolamo Cardano e il Suo Tempo.* Milan, 1947.

BELOWSKI, E. *Lukrez in der französischen Literatur der Renaissance.* Berlin, 1934.

BETZENDORFER, W. *Die Lehre von der Zweifachen Wahrheit bei Petrus Pomponazzi.* Tübingen, 1919.

BLANCHET, L. "L'Attitude Religieuse des Jesuits et les Sources du Pari de Pascal," *Revue de Metaphysique et de Moral*, XXVI (1919), 477–516, 617–47.

BLANDSHARD, B. "Early Thought on Inner Light," *Byways in Quaker History*, ed. H. H. Brinton. Wallingford, Pa., 1944.

BOASE, A. M. *The Fortunes of Montaigne.* London, 1935.

BOER, J. DE. *The Theory of Knowledge of the Cambridge Platonists.* Madras, 1931.

BONIVARD, F. *Chroniques de Genève.* Geneva, 1867.

BONNEFON, P. *Montaigne et Ses Amis.* Paris, 1898. 2 vols.

BRADBROOK, M. C. *The School of Night.* Cambridge, 1936.

BREIT, E. *Die Engel und Dämonlehre des Pomponatius und des Cäsalpinus.* Bonn, 1912.

BUCKLEY, G. T. *Rationalism in Sixteenth Century English Literature.* Chicago, 1933.

BUSSON, H. "Les Noms des Incrédules au XVIe Siècle," *Bibliothèque d'Humanisme et Renaissance*, XVI (1954), 272–83.

————. *La Pensée Religieuse Française de Charron à Pascal.* Paris, 1933.

————. *La Religion des Classiques* (1660–1685). Paris, 1948.

————. *Les Sources et le Développement du Rationalisme dans la Littérature Française de la Renaissance.* Paris, 1922. Revised edition, 1957.

CAPERAN, L. *Le Problème du Salut des Infidèles.* Toulouse, 1934.

CASSIRER, E. *Individuum und Kosmos.* Leipzig-Berlin, 1927.

————. *Die platonische Renaissance in England und die Schule von Cambridge.* Leipzig, 1932.

————, and OTHERS (eds.). *The Renaissance Philosophy of Man.* Chicago, 1948.

CHARBONNEL, J.-R. *La Pensée Italienne au XVIe Siècle et le Courant Libertin.* Paris, 1919.

CHAUVIRE, R. *Jean Bodin.* Paris, 1914.

CLARK, T. E. S. and FOXCROFT, H. C. *A Life of Gilbert Burnet.* Cambridge, 1907.

COLIE, R. L. *Light and Enlightenment.* Cambridge, 1957.

CROSSLEY, J. *The Life and Times of Cardano*. London, 1836.

D'ANGERS, J. E. *L'Apologétique en France de 1580 à 1670*. Paris, 1954.

DOUGLAS, A. H. *The Philosophy and Psychology of Pietro Pomponazzi*. Cambridge, 1910.

DRÉANO, M. *La Pensée Religieuse de Montaigne*. Paris, 1936.

DUBI, H. *Das Buch von den Drei Betrügern und das Berner Manuskript*. Bern, 1936.

DUJARDIN, B. *La Vie de Pierre Aretin*. The Hague, 1750.

EBBS, J. D. "Milton's Treatment of Poetic Justice in *Samson Agonistes*," *MLQ*, XXII (1961), 377–89.

ECKMAN, J. *Jerome Cardan*. Baltimore, 1946.

ELSON, J. H. *John Hales of Eton*. New York, 1948.

ESPOSITO, M. "Una Manifestazione d'Incredulita Religiosa nel Medioeva," *Archivio Storico Italiana*, XVI (1931), 1–48.

FEBVRE, L. *L'Incroyance au XVIe Siècle*. Paris, 1942.

FIORENTINO, F. *Studi e Ritratii della Rinascenza*. Bari, 1911.

FOXCROFT, H. C. *A Supplement to Burnet's History of My Own Time*. Oxford, 1902.

FRAME, D. *Montaigne's Discovery of Man*. New York, 1955.

GARDNER, W. *George Villers*. New York, 1903.

GARIN, E. *Giovanni Pico della Mirandola: Vita e Dottrina*. Florence, 1938.

———. "Testi Minori sull'Anima nella Cultura del 400 in Toscana," *Archivio di Filosofia*, 1951, No. 1, 1–36.

GEORGOV, I. *Montaigne als Vertreter des Relativismus in der Moral*. Leipzig, 1889.

GILSON, E. *La Philosophie au Moyen Âge*. Paris, 1947.

GRÄSSE, J. G. T. *Bibliotheca Psychologica*. Leipzig, 1845.

HAUREAU, B. *Histoire de la Philosophie Scolastique*. Paris, 1872–80. 3 vols.

HENNING, A. *Der Skepticismus Montaigne's und seine geschichtliche Stellung*. Jena, 1879.

HÖNIGSWALD, R. *Denker der Italienischen Renaissance*. Basel, 1938.

HUNT, R. N. C. *Calvin*. London, 1933.

HUNTER, W. B. "The Seventeenth Century Doctrine of Plastic Nature," *Harvard Theological Review*, XLIII (1950), 197–213.

JANSSEN, H. *Montaigne Fideiste*. Utrecht, 1930.

JENTSCH, H. C. *Henry More in Cambridge*. Göttingen, 1935.

KOCHER, P. H. *Christopher Marlowe*. Chapel Hill, N.C., 1946.
——. *Science and Religion in Renaissance England*. San Marino, Calif., 1953.
KRAEMER, W. "Ein seltener Druck des Traktats 'De Tribus Impostoribus, 1598,'" *Zeitschrift für Bücherfreunde*, N.F., XIV (1922), 101–11.
KRISTELLER, P. O. "El Mito del Ateismo Renacentista y la Tradicion Francesa del Librepensamiento," *Notas y Estudios d Filosofia* (San Miguel d Tucman), IV, 1–14.
——. "Two Unpublished Questions on the Soul of Pietro Pomponazzi," *Medievalia et Humanistica*, VIII (1955), 76–84.
——. "The Theory of Immortality in Marsilio Ficino," *JHI*, I (1940), 299–319.
LACHEVRE, E. *Mélanges*. Paris, 1920.
LAMPRECHT, S. P. "Innate Ideas in the Cambridge Platonists," *Philosophical Review*, XXXV (1926), 553–73.
LECHLER, G. V. *Geschichte des Englischen Deismus*. Stuttgart and Tübingen, 1841.
LEHNERDT, M. *Lucretius in der Renaissance*. S.l., n.d.
LENOBLE, R. *Mersenne ou la Naissance de Mécanisme*. Paris, 1943.
MACKINNON, J. *Calvin and the Reformation*. London, 1936.
MASSIGNON, L. "La Legend 'De Tribus Impostoribus' et Ses Origines Islamiques," *Revue de l'Histoire des Religions*, LXXXII (1920), 74–78.
MAUTHNER, F. *Der Atheismus und seine Geschichte im Abendlande*. Stuttgart and Berlin, 1921. 3 vols.
MAYO, T. *Epicurus in England*. Dallas, 1934.
MESNARD, P. "La Pensée Religieuse de Bodin," *Revue de Seizième Siècle*, XVI (1929), 77–121.
MOORE, J. F. "The Originality of Rochester's *Satyr Against Mankind*," *PMLA*, LVIII (1943), 393–401.
MORLEY, H. *The Life of G. Cardano of Milan*. London, 1854. 2 vols.
MUIRHEAD, J. H. *The Platonic Tradition in Anglo-Saxon Philosophy*. London, 1931.
MURDOCK, K. B. *The Sun at Noon*. New York, 1939.
PASSMORE, J. A. *Ralph Cudworth*. Cambridge, 1951.
PAULEY, W. C. DE. *The Candle of the Lord*. London, 1937.
PAWSON, G. P. H. *The Cambridge Platonists*. London, 1930.
PERRENS, F. T. *Les Libertins en France au XVIIᵉ Siècle*. Caen, 1884.

PINTO, V. DE S. *Rochester, Portrait of a Restoration Rake.* London, 1935.

PLATTARD, J. *Montaigne et Son Temps.* Paris, 1933.

POPKIN, R. *The History of Scepticism from Erasmus to Descartes.* Assen, 1960.

POWICKE, F. J. *The Cambridge Platonists.* London, 1926.

PRESSER, J. *Das Buch "De Tribus Impostoribus."* Amsterdam, 1926.

PRINZ, J. *John Wilmot, Earl of Rochester, His Life and Writings.* Leipzig, 1927.

RAGNISCO, P. "Nicoletto Vernia, Studi Storico sulla Filosofia Padovana nella Seconda Mèta del Secolo XV," *Atti del Reale Istituto Veneto di Scienze, Lettere et Arti,* XXXVIII (1890–91), 241–308, 617–79.

RENAN, E. *Averroès et l'Averroisme.* Paris, 1882.

ROGET, A. *Histoire du Peuple de Genève.* Geneva, 1870–83. 3 vols.

RUGGIERO, G. DE. *Rinascimento, Riforma, e Controriforma.* Bari, 1930. 2 vols.

SABRIÉ, J.-B. *De l'Humanisme au Rationalisme: Pierre Charron (1541–1603), l'Homme, l'Oeuvre, l'Influence.* Paris, 1913.

SAITTA, G. *Marsilio Ficino e la Filosofia dell'Umanesimo.* Bologna, 1954.

———. *Il Pensiero Italiano nell'Umanesimo e nel Rinascimento.* Bologna, 1949–51. 3 vols.

SCHMIDT, C. *Les Libertins Spirituels.* Paris, 1876.

SCHULTZ, H. *Milton and Forbidden Knowledge.* New York, 1955.

SCOTT, W. (ed.). *Somers Tracts.* London, 1812. 11 vols.

SENCHET, E. *Essai sur la Methode de Francisco Sanchez.* Paris, 1904.

SLEVA, V. E. *The Separated Soul in the Philosophy of St. Thomas Aquinas.* Washington, 1940.

SPINI, G. *Ricerca dei Libertini.* Rome, 1950.

STEFFAN, T. G. *Jeremy Taylor's Criticism of Abstract Speculation.* ("University of Texas Studies in English.") Austin, 1941. pp. 96–108.

STRATHMANN, E. *Sir Walter Raleigh.* New York, 1951.

STROWSKI, F. *Montaigne.* Paris, 1906.

TEIPEL, H. *Zur Frage des Skeptizismus bei Pierre Charron.* Eberfeld, 1912.

VERNIERE, P. *Spinoza.* Paris, 1954.

VILLEY, P. *Montaigne devant la Postérité.* Paris, 1935.

WEIL, E. "Die Philosophie des Pietro Pomponazzi," *Archiv für Geschichte der Philosophie*, XLI (1932), 127–76.

WERNER, K. *Scholastik des späteren Mittelalters.* Vienna, 1881–87. 4 vols.

WILLIAMS, C. *Rochester.* London, 1935.

WILLIAMSON, G. "Milton and the Mortalist Heresy," in *Seventeenth Century Contexts.* Chicago, 1961.

Index

DOUBT'S BOUNDLESS SEA

SKEPTICISM AND FAITH IN THE RENAISSANCE

DON CAMERON ALLEN

designer: Edward D. King
typesetter: Vail-Ballou Press, Inc.
typefaces: Janson text, Deepdene Display
printer: Vail-Ballou Press, Inc.
paper: Warren's 1854 Medium Finish
binder: Vail-Ballou Press, Inc.
cover material: Columbia Riverside Vellum